THE CATHOLIC UNIVERSITY OF AMERICA
CANON LAW STUDIES
No. 237

Dispensation from Private Vows

A Historical Synopsis and a Commentary

BY THE

REVEREND JAMES MARTIN LOWRY, B.A., J.C.L.
Priest of the Diocese of Scranton

A DISSERTATION

Submitted to the Faculty of the School of Canon Law of the Catholic University of America in Partial Fulfillment of the Requirements for the Degree of Doctor of Canon Law

THE CATHOLIC UNIVERSITY OF AMERICA PRESS
WASHINGTON, D. C.
1946

Nihil Obstat:

EDUARDUS G. ROELKER, S.T.D., J.C.D.,
Censor Deputatus.
Washingtonii, die 7 iunii 1946.

Imprimatur:

✠ GULIELMUS J. HAFEY, D.D.,
Episcopus Scrantonensis.
Scrantoniae, die 9 iunii 1946.

Printed in U.S.A.
by
Manus Langan Press, Scranton, Pa.

DEDICATED

TO

MY MOTHER AND FATHER

TABLE OF CONTENTS

CHAPTER VI

CAUSE REQUIRED FOR DISPENSATION FROM PRIVATE VOWS

CHAPTER VII

CHAPTER VIII

FOREWORD

This work proposes to treat of the juridical concept, "dispensation from vows". In this treatment, two principal divisions are observed—the first containing a historical synopsis of the doctrine on the subject before the Code of Canon Law, the second containing a commentary on the currently existing law. In these main divisions the subject is developed within definite limitations.

Except for that part of the historical synopsis which deals with the time prior to the Council of Trent (1545-1563), the writer has restricted his subject matter to the consideration of Dispensation from Private Vows, in the manner in which this point is treated in the Third Book of the Code of Canon Law. This restriction was not maintained in the treatment of the period from the *Decree of Gratian* (c. 1140) to the Council of Trent, in view of the valuable understanding to be derived from the development of the doctrine on dispensation from vows in general during that time.

Excluded from the vows to be considered are all public vows, a discussion of which properly belongs to the Second Book of the Code, and more particularly to that section of the Code which deals with the separation of a religious from a religious institute. Vows which constitute impediments to marriage insofar as they are impediments are likewise beyond the scope of this work. Consequently the various faculties which the Code grants for dispensing from these impediments do not claim any consideration in the present study.

The present work proposes, rather, to offer a discussion on private vows. The main emphasis throughout the treatment is placed on dispensation, insofar as this pertains to vows. Care, moreover, has been taken to avoid going beyond the limits of dispensation from vows except when this was prompted by the generic relationship of dispensation with the other three ways in which vows cease, namely by simple cessation, annulment, and commutation.

Among the pre-Code authors, as among those who have written since the appearance of the Code, the subject of private vows is one which both canonists and theologians have undertaken to explain. Among the two classes of writers, the moral theologians have undoubtedly been the more thorough. Despite the consequent necessity of considering the doctrine of the moral theologians, the present writer has tried to restrict his treatment to the purely legal aspects of the subject.

The writer wishes to take this occasion to express his sincere gratitude to the Most Reverend William J. Hafey, Bishop of Scranton, for making available to him the opportunity to pursue an advanced course in Canon Law; to the Faculty of the School of Canon Law at the Catholic University of America, Washington, D. C., for their many hours of instruction, capable direction, and ready assistance; and finally, to all those who in any way have helped in the preparation and editing of this dissertation.

PRELIMINARY NOTIONS

CHAPTER I

AN EXPLANATION OF THE TERMS OF THE TITLE

ARTICLE I. VOWS

For a clear understanding of the matter to be treated of in this work, the terms of the title will first be explained. These are vows, or more specifically, private vows, and dispensation in regard to vows.

A. *Definition*

The Code of Canon Law states in a rather indirect manner that a vow is a deliberate and free promise made to God of something which is possible and better than its opposite.[1] Briefly it is a promise made to God. Therein are contained implicitly the qualifications enumerated in the definition by the words deliberate, free, something possible, and better than its opposite.[2]

In examining these words separately, one will note that a vows is:

1) A *promise*. A promise is a declaration of one's will by which a person obligates himself to another who can then expect or claim the performance or forbearance

1 Canon 1307, § 1: "Votum, idest promissio deliberata ac libera Deo facta de bono possibili et meliore, ex virtute religionis impleri debet." Cf. also Augustine, *A Commentary on the New Code of Canon Law* (8 vols., Vol. VI, *Administrative Law*, 2. ed., St. Louis: B. Herder Co., 1923), VI, 295 (hereafter cited as *Commentary*).

2 Wernz-Vidal, *Ius Canonicum ad Codicis Normam Exactum* (7 tomes in 8 vols., Vol. IV, *De Rebus*, pars I, Romae: Apud Aedes Universitatis Gregorianae, 1934), IV, *De Rebus*, pars I, n. 546, p. 648 (hereafter cited as *De Rebus*).

of a specified act. Hence, it is not a *proposal* to do or omit doing something; for in a proposal another person does not acquire a right, for the simple reason that the person making the proposal does not intend to bind himself.[3]

2) A *deliberate* promise. Deliberation implies the possession of knowledge and the exercise of intellectual judgment regarding that which one is about to do. This knowledge and intellectual judgment must be at least the equivalent of that which suffices for the commission of a mortal sin. This knowledge and judgment are diminished, however, in proportion as ignorance and error influence the vowmaker. Nevertheless, the vow remains valid as long as the error or ignorance is not substantial, that is to say, if the vow would not have been made except for the error or ignorance concerning the substantial properties of the vow, its object matter, or its final cause. Hence, accidental error or ignorance does not invalidate a vow, for even if the vowmaker had not been influenced by these factors, he would nevertheless have made the vow. If, however, the accidental error or ignorance amounts to a *conditio sine qua non*, the vow is invalid.[4]

3) A *free* promise. The vowmaker must freely consent to oblige himself before God to do or omit doing something. As in the case of deliberation, so here too, the freedom which is requisite for the commission of a mortal sin suffices for the making of a vow.[5] This freedom is de-

---

[3] Noldin-Schmitt, *Summa Theologiae Moralis iuxta Codicem Iuris Canonici* (25. ed., 3 vols., Oeniponte: Fel. Rauch, 1938), II, n. 205 (hereafter cited *Theologia Moralis*).

[4] Canon 104; Wernz-Vidal, *De Rebus*, pars I, n. 549, p. 655; Noldin-Schmitt, *Theologia Moralis*, II, n. 209; Coronata, *Institutiones Iuris Canonici* (5 vols., Vols. I-IV, 2. ed., 1939-1945; Vol. V, 1936, Taurini: Marietti, 1936-1945), II, 214 (herefater cited as *Institutiones*).

[5] Wernz-Vidal, *De Rebus*, pars I, n. 550, p. 655.

stroyed and the vow rendered invalid by the infliction of an irresistible external force,[6] when this is imposed for the purpose of exacting the external expression of the vow.[7] This freedom is likewise destroyed if the vow is made because of a grave and unjust fear sustained by the vow-maker.[8] Before the Code it was the common opinion that grave and unjust fear did not vitiate a vow unless it was imposed for the purpose of exacting the vow.[9] After the Code it is the common opinion that the vitiating fear to be effective need not be inflicted on or sustained by the vow-maker specifically for the purpose of exacting the vow.[10] According to this opinion, any externally imposed unjust and grave fear invalidates a vow. But even then, fear operates with this effect only if it is actually the cause of the vow, and not if it is merely an occasion for the making of the vow. A soldier who makes a vow in the midst of battle for the reason that he fears death cannot be said to make the vow because of grave fear; rather it must be said that he is prompted in the making of his vow by the fear which innately actuates him; he hopes by respecting that fear to obtain God's protection.

Fear is the cause of a vow according to Vermeersch (1858-1936), if a person has no other choice than to make the vow in order to avoid that which he fears.[11] This opin-

---

6 Canon 103.

7 Wernz-Vidal, *loc. cit.*

8 Canon 1307, § 3: "Votum metu gravi et iniusto emissum ipso iure nullum est."

9 Ballerini-Palmieri, *Opus Theologicum Morale* (7 vols., Prati, 1889-1893), II, 444 (hereafter cited as *Theologia Moralis*); Lehmkuhl, *Theologia Moralis* (11. ed., 2 vols., Friburgi, 1910), I, n. 579.

10 Wernz-Vidal, *loc cit.*; Vermeersch-Creusen, *Epitome Iuris Canonici* (3. ed., 3 vols., Mechlinae et Romae: Dessain, 1927-1928), II, 443 (hereafter cited as *Epitome*).

11 *Loc cit.*; Coronata, *Institutiones*, II, 214.

ion is firmly founded in the law which in no place requires that the fear spoken of in Canon 1307, § 3, have as its purpose the exacting of a vow from the person subject to the fear. This understanding of Canon 1307, § 3 is also confirmed through a similar distinction which the Code makes in determining the fear which vitiates matrimonial consent.[12] It is not required that the fear be imposed in order to obtain a matrimonial consent, but rather that the person subjected to the fear be forced to give consent in order to avoid that which he fears. This is the law of the Code, though in the first formulation of the text of Canon 1087 the consultors considered demanding that the fear be inflicted for the purpose of obtaining the matrimonial consent.[13]

Furthermore, after examining the general law of the Code on fear,[14] one notes that the legislator in no way even hints at the necessity that if a grave fear is to be invalidating in its effect, it must have been thrust upon a person with the purpose of exacting a specific act.[15] Since this motivation in the act of thrusting grave fear upon someone is not mentioned in the general law as a condition which must obtain if the act motivated by the fear is to be considered as null and void, it appears that this specific motivation in the obtruded fear is not essential for the vitiation of the act committed in consequence of the implemented fear. Therefore, in order that grave and unjust fear invalidate a vow, it is not postulated that the fear which is brought to bear

---

12 Canon 1087, § 1.

13 Gasparri, *Tractatus Canonicus de Matrimonio* (editio nova ad mentem Codicis I. C., 2 vols., Romae, Typis Polyglottis Vaticanis, 1932), II, n. 856 (hereafter cited as *De Matrimonio*).

14 Canon 103, § 2.

15 Beste, *Introductio in Codicem* (2. ed., Collegeville: St. John's Abbey Press, 1944), p. 159 (hereafter cited as *Introductio*).

on the vowmaker be thrust upon him precisely for the purpose of exacting the vow from him. It is sufficient that the person making the vow regard his action as the only means available for avoiding some impending grave evil which is feared.[16]

Light fear, according to some authors,[17] annuls a vow if this fear constitutes the exclusive reason for the making of the vow. The basis for this opinion is fundamentally the same as that which is recognized as implying the invalidating effect of grave fear, namely, that God cannot accept anything which is exacted from someone by an illegal use of force or fear. Fear is the consciousness of some impending evil. To accept or exact anything under such circumstances from the person sustaining the fear is to render an injustice to that person. Thus it cannot be expected that God will accept anything as obligatory on the part of a person who is under the influence of even light fear as long as that fear is operative unjustly.[18] Moreover, fear of any kind, grave or light, diminishes the fullness of consent on the part of the vowmaker. Since this factor constitutes a reason for the invalidating effect of grave fear, it can also exist as a reason which in connection with light fear begets an invalidating effect.[19]

---

16 Cf. however Prümmer: "Metus gravis, si . . . iniuste incussus fuerit ad extorquendum votum, irritat omnia vota."—*Manuale Theologiae Moralis secundum Principia S. Thomae Aquinatis* (2. ed., recognita a P. Dr. Engelberto M. Münch, 3 vols., Friburgi Brisgoviae: Herder, 1935-1936), II, n. 397 (hereafter cited as *Theologia Moralis*).

17 Lehmkuhl, *Theologia Moralis*, I, n. 579; Noldin-Schmitt, *Theologia Moralis*, II, n. 210; Vermeersch-Crueusen, *Epitome*, II, n. 637; Coronata, *Institutiones*, II, 215.

18 Wernz-Vidal, *De Rebus*, pars I, 656, not. 43.

19 Cappello, *Tractatus Canonico—Moralis de Sacramentis* (3 vols, in 6, 1932-1939, Vol. III, Partes I et II, *De Matrimonio*, 4. ed. 1939, Romae: Marietti), III, pars I, n. 294 (hereafter cited as *De Matrimonio*).

Light fear, however, is never in the external forum presumed to have been the cause of a vow. Furthermore, it is certain that when the fear is not external or unjust, it in no way vitiates a vow, unless, although internal, it be of such a nature as to disturb the person to the point where he can no longer be held responsible. The opinion, however, which considers a vow invalid when light fear is the only cause or reason on account of which the vow was made seems to go beyond the limits intended by the legislator in this matter.

The Code asserts that grave and unjust fear annuls a vow.[20] This does not exclude directly the possibility that vows may also be vitiated when they are made in consequence of pressure sustained through the presence of light fear. On closer examination, however, it can be seen that Canon 1307, § 3, is an exception to the general rule of Canon 103, § 2, which latter canon states that grave and unjust fear does not vitiate an act performed by a physical or moral person unless the law rules otherwise.[21] The action, however, is rescissible under the terms of canons 1684-1689. This canon, therefore, states a principle: Grave fear does not annul an act. Later, in the particular section of the Code which treats of vows, the exception to this principle already indicated is found and in it the law rules otherwise than in Canon 103, § 2.[22] The exception provides that vows based on an unjust and grave fear externally created are void. From the general principle, namely, that grave fear does not annul an act, it can

20 Canon 1307, § 3.

21 Canon 103, § 2: "Actus positi ex metu gravi et iniuste incusso vel ex dolo, valent, nisi aliud iure caveatur; sed possunt ad normam can. 1684-1689 per iudicis sententiam rescindi, sive ad petitionem partis laesae sive ex officio."

22 Canon 1307, § 3.

be argued *a fortiori* that light fear does not annul an act. But from the particular principle or exception that grave fear does annul a vow, one cannot similarly argue *a fortiori* that light fear likewise does so. Before the general ruling of Canon 103, § 2, can be excluded together with the conclusions which follow from it, the Code must state that light fear annuls a vow. Unless this is specifically stated, the general principle that grave fear does not annul human acts, and *a fortiori* that light fear does not annul a vow, must be considered as prevailing.

This is the opinion of the writer, and it seems to be the doctrine which the Code intends to present. The opinion which holds for the invalidating force of light fear is, however, a solidly probable one.[23]

4) A promise *made to God.* In this way a vow differs from other promises. Inasmuch as a vow is a promise made to God it is an act of religion.[24] By this act of religion God receives a worship which is his exclusive due. Just as when a promise is made to another who accepts it, the promisor is then obligated to the promisee, so too, when a promise is made to God, the promisor places himself under a new obligation to God. In doing this, however, the vow-maker honors God, professes his belief in God's universally controlling Providence, and manifests his conviction

---

[23] St. Alphonsus, *Theologia Moralis*, ed. L. Gaudé, (4 vols., Romae, 1905-1912), lib. III, n. 197 (hereafter cited as *Theologia Moralis*); Cappello, *De Matrimonio*, pars I, n. 294.

[24] St. Thomas Aquinas, *Summa Theologica* (6 vols., Taurini: Marietti, 1937), IIa-IIae, q. 88, a. 5, 6; Suarez, *Opera Omnia* (26 vols., Parisiis, 1856-1861), Vol. XIV, *De Statu et Virtute Religionis*, tract. VI, *De Voto*, lib. I, c. XV, n. 7 (hereafter cited as *De Voto*); Noldin-Schmitt, *Theologia Moralis*, II, n. 205.

that in time of difficulty refuge is to be sought before all others with God, who alone can satisfy the needs of man.[25]

If a promise is made to a saint, it may or it may not be a vow. If it is made to the saint in so far as he reflects the holiness of God it will be a vow. If it is made to a saint absolutely and without any limitation, it will be a vow, for such a promise is virtually and implicitly made to God. It is in this way that the Church regards such promises, and it is in this way that a promise is generally made to a saint. If, however, the promise is made to a saint as an individual standing apart from the factor of his relationship to God, or if the promise is made to a saint in view of the saint's personal excellence and sanctity, then the promise cannot be regarded as a vow.[26]

5) A promise of a *possible good.* A vow must first of all be a human act, a primary requisite of which is its possibility. This possibility, however, must be not only a physical, but a moral possibility as well, i.e., it must be susceptible to performance in ordinary circumstances,[27] or without great difficulty.[28] For this reason the authors generally agree that a vow to avoid all partially deliberate venial sin is an invalid vow.[29] They agree, too, that a vow to avoid all fully deliberate venial sin is invalid if made by a person not tested in virtue.[30] They assert, on the other

---

25 Salmanticenses, *Cursus Theologiae Moralis* (6 vols, in 4, Venetiis, 1714-1728), Vol. IV, tract. XVII, *De Voto ac Juramento*, c. I, nn. 28-29 (hereafter cited as *Theologia Moralis*).

26 Salmanticenses, *loc. cit.*

27 Coronata, *loc. cit.*

28 Noldin-Schmitt, *Theologia Moralis*, II, n. 211.

29 Noldin-Schmitt, *loc. cit.*; Coronata, *Institutiones*, II, p. 216.

30 Merkelbach, *Summa Theologiae Moralis ad Mentem D. Thomae et ad Normam Iuris Novi* (2. ed., 3 vols., Parisiis: Desclée de Brouwer, 1935-1936), II, n. 719 (hereafter cited as *Theologia Moralis*); Genicot-Salsmans, *Institutiones*

hand, that a vow to avoid all mortal sin is a valid vow, though not an expedient one; and if made by a person weak in virtue, such inexpediency constitutes a sufficient cause for a dispensation.[31]

When a vow is possible of fulfillment only in part, its validity depends on the intention of the vowmaker. If the parts are intended as a unit, the vow is invalid. If the parts are intended separately, or if the intention of the vowmaker cannot be ascertained, and a presumption of this intention thus becomes necessary, the following can be stated: a). If the object of the vow cannot be divided, or if the substance of the vow does not pertain to that part which is possible, the vow is null. Thus, if a person promises to make a pilgrimage to Guadalupe, but can only go part of the way, he is not bound to make that part of the journey which is possible, for the simple reason that it is impossible to make the complete journey. If, however, the object matter of the vow is divisible, then the obligation is not contracted if the part which is possible is merely

---

Theologiae Moralis (13. ed., 2 vols., Bruxellis: L'Edition Universelle, S.A., 1936), I, n. 315; Vermeersch, *Theologiae Moralis Principia, Responsa, Consilia* (2. ed., 3 vols., Romae: Università Gregoriana, 1926-1928), II, n. 209 (hereafter cited as *Theologia Moralis*); Noldin-Schmitt, *op. cit.* II, n. 211.

31 Genicot-Salsmans. *loc. cit.*; Prümmer, *Theologia Moralis*, II, n. 399. Vermeersch accepts on the authority of other authors the invalidity of the following vows: a vow to avoid all venial sin, and a vow to avoid all deliberate sin, if made by a person lacking an experience confirmed in virtue. He accepts as probable the opinion which states that a vow to avoid all grave sin is invalid if made by a person who is normally weak. Vermeersch, however, also points out that authors speak in a manner which is too absolute when they say that a vow to avoid venial sin is invalid although such a vow merely confirms an obligation which is incumbent on everyone, of avoiding venial sin, and which continues to oblige even after a sin is committed. He shows that Suarez understood such vows as being made with a qualification, viz., to avoid venial sin in so far as this is possible, *seu de diligentia adhibenda ad omne peccatum fugiendum.* This is also the conviction of Vermeersch. Cf. *Theologia Moralis*, II, n. 209.

accessory to the principal part. Thus, if a person who is bound by a vow to fast and abstain is unable to abstain, he is at least bound to do that which he can do, namely, to fast. On the other hand, if a person promises to go to Mass every day on the journey to Guadalupe, he is not bound to go to Mass if the complete journey to Guadalupe remains impossible of fulfillment.[32]

6.) A promise of a *good which is better than its opposite*. That which is the object of the vow cannot be evil; this would be blasphemy, even if the object of the vow was a venial offense.[33] Not only, however, does an evil object vitiate a vow: even an evil purpose causes the invalidity of a vow. But here a distinction must be made. If the evil purpose is the total motivating cause of the vow, the vow is null, e.g., when a vow is used to obtain from or to thank God for something serving only a purpose which is illicit in itself. If, however, the evil purpose is only an impulsive or partial cause, as when someone externally promises in God's honor to donate a generous gift to charity, hoping thereby to be praised by men, the vow is valid.[34] Likewise, a vow is valid when it is made for a good purpose, though it be connected with something evil, as when a person vows something which is good, but on the condition of achieving or realizing something which is evil.[35]

On the other hand, a vow is invalid when that which is promised is of no spiritual utility or value, or when it is morally indifferent. But, when the object matter of the

---

32 Noldin-Schmitt, *Theologia Moralis*, II, n. 211; Prümmer, *Theologia Moralis*, II, n. 399.

33 St. Alphonsus, *Theologia Moralis*, lib. III, nn. 205-206.

34 St. Alphonsus, *loc. cit.*; Noldin-Schmitt, *Theologia Moralis*, II, n. 212.

35 St. Alphonsus, *loc. cit.*; Noldin-Schmitt, *loc. cit.*

vow is of this nature, the purpose for which or the circumstances in which the vow is made can change object matter which is useless or indifferent into a suitable matter for the vow. This, however, cannot be done at the mere whim of the vowmaker. A proportion and an appropriateness must be present between the object of the vow and the purpose for which or the circumstances in which the vow is made. Thus, if a person, while still engaged in all other forms of servile work, promises in honor of the Blessed Mother not to bake bread on Saturday, no honor is thereby paid to the Mother of God. If, however, this person promises to abstain from all servile work on a certain day or from a particular type of work which has proven an inordinate distraction to him, such indifferent matters can be transformed into a suitable object matter for a vow through the intention of the vowmaker.[36]

It is evident, then, that the object matter of a vow must be something good. More specifically, it must be a good which is better than its opposite, or better than the omission of it would be. It must be better than some other good whose attainment is hindered by the fulfillment of the vow.[37] Thus a vow to marry would ordinarily not constitute a valid vow, since it hinders the attainment of its more perfect opposite, namely observance of virginity or celibacy. On the other hand, a vow to recite the rosary would be valid, for this is obviously better than its opposite. The object of a vow, therefore, must be an act of virtue which does not impede the performance of something more virtuous.[38]

---

36 Salmanticenses, *Theologia Moralis,* tract. XVII, c. I, n. 57; St. Alphonsus, *Theologia Moralis,* lib. III, n. 204.

37 Coronata, *Institutiones,* II, 216.

38 Wernz-Vidal, *De Rebus,* pars I, n, 552, p. 657.

In addition to the acts of counsel, also the acts which already are obligatory under precept can constitute the object matter of a vow. The most frequent example of this is the vow of perfect chastity among the unmarried. The object matter of such a vow does not hinder the attainment of a greater good; rather in the case here considered the hindrance militates against evil, since the opposite of the votal object implies the violation of a precept. A person bound by a precept is still free. His obligation is a moral obligation, to which, if he so desires, he can add another. This he does when he takes as the object matter of a vow something to which he already is bound by reason of a precept.[39]

It was noted that a vow which stands in the way of the fulfillment of a greater good is not a valid vow, such as the vow not to marry, or the vow not to become a religious. In applying this to concrete cases one must point out that the comparative goodness which is required in the votal object is not necessarily to be taken in an absolute sense. Rather, it is to be taken in a relative and general way. D'Annibale (1815-1892) stated that the better good will frequently be determined by the circumstances of persons, places, and causes. The result is that in a particular case it may be better for a man to marry,[40] or better for him not to enter the religious state. Consequently, for such a person a vow relating to an objectively lesser good would be valid, since subjectively or relatively the fulfillment of the vow would imply a better good than its opposite. Thus a vow to marry would be a valid vow if the marriage was necessary

---

39 Wernz-Vidal, *loc. cit.*; Prümmer, *Theologia Moralis*, II, 401.

40 *Summula Theologiae Moralis* (5. ed., 4 vols., Romae, 1908-1909), III, n. 192, not. 3 (hereafter cited as *Theologia Moralis*).

for the sake of forestalling or avoiding scandal, or of legitimizing a child which was born out of wedlock.[41]

---

41 Aertnys-Damen, *Theologia Moralis* (11. ed., 2 vols., Taurini-Romae: Marietti, 1928), I, n. 483. The following oath was given to the students of the Propaganda College in Rome by an order of Alexander VII issued on July 20, 1660: ". . . spondeo . . . quod nullam Religionem, Societatem, aut Congregationem Regularem sine speciali Sedis Apostolicae licentia vel Sacrae Congregationis de Propaganda Fide ingrediar . . ."—*Collectanea S. Congregationis de Propaganda Fide* (2 vols., Romae, 1907), n. 143, 2 (hereafter cited as *Collect. S.C.P.F.*). Although this was not a vow, the promise was alleged by many to be invalid, since it hindered the attainment of a greater good. In response, Alexander VII (Const. *Cum circa,* 20 iul. 1660) stated that the clauses: ". . . quid fidei propagationi, et universalis Ecclesiae bono, attenta praesertim temporum et rerum circumstantia, magis conducat . . ." and ". . . gravitas muneris sacerdotum saecularium ad Missiones Apostolicas admissorum . . ." had both to be taken into consideration for any proper evaluation regarding the validity of this oath.—*Collect. S.C.P.F.*, n. 142. Later the Sacred Congregation for the Propagation of the Faith itself responded to some inquiries (8 apr. 1661, ad II et III—*Collect. S.C.P.F.*, n. 144; *Codicis Iuris Canonici Fontes cura Emi Card. Gasparri Editi* (9 vols., Romae [postea Civitate Vaticana]: Typis Polyglottis Vaticanis, 1923-1939; Vols. VII, VIII, et IX cura et studio Emi Card. Serédi), n. 4466 (hereafter referred to as *Fontes*). In its reply it stated that the student by the rules of the school was primarily responsible for the maintenance and the furtherance of the spiritual welfare of the country from which he came. If then, at any time, the Roman Pontiff permitted a student to enter the religious life, he did so with this principle in mind, otherwise he would have undermined the very principle here in question. Hence a student was permitted to enter the religious life only when the spiritual welfare of his country would benefit thereby. The granting of this permission was reserved to the Holy See inasmuch as sometimes it was, and sometimes it was not, expedient to furnish such a permission. It was further observed that this procedure was not unlike that recognized in many religious communities whereby a member could advance to a stricter order only with the permission of his present superior. So also for seculars the permission of the Holy See was necessary for their entrance upon a more perfect life. Today the Code regards as invalid the admission into the novitiate of clerics who, by the law of the Holy See, are bound by oath to serve their diocese or mission, for such time as the obligation of the oath lasts. (Canon 542, § 1.) The Code makes illicit the admission into the novitiate of clerics in major orders whose admission is unknown to their bishop, or is opposed by him when their leaving the diocese would result in grave detriment of souls, which cannot at all be averted by other arrangements. (Canon 542, § 2.)

From the foregoing it is manifest that, for a true understanding of the "better good" which must be the object of a vow, one must acknowledge that in a particular case the necessitating factors inherent in circumstances may change what would ordinarily be a "better good" into a "lesser good." Taking the "better good" in a subjective rather than in an objective sense, one can readily see that a vow which makes impossible the operation of the objectively considered greater good of the evangelical counsels, will not always be an invalid vow.[42]

B. Division

Vows are *absolute* when they are made without relation to or dependence on any uncertain future event; they are *conditional* when the obligation of fulfilling the vow is suspended until an uncertain future event takes place.[43] Conditional vows are *penal* when the vowmaker promises to inflict a punishment on himself if he incurs some predetermined future guilt.[44] Vows are *express* when they are made known by words, actions, or signs; they are *tacit* when they are attached to some freely performed action, for example, to the reception of subdiaconate, in the opinion of those who consider the vow of celibacy inseparably connected with it. Vows are *personal* when an action of the vowmaker is promised; they are *real* when something external and distinct from the action of the vowmaker is promised; they are *mixed,* when at the same time they participate in the nature of both a personal and a real vow.[45]

---

[42] Suarez, *De Voto,* lib. I, c. XI, n. 3; Wernz-Vidal, *De Rebus,* pars I, p. 658, nota 53.

[43] Suarez, *De Voto,* lib. I, c. XIX, n. 8.

[44] Prümmer, *Theologia Moralis,* II, 329.

[45] Canon 1308, § 4.

Based on the relative degree and extent of its divulgement among men, a vow is *completely occult* if only the vowmaker knows of it; *simply occult* if it is known of only by a few; *public*, if the fact of the vow is known by many witnesses.[46] A vow is *solemn* if it is recognized by the Church as such; otherwise it is *simple*.[47] Before the Code, a solemn vow seems to have been understood in the same way as in the Code. Thus Santi († 1885) spoke of a solemn vow as one which the Church recognized as such; while a simple vow was any vow which was not solemn even though it stood approved by the Church.[48]

A vow is *public* as opposed to *private* when it is received in the name of the Church by a legitimate ecclesiastical authority; it is *private* when it is made without that intervention on the part of the Church which would constitute it a public vow.[49] The ecclesiastical superior who accepts a vow in the name of the Church is not the pastor or the confessor, but that person, be he cleric or lay, man or woman, who is deputed by a statute of the Church precisely to accept vows in the name of the Church.[50]

When the last two divisions of vows are analyzed in relation to each other, it is seen that all public vows are either solemn or simple, all private vows are simple, all solemn vows are public, and all simple vows are either public or private. All private vows are simple, since it is impossible for a private vow to be a solemn vow inasmuch

46 Suarez, *De Voto*, lib. I, c. XIX, n. 20.

47 Canon 1308, § 2: "Sollemne, si ab Ecclesia uti tale fuerit agnitum; secus simplex."

48 *Praelectiones Iuris Canonici Iuxta Ordinem Decretalium Gregorii IX* (2. ed., 5 vols., Ratisbonae, 1886), III, 302 (hereafter cited as *Praelectiones*).

49 Canon 1308, § 1; Wernz-Vidal, *De Rebus*, pars I, n. 456, p. 649.

50 Beste, *Introductio*, p. 642, ad can. 1308, § 1; Vermeersch-Creusen, *Epitome*, II, n. 639.

as all solemn vows are intimately connected with religious profession, wherein all vows are public. For the reasons just explained, it is apparent that all solemn vows are public vows.

A vow is an *individual* vow when it is made by a physical person; it is a *community* vow when it is made by a moral person or a community. A vow is a *reserved* vow when its cessation by way of dispensation is made to depend on the exclusive power of the Holy See, and non-reserved when its cessation by way of dispensation does not postulate any special delegation of power from the Holy See. Finally, a vow can be made with its object accurately designated and predetermined with certitude as one particular matter (*votum determinatum*), or it can be made in such manner that several objects are promised, one of which will finally become the object of the actual vow. (*votum disiunctivum*).[51]

Article II. Dispensation from Vows

A. *The Cessation of Vows in General*

Having once made a vow, the vowmaker cannot release himself on his own authority from this obligation which he has freely undertaken.[52] This, however, does not mean that his obligation is absolutely unreleasable. Although the vowmaker is unable to release the vow on his own authority, there are four distinct ways in which vows can cease. These are simple cessation, annulment, commutation, and dispensation.

51 Lehmkuhl, *Theologia Moralis,* I, n. 582; Noldin-Schmitt, *Theologia Moralis,* II, n. 206.

52 D'Annibale, *Theologia Moralis,* III, n. 201.

Through *simple cessation* a vow ceases with the lapse of the time specified for the termination of the obligation. Likewise a vow also ceases when through the substantial change of the object matter the fulfillment of the vow becomes impossible or illicit. A vow also ceases through the non-fulfillment of the condition on which the obligation of the vow rests. A vow ceases, too, when the final cause for which the vow was made can no longer be attained by the vowmaker since, even as to purpose, a vow cannot bind beyond the intention of the vowmaker.[53] Finally, a vow ceases to a certain extent through religious profession, for by it private vows are suspended for the duration of the vowmaker's perseverance in religion.[54]

The *annulment* of a vow is effected through the intervention of those who have dominative power over the one who made the vow. Annulment is defined as an act by which one who has power over the will of the vowmaker, or over the object matter of the vow, removes the obligation of the vow.[55]

The *commutation* of a vow is the transfer of the obligation of the vow from one object matter to another. The object matter to which the obligation is transferred can be of a more perfect, an equally perfect, or also a less perfect order than that of the original object matter.[56]

Finally the *dispensation* of a vow can constitute an agency which will effect a cessation of the vow. A dispensation with reference to a vow may be defined as an act

53 Canon 1311; Wernz-Vidal, *De Rebus*, pars I, n. 555, p. 662; Suarez, *De Voto*, lib. 4, c. 18, n. 4.

54 Canon 1315; D'Annibale, *loc. cit.*

55 Suarez, *De Voto*, lib. VI, c. I, n. 3.

56 Lessius, *De Iustitia et Iure Ceterisque Virtutibus Cardinalibus* (4 vols. in 1, Antverpiae, 1617), lib. II, c. XL, n. 68 (hereafter cited as *De Iustitia et Iure*).

(*condonatio, relaxatio, remissio*) by which a competent ecclesiastical superior who has the necessary spiritual jurisdiction, for a just and legitimate cause, remits in God's name the obligation contracted through the making of a vow.[57]

B. Proof of the Authority of the Church to Dispense from Vows

An argument which is frequently used to prove the Church's authority to dispense from vows is the one which is based on the principle *ab esse ad posse.* It is an established fact that the Church has granted dispensations from vows. She has exercised this right throughout the centuries. It would be temerarious and heretical to state that the Church has throughout these centuries exercised a power beyond her competence.[58]

The most fundamental *a priori* argument, however, for establishing this power of the Church is taken from the Sacred Scripture. It is found in the words of Christ to Peter: ". . . I will give to thee the keys of the kingdom of heaven; and whatever thou shalt bind upon earth shall be bound in heaven, and whatever thou shalt loose upon earth shall be loosed in heaven."[59] Again, in another place He said: "Feed my sheep."[60] Although in these passages there is no specific mention of the power to dispense from vows, still the absolute use of the word, "feed," and the

[57] Suarez, *De Voto,* lib. VI, c. IX, n. 4; Reiffenstuel, *Ius Canonicum Universum* (7 vols., Parisiis, 1864-1870), lib. III, tit. XXXIV, n. 20 (hereafter cited as *Ius Canonicum*).

[58] St. Thomas Aquinas, *Opera Omnia* (25 vols., Parmae, 1854-1873), Vol. VII, *Commentarium in Quatuor Libros Sententiarum*, dist, 38, q. 1, a. 7 (hereafter cited as *Sent. IV*); Suarez, *De Voto,* lib. VI, c. IX, n. 4.

[59] Matt. XVI, 19.

[60] John XXI, 17.

universality of the words, "Whatever thou shalt loose," indicate sufficiently that this power is contained in them. Hence, Christ gave this power to his Church just as surely as He gave her the power to grant indulgences, and to dispense from unconsummated marriages.[61]

Finally, reason shows that, like all laws, a vow (*quasi-lex privata*) by which man binds himself will occasionally require a dispensation. In view of this not infrequent need for a dispensation from vows, together with the universal authority and power granted to Peter, it is difficult to conceive that Christ would leave his Church without this power to release her subjects from the obligation of a vow. Furthermore, human deliberation is unable to consider all future contingencies. In consequence, when one of these unforeseen circumstances does arise, it will frequently be unwise to expect the fulfillment of certain vows. Just as the observance of a general law can occasion tremendous harm unless a dispensation is granted, so, too, the observance of a private law, that is, of a vow, can under certain circumstances give rise to much harm unless it be relaxed.[62]

C. *The Nature of a Dispensation from Vows*

After the presentation of an explanation of what a dispensation from vows is and of the proof of the right of the Church to grant a dispensation, it remains now to explain the essence of a dispensation from vows.

A dispensation from a vow may seem at first glance quite impossible. A vow is a promise made to God; a dis-

---

61 Suarez, *De Voto*, lib. VI, c. IX, nn. 7, 18; Salmanticenses, *Theologia Moralis*, tract. XVII, c. III, n. 77; La Grange, *Évangile selon Saint Matthieu* (3. ed., Paris: Libraire Victor Lecoffre, 1927), commentary on Matt. XVI, 19, pp. 328-329.

62 St. Thomas, *Summa Theologica*, IIa-IIae, q. 88, art. 10; Suarez, *loc. cit.*

pensation, in its ordinary meaning, implies the relaxation of a law. A promise made to and accepted by another binds the promisor at least under fidelity. He is unable to free himself from the promise unless the promise be remitted by the promisee. When a promise is made to God, one expects it to bind to an infinitely greater degree than when it is made merely to men. Likewise, one expects that a release from the fully assumed obligation will be proportionately more difficult in view of the apparent impossibility of obtaining from God a remission of the promise made to Him.[63] Add to this the fact that fidelity to a promise, especially when this is made to God, is prescribed by the natural law, from which there can be no dispensation.[64] The resultant problem then is this: The Church, as a matter of fact, does grant dispensations. On what basis, however, can she do this, since it apparently involves the impossible factor of dispensing from the natural law?

In the solution of this problem an examination of the doctrine on the natural law is quite necessary. In the first place, a dispensation from the natural law is impossible for the reason that the author of the natural law is God. Hence the natural law is divine law, and thus it lies beyond the authority of man to relax its obligatory force even in a particular instance.[65] Divine law operates either as a divine positive or as a divine natural law. Since in regard to vows there is no divine positive law, the obligation which man assumes in making a vow, derives from and

63 St. Thomas, *Summa Theologica*, IIa-IIae, q. 88, art. 3; Vermeersch, *Theologia Moralis*, II, n. 439.

64 St. Thomas, *Summa Theologica*, IIa-IIae, q. 88, art. 10, ad 2; Suarez, *De Voto*, lib. VI, c. IX, n. 5.

65 Suarez, *Opera Omnia*, Vol. I, *De Legibus*, lib. VI, c. XIV, n. 5 (hereafter cited *De Legibus*).

rests entirely on the divine natural law.[66] Hence, when a dispensation from a vow is granted by the Church, it appears that a dispensation is thereby granted from the natural law which prescribes fidelity to one's promise made to and accepted by God. Once such a promise is made to God, He obtains a right to that which is promised. In this way He becomes a creditor in relation to the vowmaker; while the vowmaker in a new and special way becomes a debtor of God.[67]

For the purpose of reconciling the apparent contradiction contained in the idea that a dispensation from a vow is a dispensation from the natural law, a further examination of the doctrine on the natural law reveals that it can operate *preceptively* (affirmatively), *prohibitively* (negatively), or *permissively*. The natural law operates preceptively when it prescribes something, for instance, that one must honor his parents. The same law operates prohibitively when it forbids something, for instance, that one should not blaspheme. Reason tells man that these norms are necessary for a good moral life.

The natural law operates permissively in two distinct ways, that is, in a negative way, or in a positive way. The natural law permits something in a negative way when it does not establish any given norms or directions for the use of some particular right. Thus the natural law admits that man should be free, but it does not prescribe that he must always be free. The determination of this matter is left to man to dispose of according to reason. The natural law permits something in a positive way when, without actually prescribing a particular mode of action, it

66 Ballerini-Palmieri, *Theologia Moralis*, I, 380.

67 Ballerini, Palmieri, *Theologia Moralis*, I, 381.

nevertheless favors that mode of action. This is generally had in mind when something is said to be according to the natural law, or to have a foundation in the natural law, as for example, that a son should be heir to his father who dies intestate. It is true that the natural law does not prescribe such a mode of procedure; nevertheless, it does incline to such a mode of action as if it were, so to speak, the natural thing to do.[68]

When the doctrine just explained is applied to vows, it is obvious that the natural law operates preceptively. Some precepts of the natural law, however, bind antecedently to any act of the human will, as, for example, the obligation incumbent on all to be reverent to God; still other precepts of the natural law bind only subsequently to an act of consent by the human will. Thus a person is not bound by the natural law on marriage until he is actually married. So it is in the case of a vow. The natural law does not begin to bind any single individual until he has made a vow. The act of one's will through which the vow was made is the factor which causes the natural law to begin to obligate the vowmaker.[69]

Now the problem at hand is narrowed down to this: "Can a dispensation be granted from the precept of the natural law, when the obligation of that precept has depended on the previous consent of the human will?" In response it must be said that a dispensation cannot be granted *directly*. This means that a dispensation is impossible in the sense of its taking away the obligation of the natural law which dictates that a man be faithful to his

---

68 Suarez, *De Legibus*, lib. VI, c. XIV, n. 6; Ballerini-Palmieri, *Theologia Moralis*, I, 381.

69 Suarez, *De Legibus*, lib. VI, c. XIV, n. 7; Ballerini-Palmieri, *loc. cit.*

word.[70] It does not mean, however, that a dispensation from vows cannot be granted indirectly. But first let it be recalled that, once a vow is made, it is accepted by God; otherwise it would not be a vow. By thus accepting the vow God acquires a right to what is promised. Secondly, two wills enter into the making of a vow—one, that of a human being, the other, that of God.

In order to dissolve this contract by which the vowmaker obligates himself to God, it is necessary that both agree, or that a will superior to both enter into the matter to break the contract.[71] Obviously, there is no will superior to God's will. Hence, it would be quite impossible to obtain a relaxation of a vow, if God had not provided that certain of His representatives on earth were to have the power of remitting in His name obligations contracted through the making of vows. Thus, when one of these representatives on earth grants a dispensation from private vows, it is as if God were to say, "I will no longer hold you to your promise," or "I will not exact or enforce the performance of the obligation." It is similar to the manner in which men obtain a remission of those obligations which they have incurred with a fellow man.[72]

It is evident, therefore, that this dispensation is not a dispensation from the natural law precept. The vowmaker who receives such a dispensation cannot claim that he

---

70 Suarez, *ibid*, n. 8.

71 Suarez, *De Voto*, lib. VI, c. IX, n. 15.

72 Suarez, *De Legibus*, lib. VI, c. XIV, n. 11; *idem*, *De Voto*, lib. VI, c. IX, nn. 13-16; Salmanticenses, *Theologia Moralis*, tract. XVII, c. III, n. 78; Reiffenstuel, *Theologia Moralis* (2 vols., Mutinae, 1758), I, tract. II, *De Legibus*, dist, 4, q. 2, n. 27; Lehmkuhl, *Theologia Moralis*, I, n. 617; Wernz-Vidal, *De Rebus*, pars I, n. 557, p. 665; Vermeersch-Creusen, *Epitome*, II, n. 644; Rodrigo, *Praelectiones Theologico-morales Comillenses*, Tomus II, Tract. *De Legibus* (Santander: Sal Terrae, 1944), p. 346, n. 458 (hereafter cited as *De Legibus*).

was released from the obligation of being faithful to his promise made to God. Rather, God has remitted the promise to the vowmaker. It then becomes impossible for the vowmaker to keep his promise made to God, since the promise no longer exists. God has relinquished his acceptance of it.[73]

Hence, strictly considered, this is not a dispensation as a dispensation is ordinarily understood. It is rather the remission of a debt. From another point of view, it is the abrogation of a private law. A vow is a private law. When the vow ceases to exist, so also does the law. This cessation should be called an abrogation rather than a dispensation.

Suarez,[74] however, points out that in so far as God does not grant the remission of the vow personally, but through his duly authorized representatives on earth, these representatives can be called dispensers of God's favor, and the act of granting it can be called a dispensation.

At the same time, while one can call the remission of a vow the abrogation of a private law for a specific individual, nevertheless in relation to others who have similar vows which continue to bind it is properly called a dispensation, for though a vow of chastity, for example, may be relaxed for one particular vowmaker, it continues to bind all others who have made the same vow.[75]

---

73 St. Thomas: ". . . observare votum est de lege naturali, sed cessante obligatione voti non est observatio ejus de lege naturali."—*Sent. IV*, dist. 38, q. 1, art. 4, q. 1 ad 2. Suarez: "Lex . . . naturalis in praesenti est ut vota Deo reddantur, quae sicut non incipit obligare nisi postquam fit votum, ita non conservat obligationem (ut sic dicam) nisi durante voto; si autem votum semel factum auferatur, cessabit obligatio illius legis sine dispensatione in illa; hoc ergo fit per dispensationem voti."—*De Voto*, lib. VI, c. IX, n. 9.

74 *De Voto*, lib. VI, c. IX, n. 17.

75 Suarez, *loc. cit.*; Ballerini-Palmieri, *Theologia Moralis*, I, 383.

The explanation given above is the traditional explanation of the essence of a dispensation from vows. Other explanations are also to be found, but with a minimum of adherents. One of these theories maintains that a dispensation is merely a declaration or interpretation of the vow. It requires that the potential cause for the dispensation of the vow be present previous to the declaration, at the same time maintaining that the obligation ceases, not because of the declaration, but by reason of the cause.[76] This theory, however, disregards the fact that in a dispensation the obligation of the vow continues until the moment the dispensation is granted, and ceases with the granting of the dispensation. It presupposes that the obligation of the vow has already ended or has never begun. Moreover, a dispensation requires jurisdiction in him who grants it; a declaration merely requires an understanding of the circumstances and the doctrine on the obligation of vows.[77]

Another form of the same theory maintains that in a dispensation from vows the Church merely states or declares that a particular vow has become less pleasing to God, and hence has ceased to bind. This, however, places limits around the power of the Church to dispense, which, as a matter of fact, she does not observe. For not infrequently the Church dispenses when circumstances are such that it would be better and more perfect objectively to continue the observance of the vows.[78]

Another theory claims that in every vow there is contained a condition which empowers the vowmaker's super-

---

76 Fagnanus, *Commentaria in Quinque Libros Decretalium* (4 vols., Venetiis, 1708), lib. I, *De Electione*, c. XXII, n. 24.

77 Cf. Suarez, *De Voto*, lib. VI, c. IX, n. 4.

78 Cf. Lehmkuhl, *Theologia Moralis*, I, n. 617.

ior to grant a dispensation.[79] This theory, however, lacks a foundation both in fact and in law. It will be on only a rare occasion that a person will consciously make a vow under such a condition. Furthermore, there is no law which prescribes that it be done, or which prohibits vows from being made in an absolute manner.

As a conclusion to this chapter, it is pertinent to recall that a dispensation from vows differs from an annulment of vows. A dispensation requires jurisdictional power, while an annulment requires dominative power. A dispensation is given in God's name. An annulment is given in one's own name.[80] The distinction between a dispensation and a commutation must also be kept in mind. A dispensation removes the obligation of the vow completely, while a commutation links the obligation with some more perfect, equally perfect, or less perfect object matter.[81]

---

79 " . . nisi superior obligationem sustulerit," or "nisi superior ex iusta causa contradicat." Cf. Lehmkuhl, *Theologia Moralis,* I, n. 617.

80 Prümmer, *Theologia Moralis,* II, n. 420.

81 Noldin-Schmitt, *Theologia Moralis,* II, n. 236.

HISTORICAL SYNOPSIS

CHAPTER II

THE DOCTRINE ON DISPENSATION FROM VOWS PRIOR TO THE COUNCIL OF TRENT (1545-1563)

ARTICLE I. THE DOCTRINE BEFORE GRATIAN

The history of the subject of dispensation from vows before the time of Gratian is obscure and difficult to ascertain. There were dispensations from the laws of the Church from the earliest times.[1] It is also certain that vows ceased during these times, but whether they ceased through what is now recognized as a dispensation cannot be said with absolute certainty. Thomassinus (1619-1695) pointed out that though Edward, King of England (1041-1066), could have obtained from his own bishop a dispensation from a pilgrimage vow, he nevertheless approached the Holy See for the favor of being released from his promise to visit Rome. Pope Leo IX (1049-1054) relaxed the vow for the reason proposed, namely, that the Kingdom of England was in imminent danger, and the King's presence was required at home. The Pontiff, however, imposed on the King the obligation of building a monastery at Westminster.[2]

For the period before Gratian, it can be said that dispensations from law in general were granted with increasing frequency after the pontificate of Leo IX. It can also be said that included among these dispensations were dis-

[1] Stiegler, *Dispensation, Dispensationswesen, und Dispensationsrecht im Kirchenrecht* (Mainz, 1901), p. 24 (herefater cited as *Dispensation*).

[2] *Vetus et Nova Ecclesiae Disciplina circa Beneficia et Beneficiarios* (10 vols., Magontiaci, 1787), pars II, lib. III, c. 27, n. 6.

pensations from vows.[3] The actual practice, however, of granting dispensations from vows was somewhat advanced beyond the theory underlying the practice. Hence, though it can be stated that the granting of a dispensation from religious vows was reserved in practice to the Holy See, yet the very question of the possibility of granting a dispensation from religious vows and non-religious vows was disputed even at a later period.[4]

It has been stated that in the earlier centuries of the Church the Fathers of the Church were acquainted with the practice of the granting of a dispensation from a vow, but that it was called an absolution.[5] Brys, however, maintains that historically dispensation and absolution are two distinct ideas.[6]

Hence it seems safe to say that prior to Gratian there was no express law determining the jurisprudence on dispensation from vows. Custom, however, seems to have established a foundation for the laws which were subsequently established in this matter.

ARTICLE II. IN THE *Decree of Gratian*

Since Gratian did not speak about dispensations from vows, his doctrine on this matter has to be derived from his teaching on the dispensing power of the Roman Pontiff. For if the Roman Pontiff cannot dispense from vows, *a fortiori* his subordinates cannot dispense.

---

[3] Stiegler, *Dispensation*, p. 288; cf. Van Hove, *De Privilegiis—De Dispensationibus* (Mechliniae-Romae: H. Dessain, 1939), n. 314 (hereafter cited as *De Dispensationibus*); Brys, *De Dispensatione in Iure Canonico praestertim apud Decretistas et Decretalistas usque ad Medium Saeculum Decimum Quartum* (Brugis: Car. Beyaert, 1925), pp. 61-72 (hereafter cited as *De Dispensatione*).

[4] Stiegler, *Dispensation*, p. 225.

[5] Prümmer, *Theologia Moralis*, II, 355.

[6] *De Dispensatione*, p. 17.

Although Gratian recognized the fact that the Roman Pontiff possessed universal power to dispense, he nevertheless did not consider the object of that power to be universal. Rather, he regarded it to be limited to the realm of ecclesiastical law, the divine law being excluded from its exercise.[7] To him the divine law as it governed man consisted of the law of the Old Testament and the law of the Gospel.[8] From this law no dispensation could be granted.[9] This divine natural law had its origin with the creation of man. For this reason it enjoyed a primacy of time and dignity over all other laws. Throughout the course of time it had not changed, but had remained immutable.[10]

Gratian, however, perceived the difficulty which arose from the definition he had given of the natural law, and from the immutability which he attributed to it. He realized that he had defined the natural law as that which is contained in the Old and New Testaments. But he also realized that in many ways the New Law contradicted the Old Law. He knew that in the Old Law it had been prescribed that, after begetting a male child, a woman was not to enter the temple for forty days, and that after begetting a female child, a woman was not to enter the temple for eighty days.[11] He was aware of the fact that this law no longer obliged, and that a woman was not

---

7 *Brys, De Dispensatione*, p. 80.

8 *Dictum Gratiani* ad c. 1, D. I: "Ius naturae est, quod in lege et evangelio continetur."

9 *Dict. Grat.* ad c. 1, D. XIII: "Item adversus ius naturale nulla dispensatio admittitur."

10 *Dict. Grat.* ad c. 1, D. V: "Naturale ius inter omnia primatum obtinet et tempore et dignitate. Cepit enim ab exordio rationalis creaturae, nec variatur tempore, sed immutabile permanet."

11 Lev. XII, 5.

prohibited from entering a church immediately after childbirth.

He solved this difficulty by distinguishing between those laws in the Testaments which belong to the natural law and those which do not. He pointed out that all the moral precepts of the Testaments belonged to the natural law. Thus the precept not to kill was a moral precept. On the other hand mystical precepts, such as the various laws regulating the sacrifice, belonged to the natural law only in their moral sense. This meant that only the moral content of the mystical precepts belonged to the natural law. The external expression, however, of that moral content as contained in the mystical precepts, and the external manner of observing the moral content of such mystical precepts, did not belong to the natural law. Thus the various regulations for offering sacrifice were merely external modes of observing the natural moral obligation of offering worship to God. The external form of the moral content of a mystical precept did not belong to the natural law, and hence it could be changed. The moral content of the mystical precept did belong to the natural law and, in this respect, the mystical precept could not be changed.[12]

Gratian also admitted another exception to the rigorous immutability of the natural law. Thus, while he denied that a dispensation could be granted from the natural law, he immediately qualified this a dispensation could not be granted from the natural law except when one must

---

[12] *Dict. Grat.* post c. 3, D. VI: "Sunt enim in lege quedam moralia, ut non occides et cetera, quedam mistica utpote sacrifitiorum precepta, et alia his similia. Moralia mandata ad naturale ius spectant atque ideo nullam mutabilitatem recepisse monstrantur. Mistica vero, quantum ad superficiem, a naturali iure probantur aliena, quantum ad moralem intelligentiam, inveniuntur sibi annexa; ac per hoc, etsi secundum superficiem videantur esse mutata, tamen secundum moralem intelligentiam mutabilitatem nescire probantur."

necessarily choose between two evils.[13] This exception, it will be seen, was later used by Glossators and Commentators to justify the dispensation from a vow.

Article III. In the Decretists

Except Rufinus, the earlier decretists added nothing to the doctrine of Gratian.[14] Rufinus (*Summa* written about 1157--1159), however, while accepting the teaching of Gratian on the natural law, limited somewhat the extent of that term and thus made more frequent dispensation possible. He did this by omitting Gratian's distinction regarding mystical precepts "in quantum ad superficiem et in quantum ad moralem intelligentiam." Instead, he classified all mystical or ceremonial precepts as being beyond the limits of the natural law. Hence they were mutable and subject to dispensation.[15]

Rufinus, however, continued the doctrine of Gratian, namely, that a dispensation could not be granted from the moral precepts of the Testaments, for these constituted the natural law. He cited as an example of this immutability of the natural law, and of the consequent impossibility of the granting of a dispensation, a man who had made a vow in an absolute manner.[16] From such laws one could not

---

[13] *Dict. Grat.* ad c. 1, D. XIII: "Item adversus naturale ius nulla dispensatio admittitur; nisi forte duo mala ita urgeant ut alterum eorum necesse sit elegi."

[14] Brys, *De Dispensatione*, p. 122.

[15] *Die Summa Decretorum des Magister Rufinus*, hrsg. von D. Heinrich Singer (Paderborn, 1902), *ad dict. Grat.* ad c. 1, D. V, p. 16 (hereafter cited as *Summa Decretorum*).

[16] Ad. c. 6, C.I. q. 7: ". . . indispensabilia sunt illa, quorum mandata vel interdicta ex lege moralium, vel evangelica vel apostolica institutione principaliter pendent, scilicet ut qui absolutè votum fecerit reddat . . ."—*Summa Decretorum*, p. 234.

deviate without committing sin even though the exigencies of the times or any like necessity might seem to justify such deviation. The only exception he admitted was invincible ignorance. As a reason for this rigorous immutability of the foregoing statutes, Rufinus pointed out the fact that the law on keeping one's vow was a part of the natural law, and hence no dispensation could be admitted.[17]

The later decretists accepted the doctrine of Rufinus with very little change. They considered as impossible the granting of a dispensation from a vow which was made in an absolute manner, inasmuch as the law which required the fulfillment of such vows belonged to the natural law, as this was expressed in the Old Testament: "When thou has made a vow to the Lord, thy God, thou shalt not delay to pay it: because the Lord thy God will require it. And if thou delay, it shall be imputed to thee for a sin."[18] Also, "If thou has vowed anything to God, defer not to pay it. For an unfaithful and foolish promise displeaseth him: but whatsoever thou hast vowed pay it. And it is much better not to vow than after a vow not to perform the things promised."[19] Thus Huguccio (☩ ca. 1210) declared that a vow made in an absolute manner was not susceptible of a dispensation. Accordingly, he maintained that the Roman Pontiff could not grant a dispensation to one in Holy Orders for the purpose of permitting him to contract a valid marriage or to utilize a previously contracted invalid marriage. The obstacle was not the Sacred Orders as such, but the vow by

---

17 Ad. c. 6, C. I, q. 7, *Summa Decretorum*, p. 234.

18 Deut. XXIII, 21.

19 Eccles. V, 3-4.

which one in Sacred Orders was perpetually bound to continence.[20]

In conclusion to the treatment of the doctrine on the dispensation from vows as maintained during the period of the decretists, it can be said that the theory of that time had still not devised an understanding of the possibility of such a dispensation. This impasse was due to the fact that the obligation of a vow was seen to rest on the natural law, and that no explanation was discovered of the manner in which a dispensation from the latter could be granted.

Article IV. In the Decretals and Decretalists

After the first half of the twelfth century, the Roman Pontiffs were more frequently consulted for authoritative solutions of various canonical problems than ever before in history. The primary cause for this increased recourse to Rome was the change which had taken place at that time through the more manifest recognition of the supreme authority of the Roman Pontiff over the universal Church. Whereas this fact had always been recognized in theory, still the conclusions which followed from this doctrine had only infrequently been put in practice. At that time, however, the Roman Pontiff began to receive increasing practical recognition of his supreme authority from the whole Catholic world.

20 ". . . cum iam promotis ad sacrum ordinem non posset Romanus Pontifex dispensare vel constituere ut contrahant matrimonium vel contracto uterentur; non dico ratione ordinis, sed ratione voti, quo obligati sunt ad perpetuo continendum. Contra quod votum Papa non posset dispensare vel restituere cum ad reddendum votum quisque teneatur ex iure naturali, unde propheta: vovete et reddite."—Text found in Brys, *De Dispensatione,* p. 130.

To this cause must be added a closely related fact which constitutes the second cause for the more frequent appeal to Rome for solutions of problems in Canon Law. With the Decree of Gratian the science of Canon Law received a tremendous impetus to further advancement both intensively and extensively. Especially worthy of note in this regard is the fact that several of the Roman Pontiffs of that period were distinguished for their learning in this subject. The first Pontiff of this period, Alexander III (1159-1181), was outstanding for his canonical acumen, as he had been a student of Gratian.

The time between this point in the middle of the twelfth century and the Council of Trent (1545-1563) constitutes the period in the history of dispensation from private vows next to be examined in this study. In this period the doctrine on the dispensation from vows was definitely established in the general form which it retains even until today.[21]

A. *The Possibility of a Dispensation from Vows Is Established*

In the review of the doctrine on dispensations from vows during the period of the decretists, it was seen that the possibility of a dispensation from a vow was not admitted for the reason that the obligation of a vow was acknowledged as resting on the natural law, from which no dispensation could be granted. In the period of the decretalists, however, the absolute immutability of the natural law in the sense of its not yielding to a dispensation even in an individual instance was no longer maintained.

---

21 Van Hove, *Prolegomena* (2. ed., Mechliniae-Romae: H. Dessain, 1945), p. 349.

The extent and scope of the natural law likewise was appraised as comprising a more restricted sphere.[22]

Of fundamental importance in the matter of dispensation from vows are the decretals of Alexander III. The latter frequently treated of this subject in his decretals, and in a manner which very patently suggested the granting of a relaxation of vows. Thus he allowed a girl having a vow of chastity to contract marriage.[23] In a decretal to the Bishop of Exeter in England concerning subdeacons who had married, Alexander advised the Bishop to inquire into the past life of the clerics. If it had been beyond reproach, the subdeacons were to be compelled to leave the women, or to dismiss them. But if the subdeacons' life prior to the marriage had been profligate, or if it might be feared that they would fall into worse evil by being compelled to separate from the women, they were to be left unmolested.[24] In another decretal, to the Bishop of Seville in Spain, Alexander denied to deacons the liberty he had permitted the Bishop in the preceding decretal to grant to the subdeacons. Following that he added that the delinquency of subdeacons who had married could be ignored, if the previous life of the subdeacon was such that it had to be feared that greater evil would result from forcing him to separate from the woman. The reason given for this was that an evil could be tolerated, if its

---

22 Brys, *De Dispensatione*, pp. 198-199.

23 *Comp.* I, c. 8, IV, 6; c. 5, X, *qui clerci vel voventes matrimonium contrahere possunt*, IV, 6—Jaffé, *Regesta Pontificum Romanorum ab condita Ecclesia ad annum post Christum* MCXCVIII (2. ed. by Kaltenbrunner (33-590), Ewald (590-882), and Löwenfeld (882-1198) referred to as: JK, JE, JL, Lipsiae, 1885-1889), JL. n. 14165.

24 *Comp.* I, c. 3, IV, 6: Si "antea dissolutae vitae fuerunt, aut illis quas habent dismissis in deteriora lapsuri creduntur, id poterit dissimulari."

toleration served the avoidance of a greater evil. Alexander frequently during his reign also decreed that pilgrimage vows could be redeemed and commuted.[25]

The decretals of Alexander III, which have just been noted, were issued between 1159-1181. An examination will now be made of the manner in which they were received and explained by the decretalists.

Preliminary, however, to this examination, it should be noted that Alexander III regarded a solemn vow as a diriment impediment to marriage and a simple vow as a prohibitive impediment to marriage.[26] Another modification of doctrine, worthy of note for a better understanding of what is to follow, is the distinction of vows into *voluntary* and *necessary* vows. This was proposed by a few decretists, and by all the decretalists. A voluntary vow was one which was made concerning a matter which previous to the vow could be done or left undone apart from any commission of sin. A necessary vow, on the other hand, was one which was made at baptism, e.g., to keep the faith. All the decretalists admitted that a dispensation from necessary vows was impossible.[27]

When the decretals of Alexander III were analyzed by subsequent canonists, they gave rise to much discussion. Thus it was disputed whether the dissimulation which Alexander permitted the Bishop to exercise in the case of the subdeacon, was a tacit consent which excused the subdeacon from sin, or a tacit dissent which did not excuse

---

25 *Comp*, I, c. 1, III, 29; c. 1, X, *de voto et voti redemptione*, III, 34—JL, n. 13916; *Comp*. I, c. 2, III, 29; c. 2, X, *de voto et voti redemptione*, III, 34 (an. 1166-1167)—JL, n. 11339.

26 *Comp*. I, c. 6, IV, 6; c. 3, X, *qui clerici vel voventes matrimonium contrahere possunt*, IV, 6—JL, n. 13162.

27 Hostiensis, *Summa Aurea* (Venetiis, 1570), ad c. 1, X, *de voto et voti redemptione*, III, 34, n. 2 (hereafter cited as *Summa*).

him from sin. Both Tancred (✝ 1235) and Ioannes Teutonicus (✝ 1245) maintained that Alexander merely allowed the parties to live in mortal sin, and that there was no authorization of a dispensation.[28] Damasus (fl. 1215), however, taught that the permission which was granted to the subdeacon to remain with his spouse involved a dispensation. This opinion was later commonly accepted by the decretalists.[29]

Another explanation regarding Alexander's policy towards the subdeacons suggested that there was no vow connected with the reception of the subdiaconate, and instead that continence was prescribed by an ecclesiastical constitution. Hence, it was affirmed, when the Roman Pontiff granted a dispensation to clerics promoted to the subdiaconate, it was not a dispensation from a vow but rather from an ecclesiastical constitution. Vincent of Spain (✝ ca. 1240), while admitting that some canonists taught the doctrine just described, expressed his own idea as follows: A cleric who in his promotion to the subdiaconate made a vow of continence would be bound by that vow. A subsequent dispensation granted by the Pope would be a dispensation from this vow. In the case of one who in his promotion to orders did not expressly pronounce a vow, a distinction had to be made. If that person was one skilled in the law, he would have to be considered as bound by the vow of continence; if he was ignorant of the law, he would be bound not by a vow but by an ecclesiastical constitution. If the Pope dispensed in this latter case, his act would be a dispensation from an ecclesiastical constitution, and not from a vow.[30]

---

28 Texts in Brys, *De Dispensatione*, p. 177.

29 Brys, *op. cit.*, p. 180.

30 Brys, *op. cit.*, p. 211.

The canonists who immediately followed Alexander rejected his policy on dispensing from vows. His division of vows into solemn and simple[31] was not admitted by Huguccio.[32] Huguccio regarded every vow of continence as a diriment impediment to marriage, the invalidating force of which was derived not from any external solemnity, but rather from the very nature of the vow itself. The solemnity was merely added for the purpose of proving the fact lest later it be called in doubt.[33]

A vow of continence could not be made the object of a dispensation even by the Pope, if the vow had been taken in a strict sense, since every one was bound by the natural law to fulfill a vow which he had made in the strict sense of a vow, that is, absolutely, and not merely conditionally. To those who objected that the commutation or redemption of a pilgrimage vow seemed to involve a dispensation, Huguccio and his followers replied there was no dispensation from such vows but merely a declaration of law, for when a person vowed to make a pilgrimage or to abstain from flesh meat, such a vow was always understood to have been made under the condition, "if I can do it conveniently."[34]

---

31 C. 3, X, *qui clerici vel voventes matrimonium contrahere possunt,* IV, 6.

32 The opinion of Huguccio is stated by an anonymous glossator of the *Summa* of Stephen Tournai (✠ 1203).—Text in Freisen, *Geschichte des kanonischen Eherechts, bis zum Verfall der Glossenliteratur* (2. ed., Paderborn, 1893), pp. 706-707.

33 Text in Freisen, *op. cit.*, p. 706.

34 Cf. St. Raymundus de Pennaforta: "Quidam dicunt simpliciter, quod nec etiam papa potest in votis dispensare, quia redditio voti est de iure naturali sive divino, contra quod non dispensetur—Hoc tenet Hugguccio, et eius sequaces. Si opponatur eis de commutatione, vel redemptione votorum . . . respondent quod non est ibi dispensatio, sed iuris declaratio, cum enim quis vovit peregrinari vel abstinere, subintelligitur si commode fieri potest."—*Summa* (Veronae, 1744), lib. I, tit. 8, § 9.

Robert of Flamborough (✝ after 1210), English by birth and a canon of St. Victor's in Paris,[35] also stated that a vow derived its binding force from the natural law, which he understood to be the law of the Old Testament and the Gospel. Thus a dispensation from a vow was impossible. After saying this, however, Robert pointed to the fact that the Holy Father had frequently granted dispensations to subdeacons to contract marriage. In solving this difficulty he suggested that perhaps the Holy Father acted on the opinion that a vow of continence did not invalidate marriage in so far as it is a vow, but only in virtue of the solemnity which the Church attached to it. Still, he inclined to his own opinion, expressing due respect to the Pope.[36]

With Huguccio, Robert denied that a vow of continence could be commuted, for a vow could only be commuted into what was better or equally as good. There was nothing, however, better than or equal to continence in the sight of God. Robert admitted the possibility of commuting other vows, such as pilgrimage vows and vows of abstinence. He insisted, however, that the commutation had to envisage something better or equally good. When this was impossible he maintained the vow could not be subjected to a commutation.[37]

Standing alone among the decretalists of that time, so many of whom denied the possibility of a dispensation from a vow, was Bernard of Pavia (✝ 1216), who taught that a dispensation from a simple vow of chastity could be granted, while he denied that a dispensation from a

35 Kuttner, "Pierre De Roissy and Robert of Flamborough"—*Traditio* (New York, 1943—), II (1944), 493.

36 Text in Freisen, *op. cit.*, p. 756.

37 Text in Freisen, *op. cit.*, p. 757.

solemn vow of chastity could be granted. Especially noteworthy is the fact that he spoke of relaxing a simple vow of chastity without the necessity of a redemption of it.[38]

At this point a review of the early decretalists shows that while it was admitted that voluntary vows, except the vows of chastity and religion, could be commuted, it was still denied that a dispensation from them could be granted. Even the acknowledged commutation and redemption[39] of vows were declared by many to be merely an equivalent declaration of law, or an interpretation of the law in a particular case. The idea of a dispensation was excluded. Contrary to the actual practice of Alexander III, they generally maintained that a vow of perpetual chastity could not be relaxed through a dispensation. It must not be overlooked, however, that in the same period Bernard of Pavia in his *Summa*, written between 1191-1198, admitted on the authority of a decretal by Alexander III[40] the possibility of a dispensation from the simple vow of chastity,

---

38 "Sunt autem quaedam vota redemptibilia, quaedam irredemptibilia, nam ecce vota quae consistant in faciendo et votum abstinentiae redimi possunt; votum autem continentiae, i.e. castitatis, si fuerit solemne, redimi non potest; si vero fuerit simplex, etiam sine redemptione solvitur ut maius malum vitetur . . ."—*Summa Decretalium*, ed. E. A. T. Laspeyres (Ratisbonae, 1861), lib. III, tit. XXIX, n. 3 (hereafter cited as *Summa Decretalium*).

39 The *Corpus Iuris Canonici* spoke of the redemption of a vow. In a general way redemption signified liberation from the obligation of a vow. But in a more specific sense it signified that particular type of commutation of a vow whereby in place of a personal action of the vowmaker something external to him was substituted, as for example, if the pilgrimage which one promised was commuted into an alms to be given to some worthy cause. At the time of the crusades this type of commutation was not infrequent when vows which had been made to go on the Crusade were commuted into a donation of some alms in support of the Crusade. Cf. Wernz-Vidal, *De Rebus*, pars I, n. 545, p. 646, nota 1.

40 *Comp.* I, c. 8, IV, 6; c. 5, X, *qui clerici vel voventes matrimonium contrahere possunt*, IV, 6—JL, n. 14166.

although he denied the possibility of a dispensation from the solemn vow of chastity.

The most outstanding opponent to the doctrine on the relaxation of vows as presented in the decretals of Alexander III was Huguccio. In 1198 a student of his ascended the throne of Peter as Innocent III, and it seems that his teachings were not a little influenced by the opinions of his former teacher.

Thus in 1202 Pope Innocent issued a decretal in which the rigor of Huguccio was still maintained. Writing to the Abbot and the convent of Subiaco, Pope Innocent declared that the Abbot could not dispense from the vow of poverty, for the renunciation of property as well as the custody of chastity were so intimately connected with the monastic rule that not even the Supreme Pontiff "*possit licentiam indulgere.*"[41]

Before discussing the manner in which this decretal was received by the canonists after 1202, it is important to note that Innocent included this decretal in a compilation of the decretals of the first twelve years of his reign, which he ordered Peter Collivaccino to make. It was called the *Compilatio Tertia.* The most significant characteristic about this compilation was the fact that this was the first authentic collection ever made, having been promulgated

---

41 *Comp.* III, c. 2, III, 27; c. 6, X, *de statu monachorum et canonicorum regularium,* III, 35: "Nec aestimet abbas, quod super habenda proprietate possit cum aliquo monacho dispensare; quia abdicatio proprietatis, sicut et custodia castitatis, adeo est annexa regulae monachali, ut contra eam nec Summus Pontifex possit licentiam indulgere."—Potthast, *Regesta Pontificum Romanorum inde ab anno post Christum natum MCXCVIII ad annum MCCCIV* (2 vols., Berolini, 1874-1875), n. 1734 (hereafter cited as Potthast).

through the Bull *Devotioni Vestrae,* on December 28, 1210.[42]

Though Huguccio had, with only the courage of his private convictions, but with amazing facility opposed the teaching of Alexander III, it was quite unlikely that anyone would directly oppose the teaching of Innocent III after his decretal had been included in the authentic collection. Alexander had made a reply in a particular case, taking sides in the matter, as had also Innocent III. But after Innocent's decretal had been included in an official collection, it then obtained a universal binding force. Hence his doctrine could not be lightly contradicted. Yet, it must be noted that Innocent did not declare that a dispensation could not be granted from a solemn vow because the solemn vow was binding in virtue of natural law. Instead he said that the vow could not be relaxed because of its intimate connection with the monastic rule.

From the time that this decretal had been issued it became the cardinal point in the discussion on the possibility of dispensing from vows. In his *Glossa Ordinaria* to the collection of Innocent's decretals, Tancred asserted on the authority of this particular decretal that the Pope could not permit a monk to marry,[43] or dispense from any vow of continence.[44]

---

[42] Exact date is not beyond all dispute. Cf. Kuttner, *Repertorium der Kanonistik* (1140-1234) (Città del Vaticano: Bibliotheca Apostolica Vaticana, 1937), p. 355, note 2.

[43] *Glos. Ord,* ad c. 3, *Comp.* III, II, 6, s. v. *non potest:* Dominus Papa dispensare non potest ". . . in his quae sunt contra substantiam monachorum, ut monachus haberet uxorem vel proprium . . ." Cf. text in Brys, *De Dispensatione,* p. 215, note 1.

[44] *Glos. Ord,* ad c. 1, *Comp.* I, III, 29, s. v. *recompensatio*: "Mihi videtur quod circa votum continentie nullus dispensare potest, quod asserit *Vincentius* . . . et expresse habetur extra III, *De statu monachorum,* cum ad monasterium (c. 6)." Cf. text in Brys, *De Dispensatione,* p. 214, nota 2.

Likewise, St. Raymond of Pennafort in his Summa (1218-1221?) declared there could be no dispensation from the vow of continence. He admitted, however, that a dispensation could be granted from voluntary vows, since actually the relaxation of pilgrimage vows and of vows of abstinence was not a dispensation, but an interpretation.[45]

About 1212-1213, however, Vincent of Spain (✝ ca. 1240) and Ioannes Teutonicus (✝ 1245) proposed a less rigorous understanding of Innocent's decretal of 1202. They admitted that while a monk remained a monk the Pope could not dispense him from his vows. But they contended that a monk could cease to be a monk, and that the Pope had power to bring this about. To substantiate this contention, they had recourse to a law in the Code of Justinian. They claimed that just as Justinian could grant juridical existence to something which had no juridical existence and juridical validity to something which was void, so, too, the Pope could grant a juridical existence to one who lacked it, i.e., he could make a person a monk, but he could likewise take away that juridical existence and thus cause a person to cease to be a monk.[46]

In 1234 Pope Gregory IX (1227-1241) promulgated his official collection of decretals to take the place of the collections which had come into existence since the time of Gratian. In this collection, prepared by St. Raymond of Pennafort (1175-1275), the superfluous decretals of the

---

45 Lib. I. tit. 8, § 9.

46 "Si enim, cum una in instrumentis stipulatio valida inveniatur, et aliis inutilibus suam noscitur praestare fortitudinem, quare non ex nostra lege huiusmodi stipulationibus robur accedat legitimum?"—C. (5, 13) 1. Cf. *Glos. Ord*, ad c. 6. X, *de statu monachorum et canonicorum regularium*, III, 35, s. v. *abdicatio proprietatis*; Brys, *Dispensatione*, p. 216.

past were omitted.[47] Among those omitted were the decretals of Alexander III in which he had permitted subdeacons to marry. But the decisive decretal of Innocent III[48] was included. This of course took a rigorous view on the possibility of granting a dispensation from religious vows.

The same rigorous understanding of this decretal was presented in the *Glossa Ordinaria* of Bernard of Parma (✝ 1266) as was presented by most of the authors who wrote prior to the Gregorian collection. He denied that the Pope could dispense a monk from his vows, or that the Pope could dispense from the vow of continence even outside religion. He considered this the true opinion in opposition to the other solutions offered by Ioannes Teutonicus and Vincent of Spain.[49]

From the time of Innocent IV (1243--1254) the common doctrine on dispensation from vows began to undergo a more radical change. Up until this time the decretals of Alexander III had influenced the decretalists to the point where they admitted that certain voluntary vows could be commuted and redeemed. Some decretalists denied that there was any trace of a dispensation in the decretals of Alexander, affirming that it was a mere declaration of law or interpretation. However, a few did regard these decretals as containing dispensations and in consequence of this

---

47 Gregorius IX, Bulla *Rex pacificus*, 5 sept. 1234: "Sane diversas constitutiones et decretales epistolas praedecessorum nostrorum . . . quarum aliquae propter nimiam similitudinem, et quaedam propter contrarietatem, nonnullae etiam propter sui prolixitatem, confusionem inducere videbantur, . . . illas in unum volumen resecatis superfluis providimus redigendas . . ."—This is the bull by which the decretals were promulgated. Text found in Freidberg edition of the Decretals of Gregory IX.

48 C. 6, X, *de statu monachorum et canonicorum regularium*, III, 35—Potthast, n. 1734.

49 Ad c. 6, X, *de statu monachorum et canonicorum regularium*, III, 35, s. v. *abdicatio proprietatis.*

fact declared that a dispensation was possible from all vows except solemn vows and the vow allegedly taken in the reception of subdiaconate. The decretal of Innocent III further accentuated this difficulty by stating explicitly that the Pope could not permit a monk to marry or to own property.[50]

Innocent IV, however, in his commentary on the decretals of Gregory IX admitted that a dispensation could be granted from every voluntary vow, except the vow of chastity. He also conceded that vows could be commuted. In regard to dispensing from a vow, though he denied that a dispensation could be granted from the vow of chastity, he did admit that the Pope could dispense a monk from his monastic vows. This apparent contradiction is removed after one examines the doctrine of Innocent on the nature and origin of the vows of a monk. He maintained that the Pope could dispense from all positive ecclesiastical law and since the surrendering of the right to property and the obligation of chastity had been added to the religious life by positive ecclesiastic law, the Pope could grant a dispensation permitting a monk to own property and to marry; for fundamentally a monk was "nihil aliud . . . quam solitarius tristis." Innocent IV, however, did not adhere to this doctrine without fear of error. He affirmed that this dispensation should not be granted without the presence of a cause to prompt it. Later he asserted that the dispensation could be granted only for a "magna et vera causa." If a monk were permitted to marry without a cause to prompt this permission, Innocent maintained the marriage would be valid for the sake of the woman

50 Cf. Brys, *De Dispensatione*, p. 218.

who was in good faith, but that the monk could not seek the marital *debitum*.[51]

Hostiensis († 1271), who followed the doctrine of Innocent IV very closely, likewise regarded a monk as "nihil aliud quam solitarius et tristis." Anything that was added beyond these essential points was added by positive law. The Pope, however, as the supreme legislator could obviously dispense from positive law. Hence he could allow a monk to possess goods and to contract marriage. This became clearer when it was recalled that the Pope conveyed to a religious community both its juridical nature and substance, and to the religious rule its authority. Therefore, just as he gave to a religious community its juridical nature and existence, so he could take these away, and with them the rule.[52]

However, before the Pope could grant such a dispensation, a proportionate cause had to be present. But even without such a cause a papal dispensation was regarded as valid for the sake of the party in good faith when the purpose of the dispensation was to permit the contracting of a marriage. When, however, the dispensation was granted from the vow of poverty, the absence of a cause invalidated

---

51 Cf. Brys, *De Dispensatione*, pp. 218-219 for the doctrine of Innocent IV.

52 "Monachus enim nihil aliud est quam solitarius et tristis. Quidquid ergo ultra hoc additum est, de jure positivo impositum est, ex quo apparet, quod Papa potest dispensare cum monacho, ut proprium habeat, vel uxorem ducat, cum nemini dubium sit, quin ipsam religionem sive ordinem et naturam, sive substantiam, quam dedit ordini, ex toto tollere possit, secundum D.N. Etenim omnis religionis regula a sua tantum auctoritate vires sumitur. Sicut ergo religionem et eius substantialia approbat, sic et ipsa tollere potest ut patet . . . His autem subtractis subtrahatur et regula." *Commentaria in Quinque Decretalium Libros* (5 vols. in 3, Venetiis, 1581), ad c. 6, X, *de statu monarchorum et canonicorum regularium* III, 35, s. v. *quia abdicatio* (hereafter cited as *Commentaria*).

the dispensation, for the lack of a dispensation could prove prejudicial to no one but him who requested the dispensation in bad faith.[53]

Hostiensis further pointed out that every vow was made under the condition "unless something else is more pleasing to God," according to the authority of an ecclesiastical superior. No one would deny that what was more pleasing to God should be done rather than that which was less pleasing. In this regard all things being equal, what was for the common good was preferentially more pleasing to God than what was for the good of an individual. So when the common good made a demand, the execution of this demand was something more pleasing to God than the accomplishment of the materially more perfect good of a single individual. Hostiensis fundamentally subscribed to this doctrine of Innocent IV. He disagreed with him, however, on one point. The Pontiff in his Commentary on the decretals, which he had made as private teacher, taught that a monk who had received a dispensation to contract marriage when there was no cause present for granting the dispensation could render but not petition for the marital *debitum*. Hostiensis, however, denied this because, he said, it implied that the marriage in this case was only verified for the woman.[54]

Hostiensis, moreover, did not regard a vow of chastity as being of its very nature a diriment impediment to marriage, and hence incapable of being the object of a dispensation. He maintained that the diriment force which any vow obtained was derived from the ecclesiastical authority

---

53 Hostiensis, *Commentaria*, ad c. 6, X, *de statu monachorum et canonicorum regularium*, III, 35, s. v. *pontifex*, n. 29.

54 *Ibid.*, ad n. 32, he added: "matrimonium claudicare non potest."

which declared its diriment effects.[55] If, however, a vow of chastity did not by its very nature invalidate a marriage, then the one obstacle which for so long had prevented the granting of a dispensation from a vow of chastity was removed. For if the vow of chastity was not of its very nature a diriment impediment to marriage, then it was no different from other vows from which a dispensation could be granted. Moreover, the exception which Innocent IV had made for a vow of chastity, by declaring that a dispensation could not be granted from such a vow, now appears to have been without foundation.

Having established that a vow of chastity did not of its very nature invalidate a marriage, Hostiensis thus made it possible to include all vows of chastity among the other vows which such authors as Bernard of Pavia and Innocent IV had asserted were susceptible of dispensation. Hence, Hostiensis could assert that the Pope in the fullness of his power could dispense from *every* voluntary vow.[56]

Finally, Panormitanus (1386-1445 or 1453) stated that canonists generally held that the Pope could dispense from the vow of continence and from religious vows.[57]

Thus it was gradually acknowledged by the outstanding authors of the time that there were no vows which were not subject to the dispensatory power of the Roman Pontiff. The explanation, however, of what this dispensa-

---

55 *Summa* ad c. 5, X, *qui clerici vel voventes matrimonium contrahere possunt,* IV, 6, ad n. 3.

56 ". . . Papa de plentitudine potestatis in omni voto dispensare potest, quod ob initio voluntarium fuit . . ."—*Summa* ad c. 1, X, *de voto et voti redemptione,* III, 34, ad n. 16.

57 *Commentaria in Quinque Decretalium Libros* (5 vols. in 7, Venetiis, 1588), in c. 1, X, *de voto et voti redemptione,* III, 34, ad Glos. *si ibi* (hereafter cited as *Commentaria*).

tion was in its exact juridical nature was not to be offered until later.[58]

B. The Author of a Dispensation from Vows

The Roman Pontiff was regarded as having the fullness of power to dispense from all vows.[59] The residential bishop was likewise recognized as having the power to dispense from vows. In his letter to the Bishop of Exeter in England, Pope Alexander III declared that the "redemption" or "commutation" of a pilgrimage vow depended on the judgment of him who "presides." On the basis of this judgment the superior was to dispense.[60]

In the *casus* subjoined to the decretal by Bernard of Parma, Bernard concluded from this decretal that the Bishop could dispense from pilgrimage vows.[61] Hostiensis [62] and Panormitanus[63] also subscribed to this view, but they extended the bishop's power to all voluntary vows which were not reserved.

---

58 *Supra*, pp. 19-25; *infra*, pp. 57-58.

59 St. Thomas (1226-1274): "Dicendum quod quia Summus Pontifex gerit plenarie vicem Christi in tota Ecclesia, ipse habet plentitudinem potestatis dispensandi in omnibus dispensabilibus votis."—*Summa Theologica*, IIa, IIae, q. 88, art. 12, ad 3; Hostiensis: "Papa vero in omni voto voluntario dispensare potest, etiam in voto continentiae, ex magna tamen causa . . ."—*Commentaria* ad c. 1, X, *de voto et voti redemptione*, III, 34, s. v. *qui praesidet*.

60 C. 1, X, *de voto et voti redemptione*, III, 34: ". . . tibi respondemus, quod ab eius qui praesidet, pendet arbitrio, ut consideret diligentius et attendat qualitatem personae, et causam commutationis, scilicet ob id ex infirmitate, seu affluentia divitiarum contingat, an alia causa probabili peregrinatio, an recompensatio melior fuerit et Deo magis accepta; et secundum hoc debet exinde dispensare."—JL, n. 13916.

61 *Casus* ad c. 1, X, *de voto et voti redemptione*, III, 34: "Nota, quod circa votum peregrinationis potest episcopus dispensare."

62 *Summa* ad c. 1, X, *de voto et voti redemptione*, III, 34, ad n. 6; also in *Commentaria ad eumdem titulum*, s. v. *qui praesidet*.

63 *Commentaria, eodem loco.*

In addition to the bishops, superiors were also spoken of as having the power to dispense from vows.[64] Prelates inferior to bishops could not ordinarily dispense from vows unless they obtained a privilege in this regard,[65] or unless through some particular or special law they possessed episcopal jurisdiction over certain persons. In such circumstances they could be considered as coming under the term "*qui praesidet*" of the decretal, and hence could be regarded as authorized to dispense from vows.[66]

St. Thomas, speaking as a theologian, stated that all prelates inferior to the Roman Pontiff could dispense from all ordinary vows, that is, vows which were frequently made and for which, therefore, a dispensation was more often required.[67]

C. *A Cause Required for a Dispensation*

In his letter to the Bishop of Exeter in England, Alexander III pointed out that the author of the dispensation was to consider diligently the quality of the person and the reason for the commutation. He was to determine whether the commutation was sought due to the vow-

---

64 Hostiensis: "Episcopus vero et superior in omni voto voluntario . . . dispensare possunt."—*Summa* ad c. 1, X, *de voto et voti redemptione*, III, 34, ad n. 6.

65 Hostiensis, *Commentaria*, c. 1, X, *de voto et voti redemptione*, III, 34, s. v. *qui praesidet*.

66 Panormitanus: "Et potest dici quod ubicumque inferior praelatus haberet de iure speciali ius episcopale in personis, quod tunc ista litera stabit proprie ut quilibet praesidens, seu habens iurisdictionem episcopalem, possit dispensare in votis, sicut episcopus, quia talis potest exercere iura episcopalia pro hoc."—*Commentaria*, ad c. 1, X, *de voto et voti redemptione*, III, 34, *ad Glos. quod Episcopi*.

67 "Aliis autem inferioribus praelatis committitur dispensatio in votis quae communiter fiunt et indigent frequenti dispensatione, ut habeant de facili homines ad quem recurrant."—*Summa Theologica*, IIa, IIae, q. 88, art. 12, ad 3.

makers infirmity or whether the vowmaker in view of his abundant wealth wished to redeem the vow through the performance of some work of charity. Having done this, the superior was to decide which was more pleasing to God—a commutation of the vow into a shorter pilgrimage, or the redemption of the vow through the performance of some work of charity.[68]

But a cause was necessary not only when the dispensation was granted by a bishop. The presence of a cause was required also when a dispensation was granted by the Pope.[69] This cause was required not only for the licitness but also for the validity of the dispensation even when the dispensation was granted by the Roman Pontiff.[70] When the object of the dispensation was a religious vow, a graver cause was required than for the dispensation from other vows.[71]

Various causes were accepted as sufficient for a dispensation from vows. Thus the fact that a vow had been made in the tender age of youth was accepted by Alexander III as at least a partial cause for granting a dispensation from a pilgrimage vow.[72] Bernard of Parma cites Tancred for the opinion that a vow made before one's fifteenth year was invalid unless the person was "doli

68 C. 1, X, *de voto et voti redemptione*, III, 34; cf. also Hostiensis, *Commentaria in eodem titulo*, s. v. *affluentia*; and Panormitanus, *Commentaria in eodem loco*, not. 1.

69 Hostiensis: "Papa de plentitudine potestatis in omni voto dispensare potest, quod ab initio voluntarium fuit; peccat si sine causa . . ."—*Summa*, ad c. 1, X, *de voto et voti redemptione*, III, 34, ad n. 6

70 Hostiensis, *Commentaria* ad c. 6, X, *de statu monachorum et canonicorum regularium*, III, 35.

71 Panormitanus, *Commentaria* ad c. 6, X, *de statu monachorum et canonicorum regularium*, III, 35, not. 21.

72 C. 2, X, *de voto et voti redemptione*, III, 34 (an. 1166-1167)—JL, n. 11339.

capax" or unless the vow was ratified after the fifteenth year had been attained.[73] Hostiensis added that although a vow could be relaxed on account of the youthful age of the vowmaker when he made the vow, it remained with the power of the superior to commute or redeem the vow at any time.[74] Panormitanus, however, opposed the Glossator on this point by stating that a vow was binding even though made *in puerili aetate,* but that a commutation of the same could be more easily obtained.[75]

The avoidance of a greater evil was also accepted as a sufficient cause for dispensing from the vow of chastity when the purpose of granting the dispensation was to allow the vowmaker to contract marriage. The likelihood that the vow would be violated outside of marriage, if not in an illicit marriage, was sufficient reason to prompt the relaxing of the obligation derived from the vow.[76] This doctrine is found in a decretal of Alexander III to the Bishop of Lucca. It concerned a girl who, as a means of breaking an engagement with a man whom she feared to marry, had made a simple vow of chastity. Despite the fact of having taken the vow she did not enter religion, neither did she wear the garment of one with a vow. She was consequently in danger of violating her newly accepted obligation unless she was permitted to marry. Accordingly, she was granted this permission. The canonists considered the causes for this dispensation to have been the fact that the girl was

[73] *Glos. Ord,* ad c. 2, X, *de voto et voti redemptione,* III, 34, s. v. *in puerili aetate.*

[74] *Commentaria* ad c. 2, X, *de voto et voti redemptione,* III, 34, s. v. *in puerili aetate.*

[75] *Commentaria* ad c. 2 X, *de voto et voti redemptione,* III, 34, s. v. *in puerili aetate.*

[76] C. 5, X, *qui clerici vel voventes matrimonium contrahere possunt,* IV, 6—JL, 14166. Cf. *Glos. ord. ad eundem,* s. v. *non postponas.*

young and under suspicion[77] and that she had made the vow while in an agitated frame of mind.[78]

The cessation of the impulsive or accessory cause on which the vow was founded was also regarded as a sufficient cause for the granting of a dispensation from a vow.[79] Panormitanus pointed out that if the final cause for the vow had ceased, the vow itself had ceased and a dispensation or commutation would be unnecessary.[80]

Finally, the common good was looked on as furnishing a sufficient cause for dispensing from even religious vows and the vow of chastity.[81]

D. Reserved Vows

The number of vows which were considered to be reserved during the period of the decretalists was never clearly stated or unanimously agreed upon.

In his decretal to the Bishop of Norwich in 1167, Alexander III spoke of himself as the authority absolving the vowmaker from the vow. Since the petition was sent to Rome for this dispensation from a pilgrimage vow involving the Holy Land, it offers an early indication that this vow was reserved to the Holy See.[82] Another indication of this is presented in a decretal of Innocent III,[83] wherein the

---

77 Thus Goffredus de Trano (✠ 1245) and John Teutonicus (✠ 1245). Cf. Additio 6 ad *Glos. Ord.* ad c. 5, X, *qui clerici vel voventes matrimonium contrahere possunt*, IV, 6, s. v. *non postponas*.

78 *Glos. Ord., loc. cit.*

79 C. 7, X, *de voto et voti redemptione*, III, 34 (an. 1198)—Potthast, n. 48.

80 *Commentaria* ad c. 7, X, *de voto et voti redemptione*, III, 34, s. v. *cessante causa*.

81 Hostiensis, *Commentaria* ad c. 1, X, *de voto et voti redemptione*, III, 34, s. v. *melior*, n. 9; Panormitanus, *Commentaria* ad c. 6, X, *de statu monachorum et canonicorum regularium*, III, 35, not. 21.

82 C. 2, X, *de voto et voti redemptione*, III, 34.

83 C. 7, X, *de voto et voti redemptione*, III, 34 (an. 1198).

Bishop of Troyes was released from his vow to go to the Holy Land.

Later, Innocent III sent two decretals to the Archbishop of Canterbury respecting dispensations from vows involving a pilgrimage to the Holy Land.[84] In the first of these decretals the faculty was granted to dispense from a pilgrimage vow involving the Holy Land. But special note was made that it was to be executed by a religious and discerning man.[85] In the second decretal the Pope stated that the provisions of the previous decretal were to be regarded as general law. No one, however, was to claim the authority to dispense from a pilgrimage vow involving the Holy Land unless he was specially delegated to do this by the Holy See.[86]

The Glossator, Bernard of Parma, regarded this as the one case of a vow reserved to the Holy See.[87] He restricted it, however, to pilgrimage vows made for the protection of the Holy Land. Panormitanus likewise regarded this as the *unus casus reservatus Papae.* Similarly he maintained that if the pilgrimage vow was merely a devotional one it could be commuted. He also looked on

---

84 Cc. 8, 9, X, *de voto et voti redemptione,* III, 34 (an. 1200)—Potthast 1137.

85 "Unde per viros religiosos et providos dispensationes huiusmodi volumus provideri."—c. 8, *de voto et voti redemptione,* III, 34.

86 ". . . illis autem solummodo ius hoc exsequendum incumbit, qui super hoc mandatum nostrum receperint a sede apostolica speciale."—c. 9, X, *de voto et voti redemptione,* III, 34.

87 "Ecce hic unum mirabile, quod est ius . . . , ut dispensetur in voto cum debilibus et huiusmodi, et tamen eius executio non permittitur nisi cui Papa specialiter committit. Quod tamen restrigendum est circa votum huiusmodi scilicet, pro succursu terrae sanctae emissum. Ergo cum hic Papa sibi dispensationem reservet, in aliis votis episcopis dispensationem indulget."—*in eodem titulo,* s. v. *incumbit.*

the pilgrimage vow to visit the tomb of St. James as a non-reserved vow.[88]

Hostiensis, however, in his *Commentaria* written between 1270 and 1271, attributed to the bishop the power to dispense from all voluntary vows "excepto voto crucis, sive, transmarino, et excepto voto continentiae, et exceptis aliis substantialibus regulae."[89] St. Thomas Aquinas [90] spoke of the major vows being reserved. Among these major vows he placed the vow of continence, and the pilgrimage vow involving the Holy Land. The other vows which were more common and hence required a dispensation more frequently could be relaxed by an inferior prelate.

When the teaching of Panormitanus that only one vow is reserved to the Holy See is compared with his teaching on the decretal of Alexander III to the Bishop of Exeter it reveals that he regarded the vow of chastity also as reserved to the Holy See.[91] In the addition to his commentary on this chapter he mentioned the following vows as reserved to the Holy See: the vows of religion, perpetual vows, and the pilgrimage vow involving the Holy Land. Prior to this in the same context, he spoke of the vow of continence as a reserved vow, basing his assertion on the general law that all *causae maiores* are reserved to the Holy See.[92]

Accordingly, until that time it appeared that only one vow was expressly reserved by law to the Holy see.[93] This

---

88 *Commentaria* ad c. 9, X, *de voto et voti redemptione,* III, 34, n. 3.

89 Ad c. 1, X, *de voto et voti redemptione,* III 34, s. v. *qui praesidet.*

90 *Summa Theologica,* IIa-IIae, q. 88, a. 12 ad 3.

91 *Commentaria* ad c. 1, *de voto et voti redemptione,* III, 34 ad *Glos. quod Episcopi,* n. 6.

92 Ad c. 1, X, *de voto et voti redemptione,* III, 34, ad *Glos. si ibi.* Cf. also c. 3, X, *de baptismo et eius effectu,* III, 42 (an. 1201)—Potthast, n. 1479.

93 C. 9, X, *de voto et voti redemptione,* III, 34.

was the pilgrimage vow involving the Holy Land, which as it appeared was reserved only when it was a vow to visit the Holy Land for the purpose of helping to defend it. There were other reserved vows, indeed, but their reservation rested on custom, or else on the fact that they were considered *causae maiores.*[94]

In 1478 Sixtus IV (1471-1484) issued a law in which he reserved to himself the faculty of dispensing from five different vows. This law, however, expressly limited only the faculties of confessors who received from the Holy See the power to dispense from vows. This decretal did not reserve any vows absolutely to the Holy See. Consequently, if this decretal was taken at its face value, the five vows reserved in it could still be the object of the dispensatory power of those whose faculty did not come from the Holy See.[95] Despite this fact, however, the five vows were considered after that time as reserved to the Holy See. They were: 1. the pilgrimage vow to visit the Holy Land; 2. to visit the tombs of the Apostles, Peter and Paul; 3. to visit the tomb of St. James in Compostella in Spain; 4. the vow of perpetual chastity; and 5. the vows of religion.

Against those who acted contrary to the reservations of this decretal Sixtus IV issued an excommunication to be incurred *ipso facto.* Absolution from this excommunication, except at the point of death, Sixtus reserved to himself.[96]

---

94 St. Thomas, *loc. cit.*; Panormitanus, *loc cit.* Cf. c. 3, X, *de baptismo et eius effectu*, III, 42: "Maiores ecclesiae causae . . . ad Petri sedem referendas intelligit . . ."

95 C. 5, *de poenitentiis et remissionibus*, V, 9, in Extravag. com.; cf. also Lessius, *De Iustitia et Iure*, lib. II, c. XL, n. 122.

96 "Et contra facientes eo ipso excommunicationis sententiam incurrant, a qua (nisi in mortis articulo constituti) ab alio quam Romano Pontifice absolvi non possint."—C. 5, *de poenitentiis et remissionibus*, V, 9, in Extravag. com.

CHAPTER III

THE DOCTRINE ON DISPENSATION FROM PRIVATE VOWS FROM THE COUNCIL OF TRENT (1545-1563) TO THE CODE OF CANON LAW (1918)

ARTICLE I. THE CONCEPT OF DISPENSATION FROM VOWS

After it was fully established that a dispensation could be granted from every vow, the canonists and the theologians turned to a further examination of the concept of a dispensation from vows. Whereas previously this concept was vague, it began now to be understood more clearly. Thus Suarez spoke of it in the terms of the power by which the dispensation was effected: "potestas circa vota ad auferendum, quando oportuerit, illorum obligationem."[1] Again, another author stated: "Qui habet auctoritatem dispensandi, poterit omnino votum relaxare absque eo quod loco voti aliquid adiungat voventi . . ."[2] Later the dispensation from vows was defined as the "ablatio seu remissio totalis obligationis votorum ob justam et rationabilem causam facta ab habente spiritualem jurisdictionem in personam voventis."[3]

Still later another point was added: "Dispensatio est voti obligationis per id inductae Dei nomine facta remissio."[4] This definition inserted a phrase which emphasized

1 *De Voto*, lib. VI, c. IX, n. 6.

2 Navarrus (Martinus de Azpilcueta), *Opera Omnia* (6 vols. Venetiis, 1618-1621), Tom. I, comment. XII, n. 63 (hereafter cited as Navarrus).

3 Reiffenstuel, *Ius Canonicum*, lib. III, tit. XXXIV, n. 20.

4 Schmalzgrueber, *Jus Ecclesiasticum Universum* (5 vols. in 12, Romae, 1843-1845), lib. III, tit. XXXIV, n. 101 (hereafter cited as *Jus Ecclesiasticum*).

the idea that no one could grant a dispensation from a vow in his own name, not even the Roman Pontiff, for the dispensing from a vow was an act which was to be performed in the name of God. Finally, a dispensation from a vow was defined most completely as a "remissio (condonatio, relaxatio) obligationis voto contractae nomine Dei per competentem Superiorem ecclesiasticum vi iurisdictionis spiritualis ex iusta causa legitime facta."[5]

Article II. The Active Subject of Dispensation

A. *Persons Authorized with Ordinary Power*

In the period after the Council of Trent the following were mentioned and regarded as having ordinary power to dispense from vows: the Roman Pontiff,[6] a General Council,[7] and the Grand Penitentiary of the Roman Pontiff, to whose office by reason of a commission of the Supreme Pontiff this power was perpetually attached and thus existed as an ordinary power.[8] Furthermore, this power was regarded as belonging also to Legates of the Pope and to Papal Nuncios in the provinces committed to their care.[9] Others enumerated as endowed with this power were

---

5 Wernz, *Ius Decretalium* (2. ed., 6 vols., Romae et Prati, 1906-1913), III, n. 583 (hereafter cited as *Ius Decretalium*). Cf. De Angelis, *Praelectiones Juris Canonici* (5 vols. in 9, Romae, 1877-1891), Vol. II, lib. III, tit. XXXIV, p. 152 (hereafter cited as *Praelectiones*).

6 Suarez, *De Voto*, lib. VI, c. X, n. 2; St. Alphonsus, *Theologia Moralis*, lib. III, n. 256; Santi, *Praelectiones*, lib. III, tit. XXXIV, n. 16.

7 Salmanticenses, *Theologia Moralis*, tract. XVII, c. III, n. 86.

8 Suarez, *ibid.*, n. 10; Salmanticenses, *loc. cit.*; Leurenius, *Forum Ecclesiasticum in quo Jus Ecclesiasticum Universum Explanatur* (5 vols. in 3, Venetiis, 1729), Vol. III, tit. XXXIV, c. II, n. 904 (hereafter cited as *Forum Ecclesiasticum*); De Angelis, *Praelectiones*, *loc. cit.*

9 Suarez, *loc. cit.*; Tamburini, *Theologia Moralis* (3 vols. in 2, Venetiis, 1748), Vol. I, lib. III, c. XVI, § 4, n. 4; De Angelis, *loc. cit.*

archbishops and bishops in their territories,[10] the cathedral chapter when the episcopal see was vacant,[11] and, as some authors specifically mentioned, the vicar capitular who succeeded the chapter in this power.[12] Finally, the power to dispense from vows was attributed to prelates lesser than bishops in virtue of a possessed episcopal power, or, as it was also called, quasi-episcopal power in the external forum,[13] and, as some required in addition to the quasi-episcopal power, a privilege,[14] a custom, or a pontifical indult.[15] Among the prelates enjoying quasi-episcopal jurisdiction, specific mention is made of abbots who rule over independent territories,[16] and of exempt religious prelates.[17]

The extent of the archbishop's power to dispense from vows was much discussed after the Council of Trent. It was common doctrine that he could dispense his own

---

10 Suarez, *ibid*, n. 3; Navarrus, Tom. I, comment. XII, n. 75; Reiffenstuel, *Ius Canonicum*, lib. III, tit. XXXIV, n. 29; Schmalzgrueber, *Jus Ecclesiasticum*, lib. III, tit. XXXIV, n. 103.

11 Tamburini, *loc. cit.*; Salmanticenses, *Theologia Moralis*, tract. XVII, c. III, n. 86; Ferraris, *Prompta Bibliotheca Canonica, Juridica, Moralis, Theologica, nec non Ascetica, Polemica, Rubricistica, Historica* (8 vols., Parisiis, 1852-1857), s. v. "Votum", art. III, n. 70 (hereafter cited as *Prompta Bibliotheca*); Lehmkuhl, *Theologia Moralis*, I, n. 472.

12 Ferraris, *loc. cit.*; Lehmkuhl, *loc. cit.*; Bouix, *Tractatus de Episcopo* (2. ed., 2 vols. in 1, Parisiis, 1873), Vol. II, pars V, c. XXIII, § II, prop. 9.

13 Lessius, *De Iure et Iustitia Compendium* (Duaci, 1634), super quaestione 88 D. Thomae, *de voto*, q. XI, n. 3; Schmalzgrueber, *Jus Ecclesiasticum*, lib. III, tit. XXXIV, n. 103.

14 Suarez, *De Voto*, lib. VI, c. X, nn. 13-15; Wernz, *Ius Decretalium*, III, n. 584.

15 Suarez, *loc. cit.*; Navarrus, Tom. I, comment. XII, n. 75.

16 Leurenius, *Forum Ecclesiasticum*, lib. III, tit. XXXIV, q. 904; Salmanticenses, *Theologia Moralis*, tract. XVII, c. III, n. 86.

17 Leurenius, *loc. cit.*; Salmanticenses, *loc. cit.*; Ferraris, *Prompta Bibliotheca*, s. v. "Votum", art. III, n. 74; De Angelis, *Praelectiones*, lib. III, tit. XXXIV, n. 152.

subjects, but it was disputed whether he had the power to dispense from the vows of the subjects of his suffragans. It was generally accepted that he could not do this when he was not making a visitation of his suffragan's diocese.[18] If, however, an appeal was made to the archbishop by the subject of a suffragan who had been denied a dispensation unjustly, it was held as common doctrine by Ferraris († ca. 1763) that the archbishop could dispense.[19]

It was the common opinion, also, that even on the visitation of a suffragan's diocese the archbishop could not dispense from the vows of his suffragan's subjects. This denial was based on the total absence of any explicit grant of this power. Although the archbishops were expressly authorized to absolve the subjects of their suffragans from sins on the occasion of the visitation, there was no specific authorization to dispense from vows.[20]

B. Persons Authorized with Delegated Power

All those who had ordinary ecclesiastical power in the external forum were able to delegate that power. Hence those who had ordinary power to dispense from vows were likewise able to delegate that power to others qualified to receive it. If this be properly kept in mind, it

18 Suarez, *De Voto*, lib. VI, c. X, n. 8; Pirhing, *Jus Canonicum Universum secundum Titulos Decretalium Distributum Novo Methodo Explicatum* (5 vols. in 1, Dillingae, 1674-1678), lib. III, tit. XXXIV, § 25, n. 23 (hereafter cited as *Jus Canonicum*).

19 *Loc. cit.*

20 C. 5, *de censibus*, III, 20, in VI°; c. 9, X, *de officio iudicis ordinarii*, I, 31, ". . . cum sit in canonibus diffinitum, primates vel patriarchas nihil iuris prae ceteris habere, nisi quantum sacri canones concedunt, vel prisca illis consuetudo contulit ab antiquo . . ."—Potthast, n. 562; Suarez, *De Voto*, lib. VI, c. X, n. 9; Layman, *Theologia Moralis* (6. ed., 5 vols. in 2, Bambergae, 1569), lib. IV, tract. IV, c. VIII, n. 6; Ferraris, *Prompta Bibliotheca*, s. v. "Votum", art. III, n. 73.

will be seen that all those to whom ordinary power was attributed in the first section of this article were likewise recognized as being able to delegate that power.[21]

In almost all the pre-Code authors it was noted that Regular confessors had the power to dispense from the non-reserved vows of the laity.[22] This power had come to them by way of a series of privileges which had been granted to various orders. These, in turn, were shared in by others as a result of the general laws of the inter-communication of privileges as issued by Leo X (1513-1521)[23] and Pius V (1566-1572).[24]

In claiming this privilege to dispense for regular confessors, the earlier authors generally cited constitutions issued by Popes Eugene IV (1431-1447),[25] and Julius II (1503-1513),[26] and Paul III (1534-1549).[27] Yet even at the time of the Salmanticenses (1665-1724) this interpretation of these constitutions was not unanimously accepted,

---

21 Suarez, *De Voto,* lib. VI, c. XII, n. 1; Salmanticenses, *Theologia Moralis,* tract. XVII, c. III, n. 83.

22 Navarrus, Tom. I, comment. XII, n. 79; Reiffenstuel, *Ius Canonicum,* lib. III, tit. XXXIV, n. 39; Salmanticenses, *Theologia Moralis,* tract. XVII, c. III, n. 93-98; St. Alphonsus, *Theologia Moralis,* lib. III, n. 256.

23 Const. *Dudum,* 10 dec. 1519—*Bullarum Diplomatum et Privilegiorum Sanctorum Romanorum Pontificum Taurinensis Editio* (25 vols., Augustae Taurinorum, 1857-1872), V, 732. (Hereafter cited as *Bull. Rom.*)

24 Const. Et *supernae,* 16 aug. 1567—*Bull. Rom.,* VII, 586.

25 Const. *Etsi quaslibet,* 30 iun. 1436—Augustinus a Virgine Maria, *Compendium Privilegiorum Omnium Religionum* (Lugduni, 1661), p. 131 (hereafter cited as *Comp. Privil.*). Const. *Cum ad Ecclesiam,* 3 iun. 1439—*Comp. Privil.,* p. 133; Salmanticenses, *loc. cit.;* Tamburini, *Theologia Moralis,* lib. III, c. XVI, § IV, n. 39.

26 Const. *Dudum ad Sacram,* 28 iul. 1506, §§ 33, 34—Bull. Rom. V, 422; Salmanticenses, *loc. cit.*

27 Const. *Cum Inter cunctas,* 3 iun. 1545—*Comp. Privil.,* p. 150; Tamburini, *loc. cit.*

for even then some saw as contained in these privileges only the faculty to *commute* the vows of lay-persons.[28]

In 1913, Vermeersch (1858-1936) in answer to an article by Bonaventure Zugh, cited other constitutions of Roman Pontiffs in which there was given the express faculty to dispense from the vows of the laity.[29] These constitutions used practically identical words to give the approved confessors of various orders this faculty: "in alia pietatis opera commutare et desuper cum iis voventibus dispensare." Vermeersch further pointed out that, since St. Alphonsus (1696-1787) attributed this faculty to regulars, it could be safely used until the Holy See decided otherwise.[30] Thus it was held that approved regular confessors had the privilege of dispensing from the non-reserved vows of the laity, and this doctrine has passed over into the post-code doctrine.[31]

The exact extent of this power is derived from a constitution of Julius II:

> Vota per eos (fideles) pro tempore emissa in omnibus et singulis casibus locorum Ordinariis etiam per synodales seu provinciales constitutiones reservatis in alia pietatis opera

---

28 "Neoterici, qui nimis scrupulose Bullas Pontificum scrutantes, nolunt concedere posse regulares dispensare cum saecularibus in votis, quia, inquiunt, solum privilegia loquuntur de commutatione, non de dispensatione . . ."—Salmanticenses, *Theologia Moralis,* tract. XVII, c. III, n. 93.

29 Iulius II, const. *Esti ad universos,* 4 iun. 1507, § 32—*Bull. Rom.,* V, 444; Iulius II, const. *Inter caeteros,* 2 apr. 1512, § 29—*Bull. Rom.,* V, 516; Leo X, const. *Etsi a summo,* 4 iul. 1513, § 40—*Bull. Rom.,* V. 543.

30 St. Alphonsus, *Theologia Moralis,* lib. III, n. 257; Vermeersch, "De facultate confessariorum Regularium dispensandi in saecularium votis"—*Periodica* (Brugis, 1905-1906: Brugis et Romae, 1927—), V (1913), suppl., 56-59.

31 Shuler, *Privileges of Regulars to Absolve and Dispense,* The Catholic University of America Canon Law Studies, n. 186 (Washington, D. C.: The Catholic University of America Press, 1943), p. 133; cf. also Oesterle, "Die Dispensgewalt der Regularen bei einfachen Gelübden der Weltleute"—*Theologie und Glaube* (Paderborn, 1909—), III (1911), 402.

> commutare et desuper cum eis voventibus dispensare, exceptis tamen votis et casibus, super quibus esset Sedes praefata merito consulenda.[32]

Therein it is evident that the privilege of regulars to dispense extended to all vows from which the bishop himself could dispense with ordinary power.[33] The texts which contained this privilege of dispensing from the vows of the laity did not state whether the privilege was granted directly to every regular confessor or only indirectly through the superior. In view of the fact that some religious orders had a centralized organization with a supreme head, privileges took on the aspect of rights pertaining to the order and the superiors of the order, and likewise, considering that not all orders were governed by the same norms in this matter,[34] it was recommended to the individual confessor that he consult his faculties in order to ascertain to what extent he had been allowed to participate in this privilege of dispensing from private vows.[35]

C. *The Power to Dispense in Relation to the Power to Commute*

It is not the intention of the writer to enter into a discussion of the commutation of vows at this point. Nevertheless, the notion of commutation in relation to dispensation requires some consideration.

Before the Code it was disputed whether the power to dispense contained within itself the power to commute,

---

32 Const. *Etsi ad universos*, 4 iun. 1507, § 32—*Bull. Rom.*, V, 444.

33 Shuhler, *Privileges of Regulars to Absolve and Dispense*, p. 140.

34 Thus it is a general norm for the Society of Jesus that privileges are extended to the individual members through the Superior General. Thus Wernz-Vidal, *Ius Canonicum* (7 tom. in 8 vols., Tom III, *De Relegiosis*, 1933), *De Religiosis*, 390, p. 411 (hereafter cited as *De Religiosis*).

35 Wernz, *Ius Decretalium*, III, n. 584, nota 87; Wernz-Vidal, *loc. cit.*

and whether the faculty to commute contained within itself the faculty to dispense. The discussion concerned only those who had delegated power, since it was accepted as certain that those who had ordinary power to dispense from vows had also an ordinary power to commute vows.[36]

Suarez[37] spoke of some authors who contended that the power to commute vows contained within itself also the power to dispense from vows. In a later passage[38] he admitted that these authors might have been speaking of ordinary power.

Another group of authors, while opposing the doctrine just proposed, advanced the opinion that the faculty to dispense did contain the faculty to commute. They based their opinion on the idea that the faculty to dispense was related to that of commuting as the whole is related to its parts, as the perfect is related to the imperfect, as the genus is related to the species. A dispensation destroyed the obligation of the vow completely, while the commutation of a vow did so only imperfectly, in that, part of the obligation remained.[39]

A third viewpoint denied that either power was contained in the other. This opinion insisted that the faculty to dispense and the faculty to commute were two entirely different powers, and hence could not be obtained except by distinct delegations of the specific power.[40]

---

36 Salmanticenses, *Theologia Moralis*, tract. XVII, c. III, n. 80.

37 *De Voto*, lib. VI, e. XII, n. 3.

38 *Ibid.*, n. 8.

39 Suarez, *De Voto*, lib. VI, c. XII, n. 10; Tamburini, *Theologia Moralis*, lib. III, c. XVI, § 5, n. 1; Schmalzgrueber, *Jus Ecclesiasticum*, lib. III, tit. XXXIV, n. 98; Salmanticenses, *Theologia Moralis*, tract. XVII, c. III, n. 81; Ferraris, *Prompta Bibliotheca*, s. v. "Votum", art. III, n. 12C.

40 Navarrus, Tom. I, c. XII, n. 79; Sanchez, *Disputationum de Sancto Matrimonii Sacramento Libri Tres* (3 vols., Venetiis, 1614), Tom. III, lib. VIII, disp. II, nn. 14, 15 (hereafter cited as *De Matrimonio*).

This dispute has been settled by the Code which declares that he who has the power to dispense from a vow can likewise commute it into a lesser obligation.[41]

ARTICLE III. THE PASSIVE SUBJECT OF DISPENSATION

In the post-Tridentine period, although it was recognized that the Pope could dispense from the vows of all baptized persons, and bishops and lesser prelates from the vows of their subjects, the writers of this period nevertheless found several doubtful questions concerning the passive subject of dispensation from private vows.

A. The Roman Pontiff

One of the first questions concerned the Pope himself. By whom or in what manner could he obtain a dispensation from a private vow?

One opinion suggested that he could grant to his confessor the power to dispense him from his vow.[42] Another opinion pointed out that since the jurisdiction required for dispensing from a vow was of a voluntary (non-judicial) character, it could therefore be used in one's own behalf, so that the Pope could dispense himself.[43]

B. The Residential Bishop

Dispensations from vows made by a residential bishop, so some maintained, were to be granted by the arch-

41 Canon 1314: "Opus voto non reservato promissum potest in melius vel in aequale bonum ab ipso vovente commutari; in minus vero bonum ab illo cui potestas est dispensandi ad normam can. 1313." Cf. *infra*, pp. 224-226.

42 Cf. Suarez, *De Voto*, lib. VI, c. XI, nn. 1, 2.

43 Suarez, *loc. cit.*; St. Alphonsus, *Theologia Moralis*, lib. III, n. 256.

bishop whose suffragan he was.[44] Others denied that the metropolitan could dispense from the vows of a suffragan bishop, since in purely personal spiritual matters the suffragan was not subject to the metropolitan. The metropolitan's power extended simply over certain acts which pertained to the external government of the diocese.[45] Others maintained that the Pope was the sole author of dispensations from the vows of residential bishops.[46] Later authors, however, attributed to a residential bishop the power of dispensing from his own vows, or of committing the power to his confessor, who could then dispense him.[47]

C. Secular Prelates with Episcopal Jurisdiction and Exempt Prelates

For other prelates,that is for those having episcopal jurisdiction together with the specific power of dispensing from vows, the alignment of opinions was the same as it was relative to bishops, with the same authors maintaining that the archbishop could dispense a prelate from his own vows, and that the prelate could delegate to his confessor the faculty of dispensing from his vows.

For exempt prelates Suarez maintained that the lesser prelates were to have recourse to their immediate superior,

---

[44] Paludanus (1280-1342) is cited for this opinion by Suarez, *De Voto*, lib. VI, c. XI, n. 3. Cf. Ferraris, *Prompta Bibliotheca*, s. v. "Votum", art. III, n. 73; Tamburini, *Theologia Moralis*, lib. III, c. XVI, § IV, n. 5; Laymann, *Theologia Moralis*, lib. IV, c. VIII, n. 6.

[45] Suarez, *loc. cit.*; Leurenius, *Forum Ecclesiasticum*, lib. III, tit. XXXIV, q. 904.

[46] Panormitanus, *Commentaria*, ad c. 7, X, *de voto et voti redemptione*, III, 34, n. 1; Suarez, *De Voto*, lib. VI, c. XI, n. 4.

[47] Tamburini, *Theologia Moralis*, lib. III, c. XVI, § IV, nn. 5, 6; Salmanticenses, *Theologia Moralis*, tract. XVII, c. III, n. 79; St. Alphonsus, *Theologia Moralis*, lib. III, n. 256.

while for the supreme head of a religious order provision was to be made by the designation of a member of the order, who then would have the requisite power by reason of this designation. The prelate, however, could also select a confessor who in view of the papal privileges granted to that order had the power necessary for dispensing from vows.[48] Others, however, claimed that an exempt prelate could dispense himself in the same manner that anyone with ordinary jurisdiction could dispense himself, inasmuch as the exercise of the power to dispense from vows was an act of voluntary (non-judicial) jurisdiction.[49]

D. Exempt Religious

Since the privilege of exemption was a favor which was given to the religious institute as a moral person, and not directly to the religious as individual persons, it was regarded as being properly in agreement with the law that an individual religious could not renounce his privilege. Furthermore, an exempt religious was no longer a subject of the residential bishop; he was the subject of his own prelate.[50]

E. Novices

A much discussed question among the authors of the post-Tridentine period was: "Who can dispense from the

48 *De Voto,* lib. VI, c. XI, n. 5; Tamburini, *loc. cit.*

49 Tamburini, *loc. cit.* This author admitted that an exempt prelate could obtain a dispensation from his vows in any one of the three ways already explained: by seeking it from his superior, by requesting it from his confessor, or by personally granting a dispensation in his own favor. He insisted, however, that before an exempt prelate could obtain a dispensation from his confessor, he first had to grant to the confessor the necessary faculty. Cf. Salmanticenses, *loc. cit.*

50 Suarez, *De Voto,* lib. VI, c. XI, n. 7.

vows of novices?" The discussion centered around the following debatable point: Was the novice to be dispensed from his vows: 1) by the prelate of the order to which he was aspiring, or 2) by his proper bishop? There existed the probable opinion that the exempt prelate could suspend the effects of certain vows of a novice for a just cause during the period of the novitiate. But the prelate could do this only if the vows were such as to render the observance of the religious life at least more onerous if not altogether difficult or morally impossible. If the vows were not of such a character, then a dispensation in the absolute sense was indicated as necessary.[51]

Some authors maintained that it was within the exclusive power of the residential bishop to dispense a novice from his personal vows.[52] Others held that it was within the power both of the bishop and of the prelate to dispense from the vows which a novice had made while in the world or upon entering the novitiate. This opinion was based on the following considerations. The novice was not as yet a participant of the privilege of exemption, and thus was still under the jurisdiction of the residential bishop. At the same time, however, he was also living within the confines of the prelate's jurisdictional powers, and in consequence it seemed that the prelate could grant a dispensation from the vows of the novice.[53]

---

51 Cf. Suarez, *De Voto,* lib. VI, c. XI, nn. 8, 9.

52 Suarez, *De Voto,* lib. VI, c. XI, nn. 8, 9.

53 Tamburini, *Theologia Moralis,* lib. III, c. XVI, § IV, n. 7; La Croix, *Commentaria in Universam Theologiam Moralem* (3 vols., Venetiis, 1756), Tom. I, lib. III, pars I, n. 537 (hereafter cited *Theologia Moralis*); Salmanticenses, *Theologia Moralis,* tract. XVII, c. III, n. 89; Schmalzgrueber, *Jus Ecclesiasticum,* lib. III, tit. XXXIV, nn. 104-106; Leurenius, *Forum Ecclesiasticum,* lib. III, tit. XXXIV, q. 904.

F. Travelers

There were four separate opinions as to what ordinary had the authority to dispense from the vows of travelers. The first of these asserted that travelers could be dispensed by the bishop of the place where at the time they sojourned. The reason underlying this view was that by being in a place even for a day travelers had become subjects of the bishop of that place. Since, therefore, they were bound by the local laws, they were likewise entitled to enjoy the local privileges.[54]

The second opinion was directly opposed to the first. It claimed that until a true domicile[55] was acquired a traveler could not be considered as a subject of the place to which he had come. He was not bound by the laws of the place he visited. Accordingly, as a non-subject, he could not obtain a dispensation from his vows from the local bishop.[56]

A third opinion conceded that travelers could be dispensed from the common law of the Church by the bishop of the place for the reason that a traveler while in that place was bound by the common law under the authority of that member of the hierarchy in whose territory he was present. But this viewpoint did not admit a similar adaptation with regard to dispensation from vows. Rather, it asserted that the possession of the necessary jurisdiction for dispensing from vows depended for its proper sanction

---

[54] Ct. St. Alphonsus, *Theologia Moralis*, lib. I, n. 158. Lehmkuhl held as the more probable opinion that which attributed to the local bishop the authority to dispense from the vows of travelers taken in the strict sense, which was the sense of the opinion just explained.—*Theologia Moralis*, I, n. 164.

[55] I. e., a residence acquired by someone who had the intention of remaining there permanently.—St. Alphonsus, *loc. cit.*

[56] Cf. St. Alphonsus, *loc. cit.*

on custom and usage along with the agreement of the bishops.[57]

Finally, the fourth and common opinion, according to La Croix,[58] was that a traveler could be dispensed from his vow by the bishop of the place, provided that he had the intention of remaining there for the greater part of a year. In having this intention he acquired a quasi-domicile, and thus could obtain a dispensation from his vows, not by reason of custom and by usage confirmed by a mutual agreement among the bishops, but by the fact of having become a subject of the bishop of the place.[59]

This much discussed question, which in the past occasioned such a diversity of opinions among the writers, was eliminated with the advent of the present Code. The law of the present Code states quite plainly that the local ordinary can dispense from the non-reserved vows of both his subjects and travelers.[60]

Article IV. The Object of the Dispensation

In regard to certain types of vows there was much discussion before the Code of Canon Law as to who could dispense from them. These vows differed from ordinary private vows in that they contained some peculiar additional characteristic which cast doubt on the possibility of their being relaxed through a dispensation.

---

57 La Croix, *Theologia Moralis,* lib. I, n. 799.

58 *Theologia Moralis,* lib. VI, n. 721.

59 Suarez, *De Voto,* lib. VI, c. XII, n. 10; Laymann, *Theologia Moralis,* lib. I, tract. IV, c. XII, n. 1. Laymann (*loc. cit.*), however, was of the opinion that a person could be considered as an inhabitant of a place even though his intention of remaining there might have envisioned a period of time less than the greater part of a year. The Salmanticenses (*loc. cit.*) likewise supported this view.

60 Canon 1313, 1°.

A. Community Vows

A community vow was a vow made by a community. Such a vow, however, did not oblige the individual members of the community in its nature of a vow unless the individual members of the community personally made the vow and accepted it. The community, however, was regarded as having the power to oblige the individual members through a human precept to bind themselves by the vow, or at least to perform the acts which constituted the material object of the vow. Hence, if the superiors of a particular community who were capable of making a law or giving a precept consented to a community vow, this consent was regarded as imposing on all the members of the community a precept to perform all the acts which constituted the material object of the vow.

A violation, however, of such a vow was not regarded as a sin of infidelity to a promise made to God; it was thus regarded only when the individual member of the community had made or accepted the vow personally. For those who did not make the vow, the failure to perform the prescribed acts, or the failure to make the vow, was looked on as a sin of disobedience or as a sin against that virtue to which the material object of the vow pertained.

In regard to the relaxation of such community vows it can be said that, in so far as the vow constituted an obligation on the whole community, it could be revoked in the same manner that any precept could be revoked, for in relation to the community such a vow lacked all force except in the measure and to the extent in which it existed as a precept. Hence the relaxation of such a vow in relation to the community could be carried through apart from any existing cause by him who imposed it. On the other hand, for those individuals who accepted it as a vow and bound themselves to observe it in its nature of a vow, a relaxation could be brought about solely in view of a sufficient cause and by one having proper jurisdiction to grant a dispensation from a vow.[61]

B. Sworn Vows

A matter of much discussion among the authors was whether one who had delegated power[62] to dispense from vows could also dispense from sworn vows and pious oaths. In the effort to solve this difficulty the two-fold manner in which an oath could be added to a vow was naturally stressed. First an oath could be added to a vow in a purely concomitant fashion, so that there was no essential union or relation between the two. Secondly an oath and a vow could be joined in such manner that one was subordinate to the other, generally the oath to the vow, although the converse was possible.

One of the first offered solutions for this difficulty denied that the delegated power to dispense from vows could be extended to pious oaths made in conjunction with vows even when they were separable from the vows. *A fortiori*, the use of a delegated power to dispense from vows could not be extended to vows confirmed by oaths, or joined with oaths in any other manner.[63] In support of this opinion it was contended that a specific difference existed between an oath and a vow, so that the faculty

[61] Suarez, *De Voto*, lib. VI, c. IX, nn. 10, 11; Salmanticenses, *Theologia Moralis*, tract. XVII, c. III, n. 87.

[62] There was no doubt that one who had ordinary power was able to dispense from *vota iurata et pia iuramenta*.

[63] Navarrus, Tom. I, c. XXVII, n. 275, vers. 16.

to dispense from vows could not be extended to imply the power to dispense from oaths.

A second solution stated that if an oath was taken as distinct from the vow, then one who had a delegated power to dispense from vows could also dispense from the oath; not, however, if the oath confirmed the vow or was joined with it in any manner.[64]

A third solution concurred in part with the first, in so far as it stated that the use of the power to dispense from vows did not extend to the oath taken by itself. This solution admitted, however, that the power to dispense from vows did extend to an oath by means of which a vow had been confirmed. The reason for this opinion was that a confirmed vow did not cease to be a vow through the accession of an oath, and so the vow could still be dispensed. But once the vow ceased to oblige, then the oath likewise ceased to oblige.[65]

A fourth solution admitted that the power to dispense from vows contained within itself the power to dispense from an oath, when the oath was taken separately. When, however, the oath and the vow were made concerning the same material object, then a distinction was to be made. When the oath confirmed the vow, then the oath could not be directly dispensed, but the vow could, with the result that the oath also ceased. When, however, the oath and the vow were joined in a purely concomitant fashion as *connexa separabilia*,[66] that is, when apart from any mutually subordinate relationship both were pronounced directly concerning the same object, then the faculty

64 Cf. Suarez, *De Voto*, lib. VI, c. XIV, n. 3.

65 Lessius, *De Iustitia et Iure*, lib. II, c. XLII, n. 60.

66 Sanchez, *De Matrimonio*, lib. VIII, disp. I, n. 23.

to dispense from vows was not considered sufficient for breaking the double bond.[67]

A fifth solution removed, in relation to its extension to oaths, all restrictions from the power to dispense from vows. According to this explanation, one who had the power to dispense from vows could dispense from the confirmatory and the purely concomitant oath alike.[68] Hence, in view of this solution, the power to dispense from vows could be used to dispense from pious oaths even when these established a separate obligation which existed independently of that of the vow.[69] Likewise, a delegated power to dispense from vows could also be used to grant a dispensation from sworn vows.[70] Finally, according to this solution, the use of a delegated power to dispense from private vows could be extended also to an oath made concomitantly with a vow concerning the same immediate object, even though the vow and the oath had given rise to separately binding and independently incumbent obligations.[71]

After the time of Suarez, this opinion was embraced by Tamburini (1591-1675),[72] by the Salmanticenses (1665-1724),[73] and also by Lehmkuhl (1834-1918).[74]

On the other hand, though it was the practice of the Roman Congregations to grant separate faculties for the granting of dispensations from vows and from oaths, this factor could not be adduced to disprove the opposite opinion which maintained that such separate grants were not

67 Sanchez, *loc. cit.*

68 Suarez, *De Voto*, lib. VI, c. XIV, n. 6.

69 Suarez, *loc. cit.*

70 *Ibid*, n. 14.

71 *Ibid*, n. 19.

72 *Theologia Moralis*, lib. III, c. VII, n. 8.

73 *Theologia Moralis*, tract. XVII, c. III, n. 3.

74 *Theologia Moralis*, I, n. 479.

necessary. The practice was fully warranted in consideration of the ultimate effect of greater security, in view of the continuing probability of the less liberal opinion.[75]

Article V. Causes Required for Dispensation

It continued to be the common opinion in the period following the Council of Trent that a legitimate cause was necessary for the validity of a dispensation from a vow, even when the dispensation was granted by the Roman Pontiff. To free someone from the obligation of a vow was to grant a quasi-dispensation from the divine law itself, inasmuch as the proximate object matter of that law was cancelled. No human authority could do this in his own name. Hence when it was done, it was done in virtue of a divine authority and in the name of God. For this reason, a cause, and that a legitimate one, was required for the validity of the dispensation.[76]

If prior to the granting of the dispensation there was a doubt as to the sufficiency of the cause for the dispensation, it was commonly asserted that the dispensation could be granted.[77] If prior to the granting of the dispensation there was doubt not merely as to the sufficiency of a cause but also as to the existence of a cause, it was commonly denied that a dispensation could be granted, since a dispensation from a vow which was granted without a suffi-

75 Salmanticenses, *Theologia Moralis*, tract. XVII, c. III, n. 3; St. Alphonsus, *Theologia Moralis*, lib. III, n. 3.

76 Suarez, *De Voto*, lib. VI, c. XVII, nn. 1, 2, 3; Schmalzgrueber, *Jus Ecclesiasticum*, lib. tit. XXXIV, n. 102; Sägmuller, *Lehrbuch des katholischen Kirchenrechts* (2 vols., Freiburg im Breisgau: Herdische Verlag), p. 637; Wernz, *Ius Decretalium*, III, n. 584.

77 Salmanticenses, *Theologia Moralis*, tract. XVII, c. III, n. 118; Lehmkushl, *Theologia Moralis*, I, n. 623.

cient cause was invalid.[78] The Salmanticenses, however, added that if the person who sought the dispensation was doubtful concerning the existence of the cause or its sufficiency, but nevertheless explained the whole matter to the superior as it actually was, such a petitioner need not be troubled in conscience if the dispensation was granted by the superior, even though later the doubts concerning the existence or sufficiency of the cause reappeared. The reason for this assertion was that the petitioner for the dispensation needed only to speak the truth, and then submit to the judgment of the superior. Any doubts which might have been present were regarded as having been disposed of by the judgment of the superior.[79]

If, when a dispensation from a vow had been sought and granted in good faith, it was discovered that no cause or an entirely insufficient cause was present, or if the dispensation had been granted for a doubtful cause but it was later found that the doubt was without any objective basis, then it was considered as sufficiently probable by many authors that the granted dispensation was valid.[80]

---

78 Salmanticenses, *Theologia Moralis*, tract. XI, c. III, n. 76.

79 St. Thomas: ". . . in manifestis dispensatio praelati non excusaret a culpa; puta si praelatus dispensaret cum aliquo super voto de ingressu religionis, nulla apparenti causa obstante. Si autem esset causa apparens, per quam saltem in dubium verteretur, posset stare judicio praelati dispensantis vel commutantis. Non tamen judicio proprio. . ."—*Summa Theologica*, IIa IIae, q. 88, art. 12, ad 2; Salmanticenses: "Bene verum est, quod si petens dubius de causa, aut de sufficientia illius, rem totam, ut est, exponat superiori, manebit tutus in conscientia ipso dispensante, quicumque ille sit, quamvis emergant dubia circa causam, vel sufficientiam ejus: quia ad petentem solum pertinent veritatem propalare, et se judicio superioris submittere, per quod practice potest dubia emergentia deponere."—*Theologia Moralis*, tract. XI, c. V, n. 76.

80 Lessius, *De Iustitia et Iure*, lib. II, c. XL, n. 119; Salmanticenses, *Theologia Moralis*, tract. XVII, c. III, n. 119; Ferraris, *Prompta Bibliotheca*, s. v. "Votum", art. III, n. 65.

The Salmanticenses cited de Salas (1553-1612), Pontius (1569-1629), and Castropalao (1581-1633), as contending that under such conditions the granting of a dispensation was invalid. St. Alphonsus stated that, when it became known with certainty that a cause had not been present or was objectively insufficient, then the dispensation could no longer be looked on as having been valid.[81] Laymann taught that one who received a dispensation in good faith could safely remain at peace and feel secure in the possession of that dispensation "donec contraria veritas appareat," even though some doubt about the matter had later intervened.[82]

Article VI. Reserved Vows

Before the Council of Trent the number of vows recognized as reserved vows was much in dispute. Towards the end of the pre-Tridentine period, Sixtus IV (1471-1484) reserved to himself five distinct vows. These were the three pilgrimage vows, namely, of visiting Jerusalem, Rome, and Compostella, along with the vows of perfect and perpetual chastity and of entering a religious order.[83] This limitation of the power to dispense from vows had, however, restricted only those who received this faculty directly from the Holy Father.

Before the Council of Trent (1545-1563), but especially before the time of the above mentioned decretal of Sixtus IV, two or at the most three vows were commonly

---

81 *Theologia Moralis*, lib. III, n. 251.

82 *Theologia Moralis*, lib. I, tract. IV, c. XXII, n. 12.

83 Although Sixtus IV in his decretal expressly stated that the vows of religion were reserved, this was commonly accepted by the authors to mean a vow of entering an approved religious order. Thus Suarez, *Opera Omnia*, Vol. XV, tract. VII, *De Statu Perfectionis et Religionis*, lib. IV, c. VII, n. 2.

considered as reserved to the Holy See. However, subsequent to the Council of Trent the number was admitted to be the five just enumerated.

In determining the manner in which the reservation of vows arose, the authors deviated from one another. Navarrus (1493-1587)[84] attributed it to the "*stylus Curiae*" at Rome. Soto (1494-1560)[85] placed the origin of it in custom and tradition. Suarez (1548-1617), and after him most of the authors, considered the origin of the reservation of the five vows fundamentally to have been the decretal of Sixtus IV.[86] At the same time they recognized that common usage, and its acceptance by the Church, as also the common consent of the authors were contributing factors.[87]

It has already been seen that at the time of his reserving to himself the five vows Sixtus IV decreed a *latae sententiae* excommunication for anyone who attempted to dispense from the reserved vows without proper authorization. He further pointed out that the attempted grant of dispensation remained null and void in its intended effect.

The authors who wrote after Sixtus understood this penalty to apply only to those clerics who received special faculties from the Pope to dispense from vows, but in whose faculties no specific mention was made of the additional

---

84 Tom. I, comment. XII, n. 75.

85 *De Iure et Iustitia* (10 vols. in 1, Salmanticae, 1556), lib. VII, q. IV, art. 3.

86 C. 5, *de poenitentiis et remissionibus*, V, 9, in Extravag. com.

87 *De Voto*, lib. VI, c. XXI, nn. 1-4; Laymann, *Theologia Moralis*, lib. IV, tract. IV, c. VIII, n. 7; Salmanticenses, *Theologia Moralis*, tract. XVII, c. III, n. 99; Ferraris, *Prompta Bibliotheca*, s. v. "Votum", art. III, n. 78; St. Alphonsus, *Theologia Moralis*, lib. III, n. 258; Benedictus XIV, const. *Inter praeteritos*, 28 nov. 1749, n. 42—*Bullarium Ssmi Domini nostri Benedicti* XIV (ed. nova. 13 vols., Mechlinae, 1826-1827), VIII, 6 (hereafter cited as *Bullarium Benedicti XIV*).

power to dispense from the five reserved vows. If anyone who had thus received the faculties from the Pope attempted to dispense from the reserved vows, he incurred the excommunication. Sanchez (1560-1610)[88] did not consider the act of Sixtus IV as in itself establishing the reservation of vows. Rather, he felt that the enactment of Sixtus postulated that these vows were already reserved. Hence when the Pope granted faculties for dispensing from vows, the particular faculty of dispensing from reserved vows was not to be understood as included unless it was specially mentioned. Consequently, those who granted a dispensation in virtue of some other privilege or faculty did not incur the excommunication.[89]

Later writers, however, such as Reiffenstuel (1642-1703),[90] Ferraris († ca. 1763),[91] and Bouix (1808-1870)[92] spoke about this penalty as applying to anyone who presumed to dispense from a reserved vow without the special permission of the Holy Father.

On account of the omission of this penalty by Pius IX in the Constitution *Apostolicae Sedis,* it ceased to exist after October 12, 1869.[93]

---

88 *De Matrimonio,* lib. VIII, disp. IX, n. 1.

89 Sanchez, *loc. cit.*; Lessius, *De Iustitia et Iure,* lib. II, c. XL, n. 122.

90 *Ius Canonicum,* lib. III, tit. XXXIV, n. 28.

91 *Prompta Bibliotheca,* s. v., "Votum", art. III, n. 78.

92 *De Episcopo,* II, 263.

93 Wernz, *Ius Decretalium,* III, n. 572.

CANONICAL COMMENTARY

CHAPTER IV

THE AUTHOR OF DISPENSATION FROM PRIVATE VOWS

Article I. The Faculty to Dispense in General

The fact has been established that the Church can grant a dispensation from private vows. The essence of this dispensation has been explained as an act whereby the author of the dispensation remits in the name of Christ the right which Christ, as God, acquires through the making of a vow. In this chapter the writer intends to examine by a juridical rather than historical or theological method the power to grant a dispensation from private vows and to point out those who possess this power.

A. *The Jurisdiction Used in Granting a Dispensation from Vows*

The Church has a two-fold power with which it was endowed by its founder. This consists of the *power of orders* and the *power of jurisdiction*. The power of orders is exercised over the instruments instituted by Christ for the communication and the petitioning of sanctifying grace, namely, the sacraments and the sacramentals. The power of jurisdiction is exercised over the members of the Church with respect to their human acts for the purpose of directing these acts toward a correct profession of faith and conformity with Christian morals.[1] Since a vow is neither a

[1] Ottaviani, *Institutiones Iuris Publici Ecclesiastici* (2. ed., 2 vols., Romae: Typis Polyglottis Vaticanis, 1935-1936), I, 131 (hereafter cited as *Institutiones*).

sacrament nor a sacramental, the power of the Church over a vow cannot be classified under the power of orders. Accordingly, it remains for the Church to have authority over a vow in virtue of her power of jurisdiction.

The jurisdictional power which the Church possesses is spoken of as a *proper jurisdiction* when it signifies the power which flows naturally from her divine institution as a perfect society. The Church exercises this proper jurisdiction in her own name and uses it to penalize her unruly members, to adjudicate causes arising in her tribunals, and to enact legislation. The jurisdictional power which the Church possesses is spoken of as a *vicarious jurisdiction* when it signifies that power which she has received through a special authorization or commission from God to act in His Name or as His instrument, and therefore as the interpreter of His Divine Will.[2]

Proper jurisdiction exists fully and completely in the Church in the sense that the Church possesses it entirely, exercises it in her own forum, and is its principal cause. Vicarious jurisdiction, on the other hand, is possessed by the Church in the sense that she is used by God as an instrument, so to speak, in effecting certain juridical operations completely beyond her native and natural power, so that in the exercise of this vicarious jurisdiction it is rather God who is the principal cause.

The proper jurisdiction of the Church is used directly to bind the members of the Church in matters of an external character; it is used indirectly to bind in all things

[2] Wernz, *Ius Decretalium,* II, n. 4, p. 14; Wernz-Vidal, *Ius Canonicum* (7 tom. in 8 vols., Tom. II, *Ius de Personis,* 3. ed., Romae: Apud Aedes Universitatis Gregorianae, 1943), II, *De Personis,* n. 366, p. 426 (hereafter cited as *De Personis*); Ottaviani, *Institutiones,* I, 232.

which pertain in any way to the Kingdom of God. Vicarious jurisdiction, however, is used rather for the releasing of ecclesiastical subjects from obligations which can be relaxed before the tribunal of God.[3] It is this vicarious jurisdiction which the Church exercises in granting a dispensation from private vows.[4]

This distinction, however, of the jurisdiction of the Church into a vicarious and a proper jurisdiction is not found in the Code, and it must therefore be distinguished from that which the Code speaks of in canon 197, § 2: "Potestas ordinaria potest esse sive propria sive vicaria." Proper and vicarious power in the Code considers the twofold manner in which the proper jurisdiction of the Church can be exercised by individuals entrusted with its exercise. The distinction given above which is alleged not to be contained in the Code considers rather the exercise by the Church itself of a specifically communicated jurisdiction which is proper to God, but vicarious to the Church itself. The Code links this vicarious power with that jurisdictional power which is proper to the Church under the one title, "Potestas iurisdictionis seu regiminis quae ex divina institutione est in Ecclesia . . ."[5]

Hence the vicarious power by which the Church is able to grant a dispensation from private vows is included in the term, ecclesiastical jurisdiction, and, like all ecclesiastical jurisdiction, is divided into *ordinary* and *delegated.*

---

[3] Billot, *Tractatus de Ecclesia Christi* (4. ed., 2 vols., Romae: Apud Aedes Universitatis Gregorianae, 1921), I, 451 (hereafter cited as *De Ecclesia*).

[4] Suarez, *De Voto*, lib. VI, c. IX, nn. 16, 18; Reiffenstuel, *Theologia Moralis*, tract. I, *de legibus*, d. IV, q. II, n. 27; Salmanticenses, *Theologia Moralis*, tract. XVII, c. III, n. 78; St. Alphonsus, *Theologia Moralis*, lib. III, n. 250; Lehmkuhl, *Theologia Moralis*, I, n. 617; Wernz-Vidal, *De Rebus*, pars I, n. 557, p. 665; Coronata, *Institutiones*, II, 226.

[5] Canon 196.

Ordinary jurisdiction is that which is attached to some office by the law itself; delegated jurisdiction is that which is given directly to the person,[6] whether physical or moral.[7] Ordinary power is *proper* when it is attached principally to a certain office and is exercised by the occupant of that office in his own name. On the other hand, ordinary power is *vicarious* when, although attached to a particular office, it is exercised not in the name of the occupant of that office, but rather in the name of him to whose office the power is principally given.[8]

Both ordinary and delegated jurisdiction to grant a dispensation from vows is jurisdiction which is of a *voluntary* (non-judicial) character. This jurisdiction is that which is exercised at the discretion of him in whom it inheres apart from the employment of the judicial solemnities and the right of appeal. It is opposed to *judicial* jurisdiction which is used for the settling of controversies according to a judicial form.[9] Sacramental jurisdiction for administering the sacrament of penance is also classified under judicial jurisdiction, although it is exercised without the solemnities of the judicial form.[10] Voluntary jurisdiction becomes equivalent to judicial jurisdiction when a dispensation from a vow is granted in the internal sacramental forum. For voluntary jurisdiction is exercised then according to the norms governing the exercise of judicial

---

6 Canon 197, § 1.

7 Blat, *Commentarium Textus Codicis Iuris Canonici* (2. ed., 5 vols. in 6, Romae: Libreria del Collegio "Angelico", 1919-1927), II, n. 146, p. 168 (hereafter cited as *Commentarium*).

8 Wernz-Vidal, *De Personis*, n. 366, p. 426; Beste, *Introductio*, pp. 214-215.

9 Canon 201, §§ 2, 3; Wernz-Vidal, *De Personis*, n. 375, p. 436; Rodrigo, *De Legibus*, n. 54; Beste, *Introductio*, p. 218.

10 Canon 201, § 2; Blat, *Commentarium*, II, n. 150, p. 174; Beste, *Introductio*, p. 218.

jurisdiction, which is the only basis on which sacramental confession can begin, though it may not be completed by sacramental absolution.[11]

B. The Qualifications Necessary to Receive the Power to Dispense from Vows

Only clerics are qualified to receive the power of granting a dispensation from vows.[12] As has already been seen, the power of granting a dispensation from vows is not derived from the power of orders. Accordingly the reception of tonsure would suffice to qualify one for the reception of this power. For its actual acquirement, however, it would be necessary that the cleric be specially delegated, or be entrusted with some ecclesiastical office to which the power of dispensing from vows is attached.[13]

Article II. Ordinary Power to Dispense from Vows

A. Ordinary Power in General

It was said above that ordinary power to dispense from vows is that which by the law itself is attached to an office. Hence, no person directly receives ordinary power to dispense from vows; rather, one receives directly a particular office to which this power is attached. Furthermore, this power to grant a dispensation must be permanently attached to the office by the law. This attachment is verified when the law places the power in a particular office antecedently to the occupancy of that office by any particular individual.[14]

---

11 Rodrigo, *loc. cit.*

12 Canon 118.

13 Canon 109; Wernz-Vidal, *De Personis*, n. 70, p. 94; Beste, *Introductio*, p. 175; Vermeersch-Creusen, *Epitome*, I, n. 207.

14 Wernz-Vidal, *De Personis*, n. 366, p. 425.

Previous to the Code ordinary power to grant a dispensation from vows was enjoyed by those who possessed jurisdiction in the external forum.[15] The Code seems to retain this norm as the basis for the allocation of ordinary power to dispense from vows. It states:

> "Vota non reservata possunt iusta de causa dispensare dummodo dispensatio ne laedat ius aliis quaesitum:
>
> 1°. Loci Ordinarius quod attinet ad omnes suos subditos atque etiam peregrinos;
>
> 2°. Superior religionis clericalis exemptae quod attinet ad personas quae can 514, § 1, enumerantur."[16]

Certainly all local ordinaries have jurisdiction in the external forum. It is also certain that major superiors of clerical exempt religious likewise have this jurisdiction.[17] As for the local superior of clerical exempt religious, he is definitely not an ordinary but he is considered to have jurisdiction in the external forum.[18] As a consequence, ordinary power to grant a dispensation from vows under the law of the Code rests on the same foundation as it did previous to the Code, namely, on jurisdiction in the external forum.

In the period previous to the Code it was also customary for the authors to attribute ordinary power to dispense from vows to all *prelates* who had jurisdiction in the

---

[15] C. 1, X, *de voto et voti redemptione*, III, 34—JL, n. 13916; cf. *supra*, pp. 49-50, 58-60; Leurenius, *Forum Ecclesiasticum*, lib. III, tract. XXXIV, q. 904; St. Alphonsus, *Theologia Moralis*, lib. III, n. 256.

[16] Canon 1313, 1°, 2°.

[17] Wernz-Vidal, *De Personis*, n. 366, p. 426; Cappello, *Summa Iuris Canonici* (3 vols., Vols. I-II, 3. ed., Vol. III, 2. ed., Romae: Apud Aedes Universitatis Gregorianae, 1938-1940), I, 334.

[18] Canon 501, § 1: "Superiores et Capitula . . . in religione clericali exempta habent iurisdictionem ecclesiasticam tam pro foro interno quam pro foro externo."; Clancy, *The Local Religious Superior*, The Catholic University of America Canon Law Studies, n. 175 (Washington, D. C.: The Catholic University of America Press, 1943), pp. 30-36; Wernz-Vidal, *De Religiosis*, n. 95, p. 88, Vermeersch-Creusen, *Epitome*, II, n. 573.

external forum.[19] While neither the Code nor the authors writing after the promulgation of the Code speak of prelates having this authority today, nevertheless it can still be said, and for the purpose of clarity, perhaps ought to be said, that they do enjoy it. A prelate today in the strict sense is a cleric, whether secular or religious, who has ordinary jurisdiction in the external forum.[20] From the examination of the ordinary power to dispense from vows, as delineated in this article, it is seen that this power is enjoyed by all who have ordinary jurisdiction in the external forum. Among those enumerated as having this power is the local superior of clerical exempt religious, who, while possessing jurisdiction in the external forum, is not included among those listed as ordinaries in canon 198. However, he does qualify for the title of prelate, as do all those who are included under the title of local ordinary. Hence, it can be affirmed that in the present discipline all prelates in the strict sense can dispense from private vows.

When the basic reason is sought for requiring jurisdiction in the external forum as the foundation for ordinary power to dispense from vows, it must first be emphasized that ordinary power is anterior to delegated power and that, unless the law expressly provides otherwise, all ordinary power gives to him who possesses it the right to delegate that power to another cleric.[21] This faculty, however, of exercising in virtue of one's office and of conceding to others the power to dispense from vows pertains to the external forum, since it is for the good of the Church as a

---

19 Leurenius, *loc. cit.*; La Croix, *Theologia Moralis*, lib. III, pars 1, n. 537; St. Alphonsus, *op. cit.*, lib. III, n. 256.

20 Canon 110.

21 Canon 199, § 1: "Qui iurisdictionis potestatem habet ordinariam potest eam alteri ex toto vel ex parte delegare, nisi aliud expresse iure caveatur."

whole, and not for a private advantage that such a power is exercised or delegated. Neither he who exercises it in virtue of his office, nor he who delegates it, nor he who receives the delegated power derives any direct benefit from possessing this power. The benefit is received only by those who can be dispensed by one having this faculty, whether that faculty be ordinary or delegated.[22] It is evident, therefore, that in order to exercise ordinary power to dispense from vows, jurisdiction in the external forum is necessary

B. *Persons Authorized with Ordinary Power*

Besides the Roman Pontiff, those who have ordinary power to grant a dispensation from vows are the local ordinaries and the superiors of clerical exempt religious.[23]

1. *The Roman Pontiff*

As was seen above,[24] the Roman Pontiff has the power of dispensing from all vows in so far as he is the successor to St. Peter to whom Christ first committed this faculty.[25] In him it is present in its fulness and independently of anyone else. It is *ordinary* power in that he receives it in-

---

[22] Bargilliat, *Praelectiones Juris Canonici* (37. ed., 2 vols., Parisiis: Baston, Berche, et Pagis, 1923), I, n. 59; Maroto, *Institutiones Iuris Canonici* (2 vols., Romae: Apud Commentarium pro Religiosis, 1919-1921, Vol. I, 3. ed., 1921), I, 861; Ottaviani, *Institutiones,* I, 231.

[23] Canon 1313: "Vota non reservata possunt iusta de causa dispensare, dummodo dispensatio ne laedat ius aliis quaesitum:

1° Loci Ordinarius quod attinet ad omnes suos subditos atque etiam peregrinos;

2° Superior religionis clericalis exemptae quod attinet ad personas quae can. 514, § 1, enumerantur.

[24] Cf. *supra,* pp. 34-48.

[25] Matt. XVI, 19.

directly through the reception of the office of the Supreme Pontificate; it is *proper* in that it inheres in his office principally, and is not exercised in the name of any other ecclesiastical officeholder. It is *vicarious* for the reason that it is exercised in the name of God. However, it is not vicarious in the sense in which this word is used in the Code with reference to the possession of ordinary power.[26] Vicarious power in the Code is a form of ordinary power, and is opposed to proper ordinary power. This latter is attached to an office for which it is principally intended, and is exercised by the occupant of that office in his own name. Vicarious ordinary power, however, is not intended principally for the office to which it is attached by law, nor does the occupant of this office exercise it in his own name, but rather in the name of him who holds the office to which the particular power in question is primarily attached.[27] These principles of proper and vicarious power as found in the Code do not lend themselves to application in the case of the Pope's power to dispense from vows. By that is meant that this terminology when applied to the Pope's dispensing from vows, would require one to say that God holds an office in the Church to which office the power of dispensing from vows is principally attached, and in the exercise of which power God acts in His own name. It would also require one to say that when the Pope exercises his power, he does so by reason of a power which is not principally attached to his office, but only secondarily, and that in relation

---

26 The writer prefers not to speak of the ordinary power of the Supreme Pontiff to dispense from vows as *ordinary vicarious power*. Cf. Reilly, *The General Norms of Dispensation*, The Catholic University of America Canon Law Studies, n. 119 (Washington, D. C.: The Catholic University of America Press, 1939), p. 53 (hereafter cited as *Dispensations*).

27 Cf. *supra*, pp. 81-82.

to other ecclesiastical superiors he cannot exercise this power in his own name.

In other words, in canon 197, § 2, the legislator intended to speak of vicarious ordinary power as that which is exercised by one ecclesiastical superior in relation to another ecclesiastical superior. It was not the intention of the legislator to speak of the vicarious ordinary power of the Church in relation to God.[28]

For the purposes, then, of the present study, the Roman Pontiff will be spoken of as having proper ordinary power to dispense from all private vows.

However, in the exercise of this power of dispensing from private vows the Holy Father is accustomed to use the agency of the Roman Congregations and of the Sacred Penitentiary, to whom this faculty has been communicated by the Code itself. Since the local ordinary can dispense from all private vows except those by which a third party acquires a right or those which are reserved to the Holy See, it will be rather infrequent that recourse to Rome will be necessary. When, however, this must be done, then various circumstances will determine the particular office in Rome to which the petition should be sent.

First of all, when the dispensation is sought in the external forum the following norms can be followed:

1) If the petitioner lives under the jurisdiction of the Sacred Congregation for the Propagation of the Faith, the petition for the dispensation should be sent to that Congregation.[29]

---

28 Rodrigo, *De Legibus*, n. 46.

29 Canon 252, §§ 1, 3.

2) If the petitioner is a Catholic of an Oriental rite, the petition should be sent to the Sacred Congregation for the Oriental Church.[30]

3) If the petitioner is a member of the Latin rite, the petition should be sent to the Sacred Congregation of the Council.[31]

4) If the petitioner is subject to the Sacred Congregation for Religious, the petition for the dispensation from a private vow should be sent to the same Sacred Congregation.[32] In respect to this last norm, however, it should be noted that religious of the Oriental rites send their petitions for dispensations to the Sacred Congregation for the Oriental Church.[33]

The foregoing are the norms for petitioning the Holy See for a dispensation from vows in the external forum; it remains to present the norms governing the obtaining of a dispensation from the Holy See in the internal forum.

In the internal forum the Sacred Penitentiary is the competent tribunal for the granting of all dispensations from vows.[34] Its competency in this matter extends to Catholics of both the Latin and the Oriental rites.[35]

2. *The Local Ordinary*

Canon 1313, 1°, assigns to the office of the local ordinary the faculty of dispensing from all non-reserved

---

30 Canon 257, § 1.

31 Canon 250, §§ 1, 2.

32 Canon 251, § 3.

33 Canon 257, § 1; Monin, *De Curia Romana* (Lovanii: Van Linthout, 1912), p. 264.

34 Canon 258, § 1.

35 S. C. pro Eccl. Orient., resp. 26 iul., 1930—Acta Apostolicae Sedis (Romae, 1909-), XXII (1930), 394 (hereafter cited as AAS) reported in Bouscaren, *The Canon Law Digest* (2 vols., Milwaukee: Bruce, 1934, 1943), I, 174.

vows. Under the term local ordinary are included:[36] 1) residential bishops; 2) abbots and prelates *nullius*; 3) vicars general of the foregoing; 4) apostolic administrators; 5) the vicar general of a permanent apostolic administrator;[37] 6) vicars and prefects apostolic; 7) superiors of independent missions or of missions *sui iuris*;[38] and 8) vicars delegate of vicars and prefects apostolic, and of the superiors of independent missions.[39]

In addition to the above-mentioned, the following are also included under the title of local ordinary, inasmuch as they succeed those already enumerated through a *prescription of law*: 1) the cathedral chapter;[40] 2) the diocesan consultors where a cathedral chapter does not exist;[41] 3) the chapter of a prelacy or abbacy *nullius*;[42] 4) the vicar capitu-

---

36 Canon 198, § 1.

37 McDonough, *Apostolic Administrators,* The Catholic University of America Canon Law Studies, n. 139 (Washington, D. C.: The Catholic University of America Press, 1941), p. 158.

38 Although not included in the canon as a local ordinary, the superior of an independent mission or of a mission *sui iuris* seems to be regarded as such. The following is contained in an instruction of the Sacred Congregation for the Propagation of the Faith, 8 dec. 1929: "Itaque qui missioni ab Ecclesia praeponitur, sive is Vicarius fuerit sive Praefectus Apostolicus vel etiam simplex *Superior* [the italics are inserted by the writer], in gubernanda missione non iam ab Instituto sed a Sancta Sede dependet, et de ea non Instituto rationem reddere tenetur, sed Sanctae Sedi, quae eum elegit."—*AAS*, XXII (1930), 112; Cappello: "Codex silet de missionibus sui iuris earumque rectoribus de quibus complura adsunt pontificia documenta. Qui praeest missioni sui iuris habendus est iuridice tamquan loci ordinarius, ideoque iisdem gaudet iuribus et officiis, quae obtinet Vicarius vel Praefectus Apostolicus, congrua congruis referendo."—*Summa Iuris Canonici*, I, 448.

39 After the publication of the Code the Sacred Congregation for the Propagation of the Faith assigned to vicars delegate of vicars and prefects apostolic all the powers which the Code, itself, assigns to the vicar general. Cf. S. C. de Prop. Fide, letter, 8 dec. 1919—, *AAS*, XII (1920), 120; Reilly, *Dispensation*, p. 55.

40 Canons 198, 429, §§ 2, 3; 431.

41 Canon 423.

42 Canon 327.

lar elected by the chapter of a diocese, of a prelacy, or of an abbacy *nullius*, as also the administrator elected by the diocesan consultors where these exist;[43] 5) pro-vicars apostolic, pro-prefects apostolic, pro-superiors of independent missions;[44] and 6) he who succeeds to office when a vicar or a prefect apostolic, or the superior of an independent mission (or a pro-vicar, pro-prefect, or pro-superior) failed to appoint a person to succeed them according to the requirement of canon 309, §§ 1, 2, 3.[45]

Finally, there are those who do not succeed according to a prescription of the law but rather in the manner determined by approved constitutions. Thus may abbots and prelates *nullius* succeed to office when their approved constitutions determine the process of succession to a vacant office or to an office whose occupant is impeded from fulfilling his duties.[46]

An *ordinary* is primarily an ecclesiastical person having jurisdiction in the external forum. A *local ordinary* has this jurisdiction primarily and directly in the place or territory assigned to him, and as a result indirectly in respect to the people who occupy that territory. Major religious superiors are ordinaries who have ordinary power directly in respect to the persons under their charge, and not primarily in the place.[47]

---

43 Canons 429, §§ 2, 3; 432; 327.

44 Canon 309, §§ 1, 2, 3.

45 Canon 309, § 4.

46 The constitutions take precedence over the common law and must be consulted first. Canon 327, § 1; Benko, *The Abbot Nullius*, The Catholic University of America Canon Law Studies, n. 173 (Washington, D. C.: The Catholic University of America Press, 1943), pp. 119, 120; Wernz-Vidal, *De Personis*, n. 367, p. 427.

47 Wernz-Vidal, *De Personis*, n. 367, p. 426; Beste, *op. cit.*, p. 216.

a. The Residential Bishop

As was seen above,[48] the Church has received from Christ the power of jurisdiction, which is distinguished into a *proper* and a *vicarious* power.[49] The Roman Pontiff possesses this power fully and in a supreme degree. He has its fulness and not just its more important parts. He enjoys it as ordinary, immediate and truly episcopal power over all churches, all bishops, and over all the faithful taken collectively and singly.[50]

This power was given to Peter and all his successors by Christ Himself.[51] But in like manner, the office of residential bishop enjoys divine institution in respect both of the office itself and of the ordinary power which it contains.[52] It is obvious, however, that the bishop does not have

---

48 Cf. *supra*. pp. 80-81.

49 Billot: ". . . in Ecclesia uterque iurisdictionis modus vicarius et proprius ordinis supernaturalis est, et aequaliter clauditur in divina institutione quam verba evangelica exprimunt: *quaecumque alligaveritis*, etc."—*De Ecclesia*, I, 453.

50 Conc. Vat. (1869-1870), sess. IV, const. *de Ecclesia Christi*, cap. 3: "Docemus . . . Ecclesiam Romanam, disponente Domino, super omnes alias ordinariae potestatis obtinere principatum, et hanc Romani Pontificis iurisdictionis potestatem, quae vere episcopalis est, immediatam esse: erga quam cuiuscunque ritus et dignitatis pastores atque fideles, tam seorsum singuli quam simul omnes, officio hierarchiae subordinationis veraeque obedientiae obstringuntur, non solum in rebus, quae ad fidem et mores, sed etiam in iis, quae ad disciplinam et regimen Ecclesiae per totum orbem diffusae pertinent. . ."—Mansi, *Sacrorum Conciliorum Nova et Amplissima Collectio* (53 vols. in 60, Paris-Leipzig-Arnheim, 1901-1927), LII, 1332 (hereafter cited Mansi); cf. also H. Denzinger, C. Bannwart, J. B. Umberg, *Enchiridion Symbolorum, Definitionum, et Declarationum de Rebus Fidei et Morum* (21-23. ed., Friburgi Brisgoviae: Herder & Co., 1937), n. 1827 (hereafter cited as Denzinger). Canon 218; Billot, *De Ecclesia*, I, 613.

51 Matt. XVI, 19; Conc. Vat. sess. IV, const. *de Ecclesia Christi*, cap. 2, —Mansi, LII, 1331; Denzinger, n. 1824; Canon 218, § 1; Billot, *op. cit.*, pp. 567, ff.

52 Conc. Vat. sess. IV, const., *de Ecclesia Christi*, cap. 3: "Tantum autem abest, ut haec Summi Pontificis potestas officiat ordinariae ac immediatae illi

jurisdiction as extensive as that of the Roman Pontiff. Nevertheless, the bishop does receive complete jurisdiction for the governing of his diocese in doctrinal and disciplinary matters for both the internal and the external forums.[53]

The difference in extent which exists between the jurisdiction of the Roman Pontiff and that of a residential bishop is due to the limitations which have been placed on the latter by Christ Himself. The fundamental restriction is that of subordination to the Roman Pontiff, to whose primacy the subordination of the residential bishop is a correlative.[54] The fact, however, that according to divine law one bishop was to rule over a particular territory in the Church, in contrast with the universal extension of the Supreme Pontiff's power, constitutes a second fundamental limitation on the residential bishop's jurisdiction.[55]

Although the Supreme Pontificate and the Episcopacy are of divine institution, it was only the Supreme Pontificate which was altogether, both intensively and extensively, jurisdictionally determined by its Divine Institutor. Though

---

episcopalis iurisdictionis potestati, qua episcopi, qui *positi a Spiritu Sancto* (cf. Act. 20, 28) in Apostolorum locum successerunt, tanquam veri pastores assignatos sibi greges singuli singulos pascunt et regunt. . ." Mansi, LII, 1332; Denzinger, n. 1828; Canon 329, § 1; Billot, *De Ecclesia*, I, 682; Wernz-Vidal, *De Personis*, n. 573, p. 718.

53 Scherer, *Handbuch des Kirchenrechtes* (2 vols., Graz und Leipzig, 1886-1898), I, 561-562; Billot, *De Ecclesia*, I, 683; Lercher, *Institutiones Theologiae Dogmaticae* (4 vols., Oeniponte: 1927-1930), I, n. 467, p. 480 (hereafter cited as *Institutiones*).

54 Canon 329, § 1; Lercher: "Solus Petrus constitutus est claviger regni coelorum, quo claudente vel aperiente, ligante vel solvente, nemo sub Deo aperire, vel claudere, solvere vel ligare potest. Aliis apostolis data est potestas amplissima ligandi et solvendi iurisdictionis Petri subordinata."—*Institutiones*, I, 479; Ryan, *Principles of Episcopal Jurisdiction*, The Catholic University of America Canon Law Studies, n. 120 (Washington, D. C.: The Catholic University of America Press, 1939), p. 64 (hereafter cited as *Principles*).

55 Wernz-Vidal, *De Personis*, n. 610, p. 719; Ryan, *Principles*, pp. 62-63.

the jurisdictional potentiality of the subordinate episcopate was likewise objectively determined immediately and directly by the fact of its divine institution, yet its actual realization was left to be determined within certain limits according to the current circumstances by the only higher authority in the Church, the Roman Pontiff.[56]

When the Roman Pontiff actually does determine the jurisdiction of the residential bishop, this determination does not imply "that the bishop is competent only for those things which are expressly permitted him by the Pope." Rather, it means that though "the Bishop's potential capability (radical competence) may be determined by its fundamental relationship to the primatial jurisdiction of the Roman Pontiff, its actual capacity within those natural bounds was left by Christ to be more or less determined by the supreme authority of the Pope as times and circumstances, either universal or local, demand."[57]

But, although the ordinary and immediate power of the residential bishop was not determined in its divine institution as to what would constitute "its territorial and personal object, and although the same authority was only generally determined as to particular acts and matters, the fact of its (divine) institution nevertheless demands that the potential capacity of episcopal jurisdiction be left substantially perfect in its actual use."[58]

The perfection of this jurisdictional competence is substantially retained when the actual competence entails doctrinal and disciplinary faculties, the essential components of complete ecclesiastical jurisdiction. It is not required,

---

56 Ryan, *Principles*, pp. 57-58.

57 Ryan, *Principles*, p. 87.

58 Ryan, *Principles*, p. 88.

however, that these essential components be present in their "fullest possible scope or intensity" for the substantial perfection of the bishop's jurisdiction.[59]

In the actual determination of the bishop's authority, the nature of the episcopal jurisdiction excludes many matters. Thus, because the bishop has authority over only a particular flock, he cannot exercise authority over matters of a universal nature or over matters proximately connected with the universal church. These matters are the *causae maiores essentiales* or *cause maiores per se.*[60] While the Roman Pontiff may not *de facto* reserve all *causae maiores* to himself, nevertheless all such *causae maiores essentiales* are *de iure* reserved to the Holy Father, because by their very nature they are beyond the bishop's competence.

Besides the natural limitation arising from the fact that a bishop governs only a particular flock, there is another natural limitation arising out of the fact that the residential bishop is subordinate to the Roman Pontiff who at the same time enjoys immediate as well as supreme ordinary jurisdiction[61] over each and every church, and over each and every pastor as well as over the faithful.

In virtue of this last mentioned power, the Roman Pontiff can limit the bishop's jurisdiction in regard to those matters for which the ordinary power of the bishop would be independently sufficient and competent. He does this by subjecting to himself through positive law certain acts or matters which are within the potential or native competence of the residential bishop. In view of such a limitation

---

59 Ryan, *Principles*, p. 89.

60 Billot, *De Ecclesia*, pp. 684-685; Wernz-Vidal, *De Personis*, n. 429, p. 490; Ryan, *Principles*, pp. 66, 91.

61 Canons, 218; 329, § 1.

of the bishop's competence these matters are generally called *causae maiores per accidens.*[62]

Once these matters become *causae maiores per accidens* there arises the question whether the residential bishop loses his jurisdiction over them in such a way that a future action of his in these cases would be not only illicit but also invalid. In response it can be said that his action can be either invalid or illicit depending on the intention of the Roman Pontiff as expressed in the positive law by which he constitutes the particular matter a *causa maior.* In any case it would at least be illicit. That it could be invalid, or in other words that the Roman Pontiff could take away the bishop's jurisdiction over that particular matter completely, seems to be the opinion of Scherer (1845-1918),[63] Wernz (1842-1914)-Vidal (1867-1938),[64] Billot (1846-

---

62 Cavagnis, *Institutiones Iuris Publici Ecclesiastici* (2 vols., Romae, 1882-1883), II, 22; Billot, *op. cit.*, I, 685; Ryan, *Principles*, pp. 91-92.

63 ". . . durch die Reservation wird die Gewalt der untergeordneten hierarchischen Organe bezüglich der eben vorbehaltenen Belange suspendirt order völlig abolirt."—*Handbuch des Kirchenrechtes*, I, 459. "Der Papst ist ferner berechtigt nicht nur Personen sondern auch gewisse Gegenstände der Jurisdiction der Bischöfe zu entziehen und diese Angelegenheiten seiner Entscheidung zu reservieren."—*Ibid.*, 558.

64 "Episcopi . . . illam tantum partem . . . iurisdictionis ecclesiasticae obtinent ad quam a Romano Pontifice vocati sunt . . . illam solummodo habent quam Romanus Pontifex sive expresse sive tacite de iure communi vel speciali commissione ut ordinariam vel delegatam ipsis concessit."—*De Personis*, n. 609, p. 767. The writer has used this quotation from Wernz-Vidal to show that these authors are of the opinion that the Roman Pontiff can take away the bishop's jurisdiction over certain things. The writer, however, disagrees with the authors' manner of arriving at this conclusion. They seem to make their conclusion depend on their conviction that the bishop receives his jurisdiction immediately from the Pope. Because of this fact, the residential bishop receives only that jurisdiction which the Roman Pontiff concedes to him either expressly or tactitly. The writer prefers to think that such an important conclusion does not rest on a so disputed and unsettled premise. As will be seen, Billot attributes this power to the Pope because episcopal jurisdiction is particular (not universal) and subordinate to that of the Roman Pontiff. This seems the more acceptable foundation. Cf. the text in the following footnote.

1931),[65] Ryan,[66] Vermeersch (1858-1936)-Creusen,[67] and Ayrinhac (1867-1930).[68]

This is also the opinion of the writer who bases his opinion on the primacy of the Roman Pontiff and the undetermined nature of the episcopal jurisdiction. Since the episcopal jurisdiction was only objectively determined but not actually realized by Christ, it remains for the only higher authority in the Church, the Roman Pontiff, according to the circumstances of time and place, to remove from the episcopal jurisdiction certain things which he considers should be reserved to his own judgment. Furthermore,

---

65 "Caeterum apparet ista [iurisdictio Episcopi] semper intelligenda cum limitatione illa quam ipsa se importat particularitas et subordinatio episcopalis potestatis. . . Quod enim possit Pontifex a jurisdictione episcoporum subtrahere certas res vel personas quae alias ad eam pertinerent, pro certo habendum est. Nam etsi ius divinum sanxerit ut singuli greges episcopis tanquam ordinariis pastoribus regendi committerentur, adhuc tamen quaedam latitudo est intra quam episcopalis potestas restrictionem patitur, quin propterea desinat esse potestas ad pascendum populum Dei. Nec oportuit ut per ius divinum omnino immobiliter determinaretur id quod debuit manere aliqualiter mutationi obnoxium pro varietate circumstantiarum ac temporum, pro maiori vel minori facilitate recursus ad Sedem apostolicam, aliisque eiusmodi. Nunc autem, si ius divinum non assignavit in individuo fines episcopalis potestatis, constat ipsam posse plus minusve restringi per ius pontificium, quia nullos alios limites novit pontificia auctoritas praeter eos quos ei ius divinum praefixit. Hinc ergo locum habent reservationes casuum, causarum, dispensationum, et similia."—*De Ecclesia,* I, 685.

66 "Reservation . . . implies a complete withdrawal of the matters reserved from the scope of the bishop's ordinary power."—*Principles,* p. 92. This author seems to attribute a single effect to reservation, namely, that it nullifies a contrary act of the bishop.

67 These authors point out that the Pope's power to limit the bishop's jurisdiction is independent of the immediate or mediate reception of that power from the Pope. "In utroque casu certum est eam [potestatem] ita, sub auctoritate R. Pontificis exerceri, ut ipse suam cuique episcopo dioecesim assignet et, causis quibusdam sibi reservatis, iurisdictionem episcoporum restringere possit."—*Epitome,* I, pp. 268-269, n. 399.

68 "Hence the Roman Pontiff . . . could . . . fix the limits of their authority, restrict it, and even in particular cases take it way from them."—*Constitution of the Church* (New York: Benziger, 1924), p. 145.

canon 335, § 1, states that bishops are to govern their dioceses according to the norms of the sacred canons.[69] This means, according to Cappello,[70] that the bishop cannot do anything contrary to the common law by way either of derogation or of dispensation, unless he previously obtain the faculty to do so from the Holy See. Since the granting of a faculty generally implies the granting of jurisdiction, it is obvious that the obtaining of jurisdiction will ordinarily be necessary for the validity of an act. Hence it follows that unless a bishop obtain the faculty from the Holy See, he acts invalidly when he exercises his authority over a matter which has become a *causa maior per accidens*. In other words, the Holy See (the Roman Pontiff) can deprive a bishop of his jurisdiction over a certain matter, thus rendering his future action over that matter invalid.

To sum up what has been said, it has been seen that the Roman Pontiff can take away the bishop's jurisdiction over a certain matter, even though that matter belong to his native or potential competence, provided that the jurisdiction of the bishop remains substantially perfect. It remains substantially perfect as long as he retains doctrinal and disciplinary faculties, although these need not be present in their fullest scope and intensity. Once his jurisdiction over a certain matter is taken away, he acts invalidlv in that matter unless he obtains the faculty from the Holy See.

The purpose of the preceding discussion has been to facilitate an understanding of the bishop's power to grant a dispensation from private vows. In the first article of

69 "Ius ipsis et officium est gubernandi dioecesim tum in spiritualibus tum in temporalibus cum potestate legislativa, iudiciaria, coactiva ad normam sacrorum canonum exercenda."

70 *Summa Iuris Canonici*, I, n. 370, p. 475.

this chapter it was seen that the Church exercises vicarious jurisdiction in dispensing from all vows.[71] It has likewise been seen that the Roman Pontiff has this power in its fullness. It remains now to determine to what extent the residential bishop enjoys this power to dispense from vows. Is it a faculty beyond the competence of the residential bishop so as to be classified a *causa maior per se*? Or is it a faculty which belongs to the radical jurisdiction of the bishop, so that in the event of the subjection of some particular vow to the Holy See such a matter would be constituted as a *causa maior per accidens*?

In the Code the residential bishop receives the power to dispense from private vows along with all other local ordinaries.[72] The faculty attributed to him in the Code is that of being able to dispense from all non-reserved vows, provided that a third party does not suffer injury to an acquired right. In the absence of such injury, the residential bishop can thus dispense from all private vows except the vow of perfect and perpetual chastity made after the completion of one's eighteenth year, or the vow to enter a religious community with solemn vows, likewise when made after the completion of one's eighteenth year. There is no indication in canon 1313 that the bishop enjoys this power in a manner distinct from that of the other ordinaries, or that it belongs to his native competence.

However, in the period before the Code it was frequently stated either expressly or in equivalent terms that the power to dispense from private vows belonged to the residential bishop in virtue of his radical or potential competence. Hence it was held to belong to him, not by

---

71 Cf. *supra*, pp. 8C-81.

72 Canon 1313, 1°.

ecclesiastical institution, but rather by divine institution. Among those who taught this may be enumerated Suarez (1548-1617),[73] Sporer (1620-1683),[74] Reiffenstuel (1642-1703)[75] and Lehmkuhl (1834-1918).[76]

Furthermore, reason suggests that dispensing from private vows is not by its nature a matter pertaining to the universal church or proximately connected with universal church discipline. Hence it would not be a *causa maior per se*, but rather a matter perfectly within the potential or radical competence of the residential bishop. Thus it can be said that this faculty to dispense from private vows would be within the competence of the residential bishop even if the Code did not specifically attribute it to him.[77]

---

73 ". . . unusquisque episcopus in sua dioecesi habet ordinariam potestatem dispensandi et commutandi omnia vota quae specialiter reservata non sunt. . . Ratio vero est, quia haec potestas est necessario ad regimen Episcopale. . ." *De Voto*, lib. VI, c. X, n. 14.

74 "Episcopi etiam habent ordinariam potestatem dispensandi in omnibus Summo Pontifici non-reservatis votis omnium suorum subditorum dioecesanorum. Episcopi succedunt Apostolis quibus dictum est Mt. 18, 18."—*Theologia Moralis Decalogalis et Sacramentalis* (3 vols., Salisburgi, 1711), Tract. III, c. III, n. 49.

75 "Episcopi juri ordinario habent potestatem dispensandi in cunctis votis suorum subditorum, iis solis exceptis, quorum dispensationem specialiter sibi reservat Summus Pontifex . . . Ratio est: quia Episcopi succedunt Apostolis quibus dictum est Mt. 18. 'Quaecunque alligaveritis, et quaecunque solveritis.' "—*Ius Canonicum*, lib. III, tit. XXXIV, n. 27.

76 "De episcoporum autem potestate [in votis] quaeritur, num ita inhaereat eorum muneri ut specialis delegatio Romani Pontificis necessaria non sit, sive num illa potestas ab episcopali munere plene auferri nequeat. Eam auferri non posse, multis theologis probatur, ita tamen, ut a R. Pontifice possit restringi, quia nimirum ad convenientem gubernationem populi sibi commissi pertineat, ea posse, quae frequenter ex natura sua occurrant."—*Theologia Moralis*, I, n. 617.

77 "Ob hanc potestatem licet Episcopis per leges ac decreta ea omnia statuere quae ipsi in dioecesis regimine opportuniora esse censeant. Haec Episcoporum potestas nullos habet fines, nisi generales Ecclesiae leges et peculiaria Pontificum decreta. Idcirco quae neque per generales Ecclesiae leges neque per

Because this power to dispense from vows was placed in the office of the residential bishop by God Himself, to be exercised in the name of the bishop and not in the name of another ecclesiastical superior, it is proper ordinary power.[78]

In view of the established conclusion that the power to dispense from private vows is not a *causa maior per se*, but rather a matter which rests within the radical competence of the residential bishop, it is clear that the Roman Pontiff can by reason of his supreme and immediate primacy, through positive law, limit this power of the bishop to dispense from vows. Furthermore, he can limit it in such a way that the bishop would act invalidly were he to attempt to dispense from a vow subsequent to a full restriction of his jurisdiction over that vow.

As will be seen more fully in a later chapter, the Roman Pontiff does actually limit the jurisdiction of the residential bishop over private vows by reserving to himself the power to dispense from two kinds of private vow. The effect of this reservation will be discussed at that time.

b. Other Local Ordinaries

The faculty of the residential bishop to grant a dispensation from private vows has been examined. This faculty, as was already mentioned, also belongs to the numerous other local ordinaries enumerated above. These local ordinaries obtain this faculty by acquiring a particular office to which that faculty is attached, so that it is *ordinary*

---

peculiaria Pontificum decreta constituta sint, ea Episcoporum subiacent potestati."—*Signatura Apostolica*, 13 iun. 1923—*AAS*, XVI (1924), 106-107; Ryan, *Principles*, p. 115.

[78] This follows from the arguments set forth immediately above where it was shown that this faculty of granting a dispensation from vows inhered in the office of the residential bishop by divine law. Cf. also canon 197, § 1.

power. It differs, however, from the faculty of the residential bishop in that both the office and the attachment thereto of this faculty are of ecclesiastical institution, based on the full and supreme power of the Roman Pontiff[79] to dispense from vows. According as these local ordinaries exercise this faculty in their own name or in the name of another it is constituted as a proper or as a vicarious power respectively.[80]

This faculty of dispensing from private vows is a participation in the supreme power of the Roman Pontiff in the following local ordinaries: 1) vicars and prefects apostolic; 2) apostolic administrators; 3) abbots and prelates *nullius*; 4) the vicars general or vicars delegate of the above; 5) those who succeed the above mentioned prelates when their office becomes vacant or its fulfillment impeded.[81] Likewise in this group must be placed the superior of an independent mission, his vicar delegate, and he who succeeds him by reason of his vacating or being impeded in fulfilling the office. While this office is not included in the Code as deriving its power from that of the Roman Pontiff, nevertheless, since the very existence of this type of local ordinary originates in the papal documents, it is obvious that the office has as the source of its power the Roman Pontiff.

On the other hand, the vicar general of a residential bishop as well as those who succeed a residential bishop when he is impeded from fulfilling his office, or when the

79 Wernz-Vidal, *De Personis*, n. 366, p. 461.

80 Canon 197, § 2.

81 *Codex Iuris Canonici*, lib. II, pars I, sect. 2, tit. 7: "De suprema potestate deque iis qui eiusdem sunt ecclesiastico iure participes." All the above-mentioned local ordinaries are comprised under this title, except the vicar delegate who, as was seen above, has been specially designated by the Holy See since the publication of the Code as belonging to this group. Cf. *supra*, p. 91.

office becomes vacant, participate in the jurisdiction of that bishop.[82]

In any case, whether the ordinary power of these local ordinaries is a participation of the jurisdiction of the Supreme Pontiff or of the residential bishop, it is of ecclesiastical origin. It is placed in the particular office by the Supreme legislator, and hence it can be limited or taken away completely and substantially by him. Thus, when the Roman Pontiff reserves the dispensation from a particular vow to himself, it is certain that at least those local ordinaries who derive their power to dispense from vows by reason of an ecclesiastical institution originating with the Pope or the bishop, lose their jurisdiction completely and radically over that particular reserved vow. On the other hand, when a bishop reserves the dispensation from a certain vow to himself, only those local ordinaries are affected who derive their jurisdiction from the residential bishop. These would be the vicars general of the bishop who reserves the vow.[83]

3. *The Clerical Exempt Superior*

In addition to the local ordinaries, canon 1313, 2°, attributes to the superior of clerical exempt religious[84] ordinary power to dispense from private vows.[85]

It is especially significant that the legislator has utilized a distinct clause to attribute to the religious superior the power to dispense from vows. Had the legislator intended

---

82 *Codex Iuris Canonici*, lib. II, pars I, sect. 2, tit. 8: "De potestate episcopali deque iis qui de eadem participant."

83 Canon 368, § 1.

84 "Vota non reservata possunt iusta de causa dispensare, dummodo dispensatio ne laedat ius aliis quaesitum, Superior religionis clericalis exemptae quod attinet ad personas quae can. 514, § 1, enumerantur."

85 Canon 197, § 2.

to grant this faculty only to major superiors of exempt religious institutes, he could have included this grant in the immediately preceding clause by changing the wording there from "local ordinary" to "ordinary", since the major exempt superior is included under the term, "ordinary".[86] The fact, however, that the legislator has used a separate clause for this purpose, indicates that he intended to extend this power beyond those who are major superiors to those also who are minor superiors.

Of course, it is only the superiors of clerical exempt religious who possess this faculty; the superior of non-exempt religious in the matter of dispensing from vows is the local ordinary.[87] Provided, then, that a person is a superior of clerical exempt religious, he qualifies to be included under those who can dispense from private vows in so far as this power is communicated to them in canon 1313, 2°.[88] It now remains to determine who is a superior in a clerical exempt community.

The first step in this process is to determine what qualifications characterize the office of superior in the strict sense; then one can complete the process by enumerating those offices which fulfill the requirements.

Canon 501, § 1, states that superiors in clerical exempt religious communities enjoy jurisdiction for both the internal and the external forums. The jurisdiction which is thus attributed to superiors definitely meets the require-

---

[86] Canon 198, § 1.

[87] Canon 500, §§ 1-2.

[88] "Si in Codice vox Superior non habeat notam specificationis vel determinationis, ex. gr. Superior maior, generalis, provincialis, localis, comprehendit omnes qui hoc nomine gaudent in iure, proinde etiam Superiorem localem, nisi ex textu vel ex contextu patet vocem sese referre ad Superiorem maiorem."—Schaefer, *De Religiosis ad Normam Codicis Iuris Canonici* (3. ed., Romae: S.A.L.E.R., 1940), n. 103, p. 217 (hereafter cited as *De Religiosis*).

ments of ordinary power, for it is attached to the office of superior by the law itself antecedently to the possession of that office by any individual.[89] Accordingly, a superior in a clerical exempt community is one who by reason of his office has both in the external and the internal forums ordinary power which he exercises over a religious house, province, or entire religious society.[90] On the other hand, he is not a superior who is simply in charge of a certain part or certain category of clerical exempt religious, but not in charge of a complete and integral house. Nor is he a superior who does not have at least vicarious ordinary power, but only delegated power. Ordinary power of any kind suffices, whether it derives from the common or the particular law, or whether it requires a mandate almost for its every exercise.[91]

After the exposition of what are the characteristic features of the office of superior in a strict sense, it now remains to determine the particular offices which qualify under these requirements. The first source to be examined is the Code, where an enumeration of those entitled to be called major superiors is to be found.[92] They are: 1) the abbot primate; 2) the abbot president of a monastic congregation; 3) the abbot of an independent monastery, although a member of a monastic congregation; 4) the supreme head of any religious society; 5) the provincial superior, 6) the vicars of the foregoing; and 7) others who have jurisdiction equivalent to that of a provincial. All of the above mentioned religious are definitely superiors and,

---

89 Canon 197, §1.

90 Schaefer, *De Religiosis*, n. 102, p. 214; Vermeersch-Creusen, *Epitome*, I, n. 573.

91 Schaefer, *loc. cit.*

92 Canon 488, 8°.

presupposed that they are members of a clerical exempt religious group, are to be considered as having the faculty to dispense from non-reserved private vows.

Under the last heading, embracing superiors who have jurisdiction equivalent to that of a provincial, are to be found two distinct groups. The first consists of those who are in charge of potential provinces. The second group consists of those who enjoy a temporary succession to the office of provincial or who hold an office resembling that of a vice-provincial. To the first group belong those who preside over a "vice"-province, a quasi-province, a commissariat, or a vicariate, provided that they do not already have the title of provincial. In this capacity they possess vicarious ordinary power.[93] To the second group belong those who fulfill the office of the general or of the provincial, or of the abbot of an independent monastery on the occasion of the incumbent's death, or on his being impeded from fulfilling his duties. Likewise in this group are classified inspectors, visitors of a commissariat,[94] guardians, and vice-provincials.[95]

Relative to both these groups care must be taken to ascertain whether the jurisdiction of those classified therein is not merely delegated jurisdiction for a particular transaction. This will be determined by the particular constitutions of each exempt religious order or congregation.[96]

In addition to the foregoing, religious who are specifically or generically mentioned in the Code as possessing

93 Wernz-Vidal, *De Religiosis*, n. 96, pp. 88-89; Schaefer, *De Religiosis*, n. 103, p. 216, nota 9.

94 Schaefer, *De Religiosis*, n. 103, p. 216, nota 10; Wernz-Vidal, *De Religiosis*, n. 96, pp. 88-89.

95 Wernz-Vidal, *loc. cit.*

96 Wernz-Vidal, *loc. cit.*

the title of superior, abbots and priors general of a centralized monastic order are to be included under the title of supreme moderator, and therefore of major superior. In addition the superior of an independent religious house, though he may not be an abbot for the simple reason that this dignity is prohibited in his community, is also to be considered a major superior, as is also the conventual prior of a non-abbatial independent monastery, provided that the rank of priorate has been juridically conferred on the religious house.[97]

In the immediately foregoing pages, only those who as major superiors qualify for the title of superior in the strict sense have been pointed out. There are others, however, who also qualify for this title; and in the Code they are called minor superiors. They are not specifically enumerated, as are the major superiors, but the Code does explicitly refer to them. Thus canon 505 speaks of "superiores . . . minores locales." The index of the Code speaks of "superiores religiosi minores seu locales." Although thus there appears to be an identity between the local and the minor superiors, there are times when this is not true. Thus he who presides over an independent monastery is a local major superior,[98] as is also the local abbot.[99] There is, therefore, no necessary identity between the two types of superior and the Code itself speaks of the one without limiting it by reference to the other.[100] Ordinarily the Code uses the term "local superior" when speaking of those orders or congregations which have a centralized organization.[101]

97 Wernz-Vidal, *De Religiosis*, n. 96, p. 89, nota 16.

98 Schaefer, *De Religiosis*, n. 103, p. 216; Wernz-Vidal, *loc. cit.*

99 Canon 488, 8°; Schaefer, *loc. cit.*

100 Canon 509, § 2: "Curent Superiores locales . . ."

101 Canons 583, 2°; 611; 653; 668.

The next step is to determine what is the nature of the office of a minor and of a local superior. While the two are not necesarily identical, still it does seem that a minor superior is always a local superior, while a local superior is only accidentally at any time a major superior. Thus ordinarily a local superior in a centralized religious congregation or order will be a minor superior. When, however, the term local superior is used in a non-centralized religious group, the local superior is then a major superior. Hence for practical purposes the two will be spoken of as identical, and in the designation of one, the other will also be designated.

First of all, one who has charge of a filial house is not a local superior for a filial house does not constitute a distinct community, nor does it possess its own property. It remains, rather, a member of the principal house in a relationship of complete dependence on the latter, and though it has a "superior", he possesses merely a delegated power granted to him by that superior who rules and resides in the principal house.[102] Instead, a local superior is one who as regards religious discipline has other religious under his ordinary jurisdiction.[103] This authority or ordinary jurisdiction must derive either by common or particular law from the office which he holds. Hence any clerical exempt religious who has ordinary power over other religious by reason of his office must be said to be at least a local superior, or simply a superior in the strict sense of the Code.

---

102 S. C. De Religiosis, 1 febr. 1924—*AAS*, XVI (1924), 95; Schaefer, *De Religiosis*, n. 42, p. 76.

103 PCI, 2-3 iun. 1918—*AAS*, X (1918), 344.

A list of those who enjoy the title of superior among clerical exempt religious has thus been presented in the foregoing. Since the word "superior", when used in the Code of Canon Law in an unqualified sense, is to be understood as applying to a general, a provincial, a major, and a local superior alike, unless its limited sense is evident from the context, it can now be stated in conclusion that all those religious just described have ordinary power to dispense from non-reserved private vows.[104]

C. *Limited Dispensation Effected by the Law in Canons* 1111 *and* 1315

Later in this work a thorough discussion of canon 1111 will be offered. For the present it will suffice to say that in virtue of canon 1111 the legislator, at the moment a legitimate marriage is contracted, grants a limited dispensation from all vows if adherence to them would hinder the exercise of the acts proper to the marital state.

Canon 1315 states for an analogous reason, that through religious profession all vows taken previous to the profession are suspended for the time that the vowmaker remains in the religious life.

Article III. Delegated Power to Dispense from Private Vows

A. *The Nature of Delegated Power*

Delegated jurisdiction is that which is communicated directly to a person.[105] In this respect it differs from ordinary power, which is shared directly with an office and only indirectly with the incumbent.

---

[104] Canon 1313, 2°: "Superior religionis clericalis exemptae quod attinet personas quae can. 514, § 1, enumerantur . . . vota non reservata possunt iusta de causa dispensare, dummodo dispensatio ne laedat ius aliis quaesitum."

[105] Canon 197, § 1.

Delegated power to dispense from private vows can be granted to a person without regard to the office he holds, or without regard to his personal qualifications. On the other hand, it can also be granted for one of these reasons, namely, in view of the person's personal qualifications or in consideration of the office which he holds. When a person claims that he has received a delegated power in consideration of his personal qualifications, this alleged fact must be proved; it cannot be presumed.[106] Hence, if a person who is not the incumbent of an office is delegated to dispense from private vows, there is no presumption that this delegation was accorded to him on account of the personal qualifications which he possessed. Moreover, when the incumbent of an office, or the holder of some dignity or title is delegated to dispense from private vows, the idea that by way of juridical presumption the delegation was accorded on account of his personal qualifications is likewise excluded.[107]

When a person is granted power to dispense from vows on account of the office which he holds, he must not regard that power as implying the possession of the faculty as an ordinary power. Such a power lacks the stability inherent in ordinary power, since it can be recalled by him who granted it, and hence cannot be said to be contained in the office as such.[108]

Likewise, the power to dispense from private vows which is contained in the habitual faculties of the ordinary as received from the Holy See does not cease to be delegated power despite the fact that on the death of the ordi-

106 Canons 190, § 2; 57, § 2; Cappello, *Summa Iuris Canonici*, I, n. 160.

107 Cappello, *loc. cit.*

108 Canon 207, § 1.

nary the faculty is transmitted to his successor without any renewed act of delegation. Moreover, although this faculty is delegated to the ordinary, it is also enjoyed by his vicar general.[109]

In such instances and circumstances confusion can easily arise between ordinary and delegated power to dispense from private vows. Although delegated faculties be so granted as to pass from one incumbent of an office to his successor, these faculties are not contained in the office, and they belong not to all who hold the same type of office, but only to those who have received them by indult or privilege.[110]

Delegated power to dispense from private vows must also be distinguished from vicarious ordinary power to dispense from private vows. Whereas the person possessing vicarious ordinary power to dispense participates in the power of him who constitutes him as a vicar in such wise as to become the latter's representative or mandatory, the person possessing delegated power to dispense, though participating in the power of the one delegating, does not participate in that power in such wise as to become the representative or mandatory of the one delegating, unless this fact is actually stated in the delegation. Hence, a person who has delegated power to dispense from vows acts in his own name and for his own person, in contradistinction to him who for the reason that he has vicarious power necessarily acts in the name of him who constituted him as vicar.[111]

---

109 Canon 66, § 2.

110 Cappello, *ibid.*, n. 255; Coronata, *Institutiones*, I, n. 285; Vermeersch-Creusen, *Epitome*, I, n. 277.

111 Rodrigo, *De Legibus*, n. 50.

B. Persons Who Can Delegate the Power to Dispense

It is a general principle of the Code that all who have ordinary power can delegate that power completely or partially unless the law expressly provides otherwise.[112] Accordingly, all who possess ordinary power to dispense from private vows can delegate that power, for there is no provision in the Code to the contrary. In fact, canon 1313, 3°, expressly states that those who have been delegated by the Holy See can dispense from all non-reserved vows except when such a dispensation would injure the acquired right of another.

Wernz-Vidal, however, wisely recall[113] that the faculty of being able to delegate one's ordinary power is not intended as a means of shifting maliciously one's obligation to someone else though one delegate only part of one's power. Hence one who has ordinary power to dispense from vows should delegate that faculty only when in his prudent judgment there is present a grave cause.

C. Persons Who Can Subdelegate the Power to Dispense

All those who have received from the Holy See the delegated faculty of dispensing from private vows can subdelegate that power for a single act or even habitually (for a definite number of cases or for all cases within a definite period) provided that the act of subdelegating was not prohibited, or provided that the delegation was accorded not simply in view of the delegate's personal qualifications.[114] Capable also of subdelegating are all those who have received from someone intermediate in hierarchical rank to

---

112 Canon 199, § 1.

113 *De Personis*, n. 369, p. 431.

114 Canon 199, § 2.

the Roman Pontiff the power to dispense from all private vows of a certain category. It does not matter whether or not the number of cases is determined, provided that the case or cases are not determined concretely and individually.[115] In all other instances delegated faculties received from someone intermediate in rank to the Roman Pontiff can be subdelegated only when the act of subdelegation is expressly permitted.[116] If it is permitted, the extent of this faculty will be determined in accord with the express terms of the permission.

Finally, a person who has a subdelegated power to dispense from private vows cannot again subdelegate this faculty unless further subdelegation was expressly permitted.[117] This permission can be given only by him who has ordinary power.[118] A person who has ordinary power must retain control over that power, and thus it is he who determines the extent to which it is to be transferred to others. He must remain the master of his jurisdiction.[119] If a delegated person who has the power to subdelegate should add a still further power to make possible a further subdelegation, then the person who possesses the original ordinary power would immediately cease to control the extent to which his power was to be transferred to others; he would cease to be master of his jurisdiction, for the chain of jurisdiction between him and the last to exercise that jurisdiction would not exist. When finally it would be exercised, it would be done without any authority from

---

115 Canon 199, § 3; Rodrigo, *De Legibus*, n. 52.

116 Canon 199, § 4.

117 Canon 199, § 5.

118 Vermeersch-Creusen, *Epitome*, I, n. 280; Oesterle, "Subdelegation einer Dispensvollmacht"—*Theologisch-praktische Quartalschrift* (Linz 1832—), LXXXVIII (1935), 138-142 (hereafter cited as *TPQ*).

119 Oesterle, *loc. cit.*

him to whom it belonged properly and *ex officio*. Furthermore, the person who was originally delegated and empowered to subdelegate his jurisdiction would definitely exceed the limits of his mandate by attempting to communicate still further the faculty to subdelegate.[120]

D. *The Form of Delegating the Power to Dispense*

The form to be used in delegating the power to dispense from private vows is not specifically determined in the Code of Canon Law. Nevertheless, from the general norms of the Code and from the practice before the Code, certain principles can be pointed out.

For its validity, it is necessary that the act of delegation possess the following requisites: 1) It must be free from substantial error.[121] 2) The power to dispense from vows must be specifically mentioned,[122] or at least understood under an all-inclusive delegation, for since the delegated power to dispense from private vows is a privilege, it must be understood according to the strict meaning of the words.[123] Otherwise it would be quite impossible to ascertain just what was the will of the superior. One could claim, in such a hypotheses, to have the power to dispense from private vows from the fact that he had the similar power of dispensing from irregularities or of absolving from censures.[124] Furthermore, a person who has the faculty to grant a dispensation from a certain reserved vow cannot use that faculty to dispense validly from another vow, or

---

120 Canon 203, § 1.

121 Canon 104; D'Annibale, *Theologia Moralis*, I, n. 74; Cappello, *Summa Iuris Canonici*, I, n. 257; Coronata, *Institutiones*, I, n. 289, p. 343.

122 Suarez, *De Voto*, lib. VI, c. XII, n. 2.

123 Canon 67; Suarez, *loc. cit.*

124 Suarez, *loc. cit.*

from another reserved vow.[125] 3) On the part of the person who is delegated it is necessary that he accept the jurisdiction at least tacitly. If the one who is delegated is absent, he is not regarded as delegated until he has been directly informed. Accordingly, if the superior withdraws the delegation in the meantime, the jurisdiction cannot be said to have been communicated.[126] The superior, however, can grant the delegated power in such a way that it will be valid prior to and independently of its acceptance by the one who is delegated. This is also verified in the case in which the person who is delegated is absent.[127] It would seem, however, that, unless the superior expressly provided for the validity of the delegation prior to and independently of its acceptance by the person who was delegated, it would not be valid. 4) While the delegation need not be in writing,[128] it is required that the delegation be externally manifested.[129] 5) Finally, for licitness, it is required that the delegation granted be exercised freely, that it be accorded apart from simony, and that the person who is delegated be someone worthy of exercising the power committed to him.[130]

E. *The Various Ways in Which the Power to Dispense from Private Vows May Be Delegated*

Delegation of the power to dispense from private vows can be a *special* delegation or a *general* delegation. A *special* delegation is that which is given for a case or cases

125 Marc-Gestermann-Raus, *Institutiones Morales Alphonsianae* (18. ed., 2 vols., Lugduni: Vitte, 1927-1928), I, n. 646 (hereafter cited as *Institutiones*).

126 Coronata, *Institutiones*, I, n. 289, p. 349.

127 Cappello, *Summa Iuris Canonici*, I, n. 257.

128 Coronata, *loc. cit.*

129 Cappello, *Summa Iuris Canonici*, I, n. 257, p. 325.

130 Coronata, *Institutiones*, I, n. 289, p. 349.

which are previously concretely determined. A *general* delegation is that which is given for a complete category of cases, that is for all cases which occur, or for a definite number of cases not individually determined.[131] General delegation, moreover, can be limited not only in relation to the kind of vow to which it extends, but also by the appointment of a certain time after which it cannot be validly exercised.[132] When the power to dispense from vows is granted for a single and individual case, it can be validly exercised for that one act only. When the power which is granted to dispense from vows is general, it can be validly exercised depending upon the will of the superior, either for a definite number of cases not individually determined, for all cases within a prescribed time, or for all cases without any prescribed time limit.[133]

F. *Interpretation of the Faculty to Dispense from Private Vows*

Delegated power to dispense from private vows is to be interpreted broadly in the following cases: 1) when it is given for a complete category of cases, e.g., for all non-reserved vows, or for all vows of chastity, even though the delegation be limited as to time;[134] 2) when it is contained in habitual faculties (which can also be considered delegated power given for a complete category of cases) whether these were given permanently, or for a prescribed time, or for a definite number of cases;[135] 3) when the faculty to dis-

131 Rodrigo, *De Legibus*, n. 52.

132 Cappello, *Summa Iuris Canonici*, I, n. 257, p. 326.

133 Canon 66, § 1; Cappello, *Summa Iuris Canonici*, I, n. 257, pp. 326-327.

134 Canon 200, § 1.

135 Canon 66, § 1: "Facultates habituales quae conceduntur vel in perpetuum vel ad praefinitum tempus aut certum numerum casuum, accensentur privilegiis praeter ius." Canon 50: "In dubio, rescripta quae ad lites referuntur,

pense from private vows is contained in habitual faculties, even though it can be used for only one case, provided that the case is not determined concretely and individually.[136]

Delegated power to dispense from private vows is to be interpreted strictly whenever it is granted for a case or cases which are concretely and individually predetermined.[137] It must not be forgotten, however, that every delegated power is understood to contain the faculty for doing whatever is necessary for the valid and licit use of the expressly delegated power, provided that this implicit faculty does not exceed the limits of the power possessed by the one who grants the delegation.[138]

G. *The Privilege of Regulars to Dispense from Private Vows*

In the historical synopsis it was seen that regular confessors enjoyed the privilege of dispensing from non-reserved private vows.[139] In virtue of canon 4, it must be admitted that regular confessors still enjoy this privilege.[140] However, as was pointed out above,[141] the individual regu-

---

vel iura aliis quaesita laedunt, vel adversantur legi in commodum privatorum, vel denique impetrata fuerunt ad beneficii ecclesiastici assecutionem, strictam interpretationem recipiunt; *cetera omnia latam.*" (Italics inserted by the writer); cf. canon 68.

136 Rodrigo, *De Legibus*, n. 891.

137 Canon 200, § 1; Rodrigo, *De Legibus*, n. 53.

138 Canon 200, § 1: ". . . cui tamen delegata potestas est, ea quoque intelliguntur concessa, sine quibus eadem exerceri non posset."; Wernz-Vidal, *De Personis*, n. 374, p. 435; Rodrigo, *loc. cit.*

139 *Supra*, pp. 61-63.

140 "Iura aliis quaesita, itemque privilegia atque indulta quae, ab Apostolica Sede ad haec usque tempora personis sive physicis sive moralibus concessa, in usu adhuc sunt nec revocata, integra manent, nisi huius Codicis canonibus expresse revocentur."

141 Cf. *supra*, p. 63.

lar confessor, especially among the mendicant orders, should examine his faculties both as to the internal and the external forum and especially in regard to the extension of these to the laity to ascertain what privileges have been communicated to him by his superiors.[142] Moreover, since this privilege was given directly to or shared through intercommunication by regulars, it can be enjoyed by all those who make a profession of perpetual or temporary vows in a religious institute of solemn vows.[143]

H. Apostolic Legates Delegated to Dispense from Private Vows

The nuncios, internuncios, and apostolic delegates of the Holy See have been granted the faculty of dispensing from all private vows, even those reserved to the Holy See, with the exception only of those in which the rights of a third party would be prejudiced.[144] Although the apostolic legates do have ordinary power in certain matters, nevertheless this faculty of dispensing from vows is possessed by them as a delegated faculty.[145]

---

142 Wernz-Vidal, *De Rebus*, Pars I, n. 557, p. 667, nota 87.

143 Canon 488, 2°, 5°.

144 *Index Facultatum*, c. I, n. 15: "Commutandi aut dispensandi, consideratis causis, omnia vota simplicia private emissa, etiam Apostolicae Sedi reservata, exceptis votis in quibus agitur de tertii praeiudicio."—In Vermeersch-Creusen, *Epitome*, I, n. 813.

145 Canon 267, § 1, 3°; Wernz-Vidal, *De Personis*, n. 515, p. 631; Cappello, *Summa Iuris Canonici*, I, n. 343, p. 441.

CHAPTER V

THE EXTENT OF THE POWER TO DISPENSE FROM PRIVATE VOWS

The purpose of this chapter is to analyze the extent of the power to dispense from private vows. Towards this end it is the writer's intention to show *to whom* a dispensation can be granted, *in what locality* it can be granted, and *in what forum* it can be granted. Finally, it is the writer's intention to show to what extent this power of dispensing from private vows is limited in regard to certain types of vows.

ARTICLE I. THE EXTENT OF THE POWER TO DISPENSE IN REGARD TO THE PASSIVE SUBJECT OF THE DISPENSATION

A. *General Principles*

1. *The Necessity of a Superior-Subject Relationship*

The basic restriction placed on everyone having the power to dispense from private vows is contained in the principle that the power of jurisdiction can be used directly only over one's subjects.[1] When, however, a person receives either from the law itself[2] or from another authority,[3] the power to dispense from the vows of those who are not one's subjects, a person is then said to exercise his

[1] Canon 201, § 1: "Potestas iurisdictionis potest in solos subditos exerceri."

[2] E.g., canon 1313, 1°, grants to local ordinaries the power to dispense non-subjects from their private vows, i.e., the local ordinary can dispense "*peregrini*" or, as they are spoken of in this work, *travelers*.

[3] The Roman Pontiff can give to any lesser official in the Church the power to dispense any baptized person, though that person may not be a subject of the one who grants the dispensation; a person possessing ordinary power can delegate to another the faculty of dispensing from the private vows of the former's subjects.

jurisdiction indirectly,[4] and the basic restriction requiring a superior-subject relationship thus yields to a special provision of law.

Since the superior-subject relationship is so important for determining who may be given a dispensation, a brief examination of the various titles under which this relationship arises should prove valuable for determining in regard to persons dispensed the extent of the power to dispense from private vows.

First of all, the distinction between the external and the internal forums in relation to the establishment of the superior-subject relationship must be taken into consideration, since the relationship does not arise in the same manner in both forums.[5]

---

[4] Jurisdiction is exercised directly when it is exercised over a subject inasmuch as he is a subject; it is exercised indirectly when it is exercised over a non-subject in view of some special provision of law, e.g., in the case of dispensing from the vows of travelers. Cf. canon 1313, 1°; Coronata *Institutiones*, I, n. 282, p. 337.

[5] The *internal forum* takes cognizance of things which concern men and women as individuals. It primarily and directly attends to the spiritual welfare and the relation of the individual to God. To this forum pertain matters which by divine law must always be acted upon in the sacrament of penance, e.g., absolution from sins; or which by human law must sometimes be treated in the sacrament of penance, e.g., absolution from censures. On the other hand, some matters pertaining to this forum can be acted on outside of the sacrament of penance, unless a particular law or prescript requires otherwise. As a result of the indicated distinctions, the internal forum is divided into the *internal sacramental* and the *internal extra-sacramental forums.*

The external forum is primarily concerned with the public and common good of the Church. It embraces the individual as a member of the Church and in his relation to the other members of the Church.

The internal forum requires secrecy in its operation, even though the matter involved in a given instance be publicly known; the external forum, on the other hand, operates in a manner which makes it possible according to the nature of the matter to establish sufficiently before the visible body of the Church the exercise of ecclesiastical jurisdiction. Maroto, *Institutiones*, I, pp. 857-858.

a. The Titles Underlying the Superior-Subject Relationship in the Internal Forum

The superior-subject relationship requisite for dispensing from private vows in the internal sacramental forum arises at the moment a priest endowed with the faculty to dispense from private vows in the internal sacramental forum is approached by a penitent, provided that the penitent begins his confession, and provided that the priest at that moment can validly accept it.[6] It is not, however, required for the existence of the superior-subject relationship that absolution follow. Accordingly, if the absolution is denied or given invalidly, the superior-subject relationship must still be said to have arisen.[7]

In regard to the titles underlying the superior-subject relationship in the internal extra-sacramental forum, a distinction must be made. If the faculty to grant the dispensation is directed to be used for one's penitents, or if it is given to one in the capacity of a confessor, the sole requirement for the existence of the superior-subject relationship is that the author of the dispensation possess confessional jurisdiction over the person to be dispensed, even though confession is not begun or intended. If such terms, or terms equivalent to them, were not used in the granting of the faculty to dispense from private vows, then the norms—to be explained later—for determining the use of ordinary and delegated power over subjects and non-subjects must be applied.[8]

---

[6] Rodrigo, *De Legibus*, n. 475.

[7] Cappello, *De Matrimonio*, pars I, n. 238, p. 301.

[8] Rodrigo, *De Legibus*, n. 475; Michiels, *Normae Generales Juris Canonici* (2 vols., Lublin-Polonia: Universitas Catholica, 1929), II, 492 (hereafter cited as *Normae Generales*).

b. The Titles Underlying the Superior-Subject Relationship in the External Forum

The superior-subject relationship in the external forum takes its origin from the following titles: from baptism, which constitutes a person primarily a subject of the Roman Pontiff;[9] from domicile, quasi-domicile, or an actual presence in a particular territory, for those who are without a domicile or quasi-domicile,[10] which factors constitute a person a subject of the local ordinary, of the pastor, or of other superiors who have charge over a particular territory;[11] from entrance into the novitiate of a clerical exempt institute, which constitutes the novice a subject of the major and local superior of that community;[12] from religious profession, which constitutes the professed person a subject of the exempt major and minor superiors;[13] from the assignment, even though transitory, of a professed religious, of a novice, or of a postulant to a particular exempt house, which fact constitutes him a subject of the local superior of that house;[14] and from the residence in an exempt religious house by day and by night, which constitutes servants, guests, students, convalescents, and the infirm as subjects of the clerical exempt local superior.[15]

In designating, in the foregoing, the titles by which a person becomes a subject of a clerical exempt superior, the

---

9 Canons 12; 87.

10 Canons 91; 94, § 2.

11 Canon 94, § 1.

12 Canons 615; 514, § 1; Rodrigo, *De Legibus*, n. 475.

13 Canons 501, § 1; 578, 2°; 615.

14 Canon 514, § 1.

15 Canon 514, § 1; Michiels, *Normae Generales*, II, 494; Rodrigo, *De Legibus*, n. 475.

present analysis was restricted to the religious society with a centralized organization. In the case of independent monasteries and monastic congregations, the designation is necessarily somewhat different. Thus, while the clerical exempt superior in an individual monastery governs the members of that monastery (professed, novices, postulants, and others according to the enumeration of canon 514, § 1) as his subjects, yet in the case of monastic congregations the Abbot Primate and the Abbot President do not have power and jurisdiction as complete and extensive as that which the law communicates to the major superiors of other religious institutes. Consequently, in determining what actually are the powers of the Abbot Primate and the Abbot President over the members of a monastic congregation or an independent monastery, an examination must be made of their own constitutions and the special decrees of the Holy See.[16]

2. *Dispensation from One's Own Vow*

As was seen in the historical synopsis,[17] there was extensive speculation before the Code as to the manner in which a cleric with the faculty to dispense from the vows of others might obtain a dispensation from his own vows. Once again, in the matter of vows, the Code has settled the pre-Code dispute and uncertainty. Under the Code one endowed with the faculty to dispense from private vows in the external forum or in the internal extra-sacramental forum can use that faculty to dispense from his own private non-reserved vow, provided that the dispensation does not violate the acquired right of another.

---

[16] Canon 501, § 3; Reilly, *Dispensations*, p. 98.

[17] Cf. *supra*, pp. 65-68.

This exercise of the dispensing power in one's own favor is possible, for the granting of a dispensation from a private vow is an act of voluntary jurisdiction, in the exercise of which a distinction of persons is not required as in the exercise of judicial jurisdiction.[18]

It has been pointed out that this faculty can be exercised in one's own favor only when the jurisdiction which one possesses over the private vows was granted for the external or the internal extra-sacramental forum. One cannot dispense from his own private vows if his faculty over private vows can be exercised only in the internal sacramental forum. Canon 201, § 3, states:

> "Nisi aliud ex natura rei aut ex iure constet, potestatem iurisdictionis voluntariam seu non iudicialem quis exercere potest etiam in proprium commodum, aut extra territorium exsistens, aut in subditum e territorio absentem."

There is, indeed, no prescription of law prohibiting the use of the faculty to dispense from private vows in one's own favor when the faculty which one has to dispense from vows is restricted to the internal sacramental forum. But, while there is no law to that effect, the nature of things, that is, of the forum in which jurisdiction is to be exercised, does prohibit it. It has been seen that when voluntary jurisdiction is attached to judicial sacramental jurisdiction, it becomes subordinate to the judicial jurisdiction, and follows the rules for the exercise of the latter.[19] Furthermore, it has been seen that when the faculty of dispensing from private vows is granted for the internal sacramental forum, it cannot be used until the person seeking the dispensation begins his confession in the pres-

---

[18] Canons 201, §§ 2-3; 1313; Reilly, *Dispensations*, p. 102.

[19] Cf. *supra*, pp. 83-84, 122.

ence of a priest who can validly accept it.[20] Since, however, no one can validly accept his own confession,[21] so no one whose jurisdiction over vows is restricted to the internal sacramental forum can dispense himself from a vow.[22]

B. *The Extent of Ordinary Power in Regard to the Passive Subject*

Ordinary power is that which by law is attached to an office. In this way it becomes an integral part of the office, and, unless the law specially decrees otherwise, it extends only to those persons to whom the office itself extends. For example, the local ordinary's power extends not only to all who have a domicile or quasi-domicile in his territory but also to wanderers (*vagi*).[23] It does not extend to travelers (*peregrini*), for his office, which does not comprise them as subjects, does not extend to them, except in the few instances wherein the law specifically states that it does.[24]

1. *The Extent of the Roman Pontiff's Power*

As has been seen,[25] a person is constituted a subject of the Roman Pontiff through the valid reception of the sacrament of baptism. Once this relationship of superior and subject is established by the fact of a valid baptism, the Roman Pontiff can dispense the baptized person from his private vows anywhere in the world.[26]

---

20 Cf. *supra*, p. 122.
21 Canon 201, § 2.
22 Rodrigo, *op cit.*, n. 54.
23 Canon 94, §§ 1-2.
24 Canons 14, § 1; 1313, 1°; Rodrigo, *De Legibus*, n. 55.
25 Cf. *supra*, p. 123.
26 Canon 218; Prümmer, *Theologia Moralis*, III, n. 423.

2. *The Extent of the Local Ordinary's Power*

It has also just been seen that a baptized person is constituted a subject of a local ordinary through domicile, quasi-domicile, and, in the case of wanderers, through their actual presence in the territory of the local ordinary. To all these duly constituted subjects the local ordinary can grant a dispensation from private vows by reason of the faculty attributed to him in canon 1313, 1°.[27] In addition, however, the local ordinary has received through the Code the power to grant to certain non-subjects, namely, to travelers, a dispensation from private vows;[28] and, although the local ordinary derives this power over travelers from the Code, it is not a delegated power, but rather an ordinary power, to dispense from private vows.[29] By thus granting to the local ordinary this faculty to dispense travelers from their private vows, the Code has settled a dispute of long standing.

3. *The Local Ordinary's Power to Dispense from the Private Vows of Professed Religious, Novices, and Postulants in an Exempt Institute*

That which constitutes a baptized person the subject of a local ordinary or of other territorial superiors is domicile, quasi-domicile, and, in respect of those who are wanderers, an actual presence. In regard to religious, however,

27 As was seen above, the residential bishop derives this power from Christ Himself. Cf. *supra*, pp. 93-102.

28 Canon 1313, 1°: "Loci Ordinarius quod attinet ad omnes suos subditos atque *etiam peregrinos* vota non-reservata potest . . . dispensare. . ." (Italics inserted by the writer.)

29 Cappello: ". . . hodie ordinariae censendae sunt omnes facultates quae a Codice statuuntur. . ."—*Summa Iuris Canonici*, I, n. 255, p. 323; Wernz-Vidal, *De Rebus*, pars I, n. 557, p. 666.

it is disputed whether they can acquire a domicile or a quasi-domicile. As a result their subjection to the local ordinary is placed in question. In the case of non-exempt religious, the Code takes care of this difficulty by placing them all under the local ordinary.[30] Accordingly, whether non-exempt religious have or do not have a domicile or a quasi-domicile, they are subject to the local ordinary. In consequence of this fact the local ordinary can grant non-exempt religious a dispensation from private vows according to canon 1313, 1°.

Now it remains to examine the extent of the local ordinary's dispensatory power over exempt religious, with consideration being given first to the perpetually professed, then to the novices, and finally to the postulants.

a. Religious

Through the privilege of exemption religious are removed from the authority of the local ordinary except in those matters to which express mention is given in the Code as bringing even exempt religious under the local ordinary's authority.[31] Subsidiary to and in relation to this personal exemption canon 615 adds a local exemption whereby the houses and the churches of those who are personally exempt likewise participate in the privilege.

As is obvious, the privilege of exemption removes the title underlying subjection to the local ordinary. Therefore, even if the exempt religious had a domicile, that, in itself, would not place them under the local ordinary's

---

30 Canon 500, § 1: "Subduntur quoque religiosi Ordinario loci iis exceptis qui a Sede Apostolica exemptionis privilegium consecuti sunt, salva semper potestate quam ius etiam in eos locorum Ordinariis concedit."

31 Canon 615.

power to dispense them from their private vows. However, if they had a domicile, they could become travelers in the canonical sense and thus come under the local ordinary's power by reason of canon 1313, 1°. The question then to be decided is whether they can acquire a domicile.

In this matter there are three opinions, or rather three divergent solutions. Some authors expressly disqualify all religious from acquiring any but a necessary domicile. This necessary domicile is neither parochial nor diocesan; it is a domicile in the place where the monastery or the religious house actually exists,[32] and for its acquisition the mere assignment of the religious to the religious house suffices. In support of this solution it is maintained that this was the law prior to the Code. An analogy of law is also resorted to. These authors point out that since religious are not *sui iuris*, they are to be considered as equivalent to minors and must therefore be assigned a necessary domicile.[33] Finally, it is asserted that, since exempt professed religious lose their proper domicile and diocese by perpetual profession, they must be granted one to take its place. Because, however, they lack the power of choosing for themselves, the substitute domicile can only be a necessary domicile.[34]

A second solution to this problem comes from a few authors who seem to indicate that exempt professed religious can obtain a voluntary domicile by means of a de-

---

32 Vermeersch-Creusen: ". . . in loco conventus. . ."—*Epitome*, I, p. 142, n. 188; Beste, *Introductio*, p. 139; Wernz-Vidal, *De Personis*, n. 12, p. 16, nota 12; cf. Coronata, *Institutiones*, I, n. 128, p. 146; Rodrigo, *De Legibus*, p. 101, n. 133; Cappello, *Summa Iuris Canonici*, I, n. 195, p. 229.

33 Vermeersch-Creusen, *loc. cit.*; Meysztowicz, "Domicilium et Quasi-Domicilium,"—*Jus Pontificium* (Romae, 1921—), VI (1926), 47.

34 Coronata, *Institutiones*, I, n. 128, p. 146; Meysztowicz, *loc. cit.*

cennial residence in a certain place apart from any previous intention of remaining there.[35] At the same time some authors say that religious can acquire a quasi-domicile. Thus Vermeersch[36] and Coronata[37] speak of religious acquiring a quasi-domicile, the latter even conceding that they can acquire a parochial quasi-domicile.[38]

Finally, there is a third group which denies that an exempt professed religious can acquire any domicile. An outstanding proponent of this opinion is Oesterle, who proposed his doctrine for the first time in an article entitled "De Domicilio Religiosorum."[39] This opinion begins with the premise that a domicile or quasi-domicile can only be acquired in a parish, or in a quasi-parish, or at least in a diocese, a vicariate apostolic, or a prefecture

---

35 Kinane, "Legal or Necessary Domicile"—*The Irish Ecclesiastical Record* (1864—), 5th series, XXVII (1926), 647-648 (hereafter cited as *IER*). Coronata: "In religionibus antiquis, ubi singuli monachi determinatae domui seu monasterio ab ingressu in religionem adscribuntur, ibidem semel ac professionem emiserint domicilium obtinent; habent enim animum, obedientiae subordinatum, ibidem permanendi in perpetuum. In aliis vero religionibus difficilius domicilium, facilius quasi-domicilium acquiri poterit, cum enim quaelibet assignatio domui determinatae precaria sit a voluntate superiorum pendens, ita assignatus animum perpetuo ibi manendi habere nequit et domicilium solummodo ex decennali commoratione completa ibidem acquirere poterit . . . Potest insuper religiosus domicilium habere dioecesanum et quasi-domicilium paroeciale; si nempe in dioecesi a decennio commoretur cum animo ibidem perpetuo manendi, at non commoretur in determinata paroecia."—*Institutiones*, I, n. 128, p. 147.

36 This author, after having denied that there can be a necessary or legal quasi-domicile, asserts: "Religiosi quoque quasi-domicilium habebunt in loco ubi ultra sex menses residere iubentur [necessary or legal domicile?] vel revera sedem habuerunt [voluntary?]."—*Epitome*, I, p. 142, n. 188.

37 ". . . facilius tamen acquiri potest quasi-domicilium (quam domicilium), quia assignationes singulorum religiosorum domui determinatae licet precariae sint, generatim tamen ad tempus determinatum ultra maiorem anni parte fieri consueverunt, e.g., ad triennium, ad annum, etc." *Loc. cit.*

38 Coronata, *loc. cit.*

39 *Commentarium pro Religiosis et Missionariis* (prior to 1935, *Commentarium pro Religiosis*) (Romae, 1920—), V (1924), 167-178 (hereafter cited CpR(M).

apostolic.[40] When the domicile or quasi-domicile is in a parish or a quasi-parish, it is a parochial domicile; when it is in a diocese, in a vicariate, or in a prefecture, and not in a parish, it is known as a diocesan domicile.[41] With the foregoing introductory conclusion as a premise, Oesterle then advances his view by recalling that exempt religious are exempt from parochial and diocesan jurisdiction together with their houses and churches.[42] Through this exemption they are removed from the authority of the bishop and *a fortiori* from the authority of the pastor. If, then, they are juridically neither in the parish nor in the diocese, and if they belong juridically neither to the parish nor to the diocese, how can they acquire a domicile or a quasi-domicile in the parish or in the diocese? In this regard it must not be overlooked that a mere physical presence in a parish or in a diocese does not constitute a parochial or a diocesan domicile for a person. In addition to the physical presence a juridical presence is also necessary. By a juridical presence is meant that a person is actually present within a diocese in such a manner that according to the existing norms of Canon Law there can arise between him and the pastor or the local ordinary a relationship from which may result a jurisdictional or juridical bond.[43]

This may become clearer through the use of illustrations. If a Catholic of the Oriental Ruthenian Rite resides for ten years within the boundaries of a parish of the Latin Rite, does the Latin pastor thus become his proper pastor? Likewise, if a Catholic of the Latin Rite

---

40 Canon 92, § 1.

41 Canon 92, § 3.

42 Canon 615.

43 Oesterle, *ibid.*, p. 171.

belongs to a personal parish, all affiliation with a territorial parish being excluded, does he become a subject of the territorial pastor in whose parish he has lived for twenty years? It is the same with exempt religious; for as they are not able to renounce their privilege of exemption, so, too, they cannot acquire by their mere physical presence a jurisdictional or juridical status in a parish or a diocese, the result of which would be to give them a domicile or a quasi-domicile there, thus making the territorial pastor or bishop their proper pastor or bishop.[44]

Furthermore, a legal or a necessary domicile is a fiction of law; for this reason it cannot be said to embrace either persons or cases except those expressed in the law. Accordingly, its extension to the persons or cases not mentioned in the law must be considered unwarranted in law. Because the law has not included religious among those who have a necessary quasi-domicile, any attempt to include them among those who do have a necessary quasi-domicile must necessarily be considered as legally unwarranted.[45]

After thus examining the various solutions offered with relation to the problem of whether exempt professed religious can obtain a domicile, it is the conviction of the writer that the solution which denies religious this capacity is the more probable.[46] The writer, however, does not deny

---

[44] Oesterle, *loc. cit.*

[45] Reiffenstuel, *Ius Canonicum*, lib. I, tit. II, n. 184; Roberti, *De Processibus* (2 vols., Romae: Apud Aedes Facultatis Iuridicae ad S. Appollinaris, 1926), II, n. 376, nota 1; Costello, *Domicile and Quasi-Domicile*, The Catholic University of America Canon Law Studies, n. 60 (Washington, D. C.: The Catholic University of America, 1930) p. 174; Schaefer, *De Religiosis*, n. 598, p. 1028.

[46] In addition to Oesterle, it seems that also Schaefer (*loc. cit.*) prefers this opinion, though he admits that the common opinion attributes to religious a capacity for the acquisition of a necessary domicile and a necessary quasi-domicile.

the probability of the opinion which claims for exempt professed religious the capacity of acquiring a necessary domicile or a necessary quasi-domicile. Under the view that professed exempt religious cannot acquire a domicile or a quasi-domicile, the same professed religious must be denied the capacity for the juridical status of a traveler, since a traveler in the canonical sense is one who is outside the place of his domicile or quasi-domicile.[47] Nevertheless, even if exempt professed religious be denied the capacity for acquiring a domicile or a quasi-domicile, and consequently for gaining the juridical status of a traveler, there still remains a well founded opinion which attributes to exempt professed religious the right to petition for and to receive the fruits of the local ordinary's benign power.

In the case at hand, there is no positive law which expressly forbids or permits exempt professed religious to petition and receive from the local ordinary a dispensation from their private vows. There is, however, an obstacle to their doing this. It consists in their enjoying the privilege of exemption, whereby they are removed from the authority of the local ordinary. If they were not so favored, they, like non-exempt religious, could obtain from the local ordinary a dispensation from their private vows. It is true that they can receive from their own superiors a dispensation from their private vows; nevertheless, their condition thereby is hardly equal to that of the non-exempt religious. For even this approximately equal condition ceases when the religious superior cannot be reached. Then their condition, because of the favor they enjoy through the privilege of exemption, becomes less advantageous than that of the non-exempt.

47 Canon 91.

In the absence of any positive law to cover this situation, it seems perfectly legitimate under the authority of Canon 20 to apply the general principle of law, "Quod ob gratiam alicuius conceditur, non est in eius dispendium retorquendum."[48] When because of their exemption exempt religious find themselves unable to obtain a dispensation from their private vows at the hands of the local ordinary, it is clear that their privilege is working to their detriment, and as a consequence the general principle stated above must be put into effect.

Once the above-given general principle is put into effect, it must be admitted that exempt religious are subject to the exclusively benign power of the local ordinary to the extent that the exercise of this benign power in their favor is not in opposition to the obligations of the rules and constitutions of the exempt religious institute.[49]

The reasonableness of the proffered opinion becomes more apparent when it is recalled that the exemption of religious is not so complete that it does not admit of exceptions whereby they are made subject to the burden-imposing power of the local ordinary in many matters. Actually exempt religious are subject to the local ordinary in many more matters than are travelers.[50] Yet, travelers are expressly placed under the benign power of the local ordinary in regard to vows,[51] while exempt religious, though not entirely free of subjection to the burden-imposing power,

---

48 Reg. 61, R.J., in VI°. Text from Friedberg, *Corpus Iuris Canonici*.

49 Rodrigo, *De Legibus*, p. 361, n. 481.

50 Beste (*Introductio*, pp. 419-420) enumerates approximately sixty-one different ways in which exempt religious are subject to the local ordinary. Travelers, on the other hand, are subject to the burden-imposing power of the local ordinary only in those laws which are intended for the protection of the public order or which determine the formalities of certain acts (Canon 14, 2°).

51 Canon 1313, 1°.

would be hindered from enjoying the advantage of the benign power of the local ordinary because of their privilege of exemption. The application, therefore, of the general principle stated above, as a means of supplying for the lacuna in the Code, seems perfectly lawful as a juridic analogy.[52]

As a result of this study of the capacity of exempt professed religious to seek from the local ordinary a dispensation from their private vows, it can be stated that exempt professed religious have the right to seek and the local ordinary has the power to grant such a dispensation.[53]

b. Novices

Although here only novices in exempt communities will be spoken of expressly, under this title exempt religious with temporary vows are also understood to be included, since their status for the purpose of this discussion is practically identical with that of the novices.

In virtue of canon 615, novices in the communities of regulars participate in the privilege of exemption. Since, however, they are not perpetually professed, they can still retain their domicile.[54] In one respect, therefore, their juridical status is the same as that of the perpetually professed; in another, their status is different. In so far as novices are not perpetually professed, they retain as minors their necessary or legal domicile, and they can, if they wish, retain their voluntary quasi-domicile; if they are adults they can retain their voluntary domicile.[55] In so far as

52 Canon 20.

53 Rodrigo, *De Legibus*, n. 481; cf. Van Hove, *De Dispensationibus*, n. 434.

54 Canon 585.

55 Oesterle, *ibid.*, p. 172; cf. Canon 93, § 2.

novices are exempt, they cannot, under one view, acquire a domicile or a quasi-domicile for the same reasons which were given above for denying this capacity to religious under perpetual profession in an exempt community.[56] If, however, a novice retains the domicile or quasi-domicile which he had prior to his entrance into the novitiate, he can be classified as a traveler outside his domicile or quasi-domicile. In this capacity of traveler he can rightfully seek a dispensation from his private vows, and the local ordinary can grant him the dispensation by reason of canon 1313, 1°. The only local ordinary who could not dispense him from his vows would be the proper ordinary of his domicile or quasi-domicile, because in the territory of this proper local ordinary the novice is not a traveler, while at the same time he is removed from the authority of that proper ordinary by reason of his exemption.

As in the case of the perpetually professed, however, and by reason of the general principle of law enunciated above, the novices of an exempt order or congregation enjoy subjection to the benign power of the local ordinary even of the diocese of their domicile or quasi-domicile, and can accordingly petition and receive from him a dispensation from private vows.

c. *Postulants*

Since postulants in exempt communities do not participate in the privilege of exemption,[57] and since they retain their freedom of choice,[58] they can as minors acquire a voluntary quasi-domicile[59] while retaining their necessary

56 Oesterle, *loc. cit.*

57 Canon 615.

58 Rodrigo, *De Legibus*, p. 101, n. 133.

59 Canons 92, § 2; 93 § 2.

domicile.[60] When a postulant is in his majority, or when he gains his majority during his postulancy, he can acquire a voluntary domicile or quasi-domicile. Both the postulant, therefore, who is a minor, and the postulant who is in his majority are subjects of the local ordinary where they have their domicile and quasi-domicile. On the basis of this title of superior-subject relationship, the proper local ordinary, or simply the local ordinary can dispense them from their private vows according to canon 1313, 1°.

4. *The Clerical Exempt Superior's Power*

In determining those to whom a clerical exempt superior can grant a dispensation from their private vows, canon 1313, 2°, states that the superior can grant this dispensation to all persons who are enumerated in canon 514, § 1.[61] In this latter canon the following persons are enumerated:

1). Professed religious. This evidently refers to the professed religious of the institute over which the superior has charge.

2). Novices. These too would be of the same institute as the superior in question.

3). "Others who live day and night in the religious house, either as servants, or for the purpose of education, or as guests, or on account of health."[62]

---

60 Canon 93, § 1.

61 "Vota non reservata potest iusta de causa dispensare, dummodo dispensatio ne laedat ius aliis quaesitum . . . Superior religionis clericalis exemptae quod attinet ad personas quae can. 514, § 1, enumerantur."

62 Canon 514, § 1: "In omni religione clericali ius et officium Superioribus est per se vel per alium aegrotis professis, novitiis, aliisve in religiosa domo diu noctuque degentibus causa famulatus aut educationis aut hospitii aut infirmae valetudinis Eucharisticum Viaticum et extremam unctionem minis-

When the Code speaks of those who live day and night in the religious house, it is generally understood to include those who have actually stayed there one full day, that is, at least a day and a night, and also those who, having the intention of remaining in the religious house a day and a night, have already begun their stay.[63]

The term "religious house", as used in canon 514, § 1, is generally understood to be surrounded with certain definite limitations. Hence, it must be a religious house in which the religious institute retains a permanently organized community which under the authority of a superior carries on in a stable manner the work proper to that order or congregation.[64] While it is not required that the religious house consist of one physically distinct building, but may even consist of a group of buildings provided that they are in the possession of and inhabited by the religious,[65] nevertheless the religious house must not be thought to extend to schools and colleges, or to summer homes and similar buildings, when these cannot be considered formally a part of the religious house and with it to constitute one complex of buildings.[66]

Among those enumerated in canon 514, § 1, no mention is made of the postulants of exempt orders or congregations, or of nuns subject to clerical exempt superiors. They should not, however, for this reason be excluded

---

trandi."; Woywod, *A Practical Commentary on the Code of Canon Law*, cf. 7. ed. revised by Callistus Smith (2 vols., New York: Wagner, 1943), I, 191-192 (hereafter cited as *Commentary*).

63 Coronata, *Institutiones*, I, n. 540, p. 669; Vermeersch-Creusen, *Epitome*, I, p. 366, n. 582; Beste, *Introductio*, p. 336.

64 Beste, *op. cit.*, p. 321.

65 Coronata, *op. cit.*, n. 540, p. 670; Beste, *op. cit.*, p. 336.

66 Vermeersch-Creusen, *loc. cit.*; Beste, *loc. cit.*; Coronata, *loc. cit.*

from among those who can receive a dispensation from their private vows from their clerical exempt superior.

Postulants, inasmuch as they are not exempt,[67] do not come under the authority of the superior of a clerical exempt institute in the same exclusive manner as do novices, and especially the professed. They can, however, benefit from the dispensatory power of their superior over private vows in the same manner as those who remain night and day in the religious house for the purpose of obtaining an education.[68] Postulants can, therefore, seek from their clerical exempt superior a dispensation from their private vows, and he in virtue of canons 1313, 2°, and 514, § 1, can grant it to them.

In regard to nuns, it must be recalled that the fundamental requirement for granting a dispensation from their private vows is that there exist a superior-subject relationship.[69] Although neither canon 1313, § 1, nor canon 514, § 1, includes nuns among those who may obtain from a clerical exempt superior a dispensation from their private vows, and although these same canons do not use the general term "subjects" to designate those who can be dispensed, nevertheless there are times when, according to the

67 Canon 615.

68 Berutti, (*Institutiones Iuris Canonici* [6 vols., Vol. III, Taurini-Romae: Marietti, 1936], III, n. 27, p. 54) states that postulants can be classified with either the novices or with those who remain day and night in the religious house. Such an arbitrary classification, however, seems to be untenable in view of a response of the Pontifical Commission for the Interpretation of the Code. This response states that if anyone among those mentioned in canon 514, § 1, is ill outside of the religious house, the religious superior can administer the last sacraments only if the person who is thus ill outside of the religious house is a professed religious or a novice. (*PCI*, 16 iun. 1931—*AAS*, XXXIII [1931], 353.) Accordingly, if postulants cannot receive the last sacraments from the hands of the superior outside of the religious house, it seems illogical to classify them with those who can.

69 Canon 201, § 1.

prescripts of their constitutions, exempt women religious[70] are committed to the jurisdiction of regular superiors, and are thus removed from the authority of the local ordinary, except in those matters wherein the Code expressly states otherwise.[71] When this superior-subject relationship arises between clerical exempt superiors and nuns, the clerical superior takes the place of the local ordinary.[72] For that reason it is the conviction of the writer that the exempt superior can grant to the nuns subject to him a dispensation from their private vows.

C. *The Extent of Delegated Power in Regard to the Passive Subject*

1. *General Principles*

In the first place it may be said that delegated power to dispense from private vows can be exercised over all the subjects of him who delegated the faculty.[73] In this regard, however, travelers are not to be excluded from those in whose favor this delegated power can be exercised, provided that the delegated power has been obtained from the local ordinary.[74] The power of the local ordinary to dispense travelers from their vows is ordinary power.[75] Hence, when he grants the faculty to dispense from private vows without in any way limiting the extent of that faculty, it must be

---

70 Canon 500, § 2.

71 Canons 500, § 2; 615.

72 Regatillo, *Institutiones Iuris Canonici* (2 vols., Santander: Sal Terrae, 1941-1942), I, p. 322, n. 652 (hereafter to be cited as *Institutiones*).

73 Canon 201, § 1; Wernz-Vidal, *De Personis*, n. 375, p. 435; Rodrigo, *De Legibus*, p. 36, n. 55.

74 Canon 1313, 1°; 199, § 1.

75 Wernz-Vidal, *De Rebus*, pars 1, n. 557, p. 666.

understood that he has delegated the complete faculty which he himself enjoys.[76]

It not infrequently happens, however, that the delegated faculty to dispense from private vows is somewhat restricted by the delegating superior. The extent of the delegated power is then determined by the limits placed on the faculty by the superior as to what persons can be licitly or validly dispensed. Thus there may be granted the faculty to dispense one specified person from his private vows, or it may be granted to dispense all one's penitents. When the faculty is thus restricted in regard to persons, any exercise of it beyond the prescribed limits is invalid.[77]

2. *The Extent of the Regular Confessor's Power*

It has been seen that approved regular confessors may enjoy the privilege of dispensing from private vows. In the period before the Code it was the common opinion that with this faculty the regular confessors could dispense from the non-reserved vows of even the laity.[78] Inasmuch as the Code has not recalled this privilege or in any way restricted it, it must be admitted in virtue of canon 4 that approved regular confessors still retain the faculty to dispense the laity from non-reserved vows, provided that the dispensation does not violate the rights of a third party.[79]

In so far as this privilege is granted by the Roman Pontiff without any limitation as to the persons who can

---

76 Canon 200, § 1: "Potestas iurisdictionis ordinaria et ad universitatem negotiorum delegata late interpretanda est."

77 Canon 203, § 1.

78 Cf. *supra*, pp. 61-63.

79 Prümmer, *Theologia Moralis*, II, p. 359, n. 426; Coronata, *Institutiones*, II, p. 227, n. 897; Wernz-Vidal, *De Rebus*, pars I, n. 557, p. 667; Shuhler, *Privileges of Regulars to Absolve and Dispense*, pp. 140-141.

be dispensed, it follows that the regular confessor can dispense all subjects of the Roman Pontiff in that place where he is approved to hear the confessions of seculars.[80]

In view of the fact, however, that a regular confessor can hear the confession of the laity only when approved and delegated by the local ordinary,[81] it is evident that he cannot dispense from the private vows of the laity unless he is approved and delegated to hear such confessions by the local ordinary. For until he is so delegated, the regular cannot be regarded as a confessor for the laity. It is, however, only as a confessor that he possesses the privilege. Moreover, as was said previously, the regular confessor should examine the faculties which his superior has granted him in order to determine the extent to which he has been granted participation in this privilege.[82]

3. *The Extent of the Apostolic Legate's Power*

In addition to their faculties which are ordinary to their office, apostolic legates (nuncios, internuncios, and apostolic delegates) generally receive from the Roman Pontiff other faculties, all of which are delegated.[83] Among these delegated faculties is included the power to dispense from all private vows, even those which are reserved to the Holy See, except when the vow concerns the right of a third party.[84]

---

80 Shuhler, *op. cit.*, p. 140.

81 Canon 874, § 1.

82 Wernz-Vidal, *De Rebus*, pars I, n. 557, p. 667, nota 87; Vermeersch-Creusen, *Epitome*, II, n. 644.

83 Canon 267, §§ 1, 3°, and 2.

84 *Index Facultatum*, c. I, n. 15: "Commutandi aut dispensandi, consideratis causis, omnia vota simplicia private emissa, etiam Apostolicae Sedi reservata, exceptis votis in quibus agitur de tertii praeiudicio."—In Vermeersch-Creusen, *Epitome*, I, n. 813.

Because these faculties derive from the Roman Pontiff, they can be used for all the subjects of the Roman Pontiff, if no restriction is placed on their exercise. In so far as they are to be used for the territory to which the apostolic legate is assigned, it seems that as long as he is in that territory he can grant a dispensation there from the vows of all baptized persons. Furthermore, while he remains in his territory he can grant a dispensation to his subject who is absent from his territory. When the apostolic legate leaves the territory of his assignment, he can still dispense from the vows of his subjects and travelers who are within his territory, as well as from his own vows, and the vows of his subjects who are absent from his territory. While, however, he is outside of his territory, he cannot dispense from the vows of travelers or non-subjects who are outside his territory.[85]

Article II. The Extent of the Power to Dispense in Regard to the Place of the Dispensation

A. *General Principles*

Inasmuch as a dispensation from private vows is an act of voluntary jurisdiction,[86] the extent to which it can be used in regard to place is somewhat broader than the extent of judicial jurisdiction in the same regard. Thus, both ordinary and delegated power to dispense from private vows in the *external forum* can be exercised over one's subjects anywhere in the world. This means that, if a subject is outside the territory of his proper local ordinary, the local ordinary can nevertheless dispense him from his private vows. Likewise, a pastor endowed with the dele-

[85] Canon 201, § 3.

[86] *Supra*, p. 83.

gated faculty to dispense from private vows can grant a dispensation to his subjects or the subjects of his delegating superior who are outside of the parish or the territory of the local ordinary. This personal character of voluntary jurisdiction also enables the author of the dispensation to dispense his subjects and travelers even when he himself is outside his territory while the subject and travelers are within it, or when both he and his subjects are simultaneously outside the territory.[87]

In conceding this freedom of operation to those who exercise voluntary jurisdiction, canon 201, § 3, prefaces the concession with the following proviso: "Nisi aliud ex rerum natura aut ex iure constet . . ." On closer examination it becomes evident that the use of voluntary jurisdiction to dispense from vows does not always entail such freedom of operation. Actually this freedom of dispensing one's subjects anywhere in the world is permitted unqualifiedly only when one enjoys the faculty to dispense in the external forum. When the faculty to dispense from private vows is granted for the internal forum there is less freedom of operation.

Thus, if the faculty to dispense from private vows is granted for the internal sacramental forum, or if it is granted for the internal extra-sacramental forum in terms which state that it is granted to the person in his capacity of confessor, or that it is to be used in favor of one's penitents, or in equivalent terms, a distinction is necessary. If the person receiving the faculty possesses ordinary power to

87 Canon 201, § 3: "Nisi aliud ex rerum natura aut ex iure constet, potestatem iurisdictionis voluntariam seu non-iudicialem quis exercere potest etiam in proprium commodum, aut extra territorium exsistens, aut in subditum e territorio absentem."

absolve from sins, then the faculty to dispense one's subjects from private vows can be used in their favor anywhere in the world. This follows from the fact that a person who possesses ordinary power to absolve from sin can absolve his subjects anywhere in the world.[88]

If, however, the person who receives the faculty possesses only delegated power to absolve from sin, then the faculty to dispense from the private vows of those whose confessions one can validly hear is restricted to the territory in which one can validly hear their confessions. This follows from the fact that delegated power to absolve from sin can be used only in the territory for which one is approved for the hearing of confessions.[89]

B. *The Extent of the Clerical Exempt Superior's Power*

The extent of the clerical exempt superior's power to dispense from private vows with respect to the place of the dispensation requires special consideration in view of the fact that there appears to be a lacuna in the law in this regard. Canon 1313, 2°, states:

> "Vota non reservata potest iusta de causa dispensare, dummodo dispensatio ne laedat ius aliis quaesitum . . .Superior religionis clericalis exemptae quod attinet ad personas quae can. 514, § 1, enumerantur."

When the persons enumerated in canon 514, § 1, are included in the provisions of canon 1313, 2°, the latter canon is then exhibited in its completed sense and full meaning as intended by the legislator. Then it becomes manifest that the clerical exempt superior can dispense from the private vows of those who remain day and night

---

88 Canon 881, § 2: "Qui ordinariam habent absolvendi potestatem, possunt subditos absolvere ubique terrarum."

89 Canon 874, § 1.

in the religious house, whether as students, servants, guests, or convalecents. While, however, the law states that the clerical exempt superior can dispense the persons just enumerated from their private vows, it does not state the precise place in which they must be in order that he may be able to dispense them.

It is certain that, as long as those enumerated in canon 514, § 1, are physically inside the religious house,[90] the clerical exempt superior can dispense them from their private vows. That is the minimum which the law could mean; whether it means more is difficult to determine from the law itself. Canon 1313, 2°, does not provide any norm for indicating, in regard to the factor of place, the extent of the clerical exempt superior's power to dispense from the private vows of the persons enumerated in canon 514, § 1.

In a matter, however, which is very similar, namely, in the administration of the last sacraments to the persons mentioned in canon 514, § 1, the Pontifical Commission for the Interpretation of the Code was asked:

> An canon 514, § 1, ita intelligendus sit ut in religione clericali Superioribus ius et officium sit omnibus, de quibus in eodem canone, extra religiosam domum aegrotis Eucharisticum viaticum et Extremam Unctionem ministrandi.

To this question the Commission replied:

> R. Affirmative, si agatur de religiosis professis vel novitiis, firmo tamen praecriptis canonis 848; secus negative.[91]

From this response it is clear that the power of the religious superior over professed religious and novices is so firmly established by reason of their religious subjection to him[92] that it endures even outside the religious house. On the

---

90 *Supra*, pp. 137-138.

91 16 iun. 1931—*AAS*, XXIII (1930), 353.

92 Canons 561; 578, 2°.

other hand, the power of the religious superior over the others enumerated in canon 514, § 1, must necessarily cease when they are physically outside of the religious house, since their subjection to him is based on their actual presence in the house night and day.[93] As a corollary, it follows that canon 514, § 1, is limited by the response of the Pontifical Commission in regard to the extent of the religious superior's right to administer the last sacraments both as to persons and places. In canon 1313, 2°, the extent, in regard to place, of a clerical exempt superior's power to dispense from the private vows of the same persons is left undetermined. Certainly a norm is needed for determining where the superior can dispense from vows as well as for determining where he can administer the last sacraments.

This norm, in the writer's opinion, must be the same for both cases, and is to be obtained through a legal analogy. In both cases the persons concerned are for all practical purposes the same;[94] their juridical relationship is identical. In both cases it is an act of authorization regarding the exercise of which, limits must be established.[95] Furthermore, the authentic interpretation of canon 514, § 1, clearly showed that the superior's jurisdiction over professed religious and novices continues even when the professed religious and novices are outside the religious house. At the same time it showed that the superior's

93 Clancy, *The Local Religious Superior*, pp. 143-144; Beste, *Introductio*, p. 337.

94 In canon 514, § 1, the superior is any clerical superior; in canon 1313, 2°, it is a clerical exempt superior.

95 For the administration of the last sacraments, this authorization is necessary for the licitness of the act (canons 850; 939); for a dispensation from a vow, jurisdiction is necessary for validity (canon 1313).

jurisdiction over the other persons enumerated in canon 514, § 1, ceases when they are outside the religious house. This was obviously the juridical basis for the authentic interpretation. Since, however, canon 1313, 2°, clearly rests on the same juridical foundation, there is ample justification for asserting that the same norms can and should be applied.[96]

Hence, it can be said that the clerical exempt superior can anywhere in the world dispense from their private vows the professed religious and novices who are subject to him. To the others mentioned in canon 514, § 1, the same superior can grant a dispensation from their private vows only when they are actually inside the religious house.

In regard to nuns who have been made subject to a particular clerical exempt superior by their own constitutions, it appears that they participate in the same juridical status as the professed religious and novices. Consequently, they can be dispensed from their private vows by their clerical superior wherever in the world they may be.

When it is asked, where must the superior be when he actually exercises his power to dispense, it can be said that the superior can exercise this power even when he is outside the established limits of the religious house.[97]

C. *The Extent of the Regular Confessor's Power*

It has been seen that the regular confessor who is approved by the local ordinary for the hearing of the confessions of the faithful can dispense from the vows of the

---

96 Canon 20.

97 Canon 201, § 3: "Nisi aliud ex rerum natura aut ex iure constet, potestatem iurisdictionis voluntariam seu non-iudicialem quis exercere potest etiam in propriam commodum, *aut extra territorium existens* (italics are inserted by the writer), aut in subditum e territorio absentem.

laity.[98] Because this power to dispense is made to depend on the local ordinary's approval for the hearing of confessions, it is evident that the regular confessor can dispense from private vows of the laity in that territory only in which he can validly hear the confessions of the faithful.[99]

D. *The Extent of the Apostolic Legate's Power*

The title to the Index of Faculties granted to apostolic legates indicates that they are "pro locis missionis suae."[100] This indicates that they are to be used only inside the territory of their particular assignment. At the same time, however, canon 201, § 3, permits the use of delegated power both inside and outside of the territory of one's jurisdiction, if the use is to favor one's subjects. Consequently, the apostolic legate can dispense from private vows within the territory of his assignment. Furthermore, while he is in his territory he can grant a dispensation from the private vows of a subject who is absent from his territory. When he himself leaves his territory, he can dispense from the private vows of his subjects and travelers within his territory, and even from the vows of his subjects who are absent from his territory.[101]

Article III. The Extent of the Power to Dispense in Regard to the Forum of Dispensation

The purpose of this brief article is to determine in what forum the power to dispense from private vows can be used.

---

98 *Supra*, pp. 61-63.

99 Cf. Shuhler, *Privileges of Regulars to Absolve and Dispense*, p. 141.

100 Text in Vermeersch-Creusen, *Epitome*, I, n. 813.

101 Canon 201, § 3.

A. Ordinary Power

Ordinary power to dispense from private vows is attributed to the local ordinary and to clerical exempt superiors by canon 1313. Since no limitation is set in that canon as to the forum in which the faculty can be used, it is to be understood that this ordinary power can be exercised in both the internal and the external forums.[102]

Furthermore, canon 199, § 1, states that those who have ordinary power can delegate it unless the law prohibits delegation in certain instances. In view of the absence of any such prohibition in regard to private vows, it follows that those who have ordinary power to dispense from private vows can delegate this faculty to others. The faculty, however, by which one is authorized to delegate a particular power, belongs by its very nature to the external forum since it has for its purpose the common good.[103] Since, however, it is certain that all those who possess ordinary power to dispense from private vows have the faculty to delegate that power, it follows that they must have ordinary power in the external forum.

B. Delegated Power

The forum in which delegated power can be used is determined by the limits placed on that power in the act of the delegation. If no limits are placed on it, it can be used in both forums, although not with the same effects.[104] For if an act of jurisdiction by which a dispensation is granted from a vow is exercised in the external forum, it is

---

102 Canon 202, § 3.

103 Bargilliat, *Praelectiones Juris Canonici*, I, n. 59; Maroto, *Institutiones*, I, 861.

104 Canon 202, §§ 1, 3.

effective in the internal forum; but if a dispensation from the same vow is given only in the internal forum, it is not valid for the external forum.[105]

1. *The Forum in Which the Regular Confessor Can Dispense from Private Vows*

It has been seen that the privilege of dispensing from private vows belongs to regulars in so far as they are approved confessors.[106] If this approval proceeds from the local ordinary, regular confessors can dispense from the vows of all the faithful in the territory of the local ordinary who approves them. Despite the fact, however, that the privilege has been given to regulars who are approved confessors, it has never been understood to be restricted to the sacramental forum. On the contrary, a continuous succession of authors has asserted that this power can be used "tam intra quam extra confessionem."[107] The extent of the term "extra confessionem" has not, however, been discussed by them. The delegation of any faculty to a priest in his capacity as a confessor is generally understood to be intended only for the internal forum both intra and extra-sacramental, unless the sacramental forum is expressly designated.[108] Regular confessors, therefore, can exercise their faculty to dispense from private vows only in the internal forum whether intra or extra-sacramental.

---

105 Maroto, *Institutiones*, I, 862.

106 *Supra*, p. 62.

107 Salmanticenses, *Theologia Moralis*, tract. XVII, c. III, n. 92; St. Alphonsus, *Theologia Moralis*, lib. III, n. 257; Ballerini-Palmieri, *Theologia Moralis*, II, 504; Lehmkuhl, *Theologia Moralis*, I, n. 620; Noldin-Schmitt, *Theologia Moralis*, p. 217, n. 233; Vermeersch-Creusen, *Epitome*, II, p. 450, n. 644; Augustine, *Commentary*, VI, 307.

108 Cappello, *Summa Iuris Canonici*, I n. 131, p. 145; Vermeersch-Creusen, *Epitome*, I, p. 130, n. 164; Rodrigo, *De Legibus*, p. 38, n. 57.

2. *The Forum in Which Apostolic Legates Can Dispense from Private Vows*

As has been seen, apostolic legates possess delegated power to dispense from private vows. At present, however, the faculty of the apostolic legates to dispense from private vows does not mention the forum in which it can be used.[109] Hence, in virtue of canon 202, § 3, it can be used in both the internal and the external forums.

Article IV. The Extent of the Power to Dispense in Regard to the Object of the Dispensation

In the foregoing pages of this chapter, the discussion has dealt with the persons who can be dispensed from private vows, the places where such dispensations can be granted, both in regard to the superior dispensing and the person dispensed, as well as the forum in which the dispensation is granted. It remains now to examine the extent of the power to dispense from private vows as limited by the circumstances of the vows themselves.

A. *Private Vows Made in Favor of a Third Party*

Through the reservation of certain vows to the Holy See the faculty of those subordinate to the Roman Pontiff is restricted. This restriction, however, will be treated in the chapter on reserved vows which follows. At this point it is the writer's intention to investigate the question of private vows in which there is inherent a factor which causes them to be removed from the dispensing power of the local ordinaries, clerical exempt superiors, and those having delegated power to dispense from private vows. These are vows which are made in favor of a third party.

---

[109] Cf. *Index Facultatum*, c. 1, n. 15, in Vermeersch-Creusen, *Epitome*, I, n. 813.

In stating that local ordinaries, clerical exempt superiors, and those having delegated power can dispense from non-reserved private vows, canon 1313 places one limitation on that power, that is, "dummodo dispensatio ne laedat ius aliis quaesitum." From this it follows that, if the acquired right of another is not violated, those who have ordinary or delegated power to dispense from private vows can use this power to dispense from private vows which are made in favor of a third party.

It remains, then, to determine the circumstances under which a dispensation from a private vow violates the acquired rights of another. This, one can best do by first examining the various ways in which a vow can be made in favor of a third party, and then by ascertaining the various vows in which the third party acquires a right.

A vow can be made in favor of a third party in at least five ways. Thus:

1) a promise in favor of another specified person can be made to God without the promise being manifested to that third party;

2) a promise in favor of a generically determined third party, e.g., the poor, can be made to God and later manifested to several of this unspecified group who accept it;

3) a promise in favor of a specified third party can be made to that party, who accepts it, and to God, but in such a way that God's honor rather than the third party's convenience is the principal reason of the promise made;

4) a promise in favor of a specified third party can be made to that party, who accepts it, and to God, but in such a way that the third party's convenience and not God's honor is the principal reason of the promise made;

5) a promise in favor of a specified third party can be made to that party, who accepts it, and to God, but in such a way that God's honor rather than the third party's convenience is the principal reason of the promise made, but with this added circumstance, that the third party also obligates himself to the vowmaker, as e.g., in some religious congregations a promise of perseverance is made to God and the congregation by the professed, and in turn the congregation obligates itself to support the promisor by accepting his promise.

The list here given of the various ways in which a vow can be made in favor of a third party has been deduced from the doctrine on this matter as contained in various authors since the Council of Trent, such as Suarez,[110] the Salmanticenses,[111] St. Alphonsus,[112] and Lehmkuhl.[113] From even a cursory examination of that list, it is evident that a human promise plays an important role in vows favoring a third party. For this reason a brief examination of the moral doctrine on human promises is considered necessary before an attempt is made to ascertain in which type of vow the third party acquires a right.

A promise is defined as an accepted offer whereby the promisor freely binds himself to do or to omit doing something for the promisee.[114] In order to have a valid promise, it is necessary that the promisor have the intention of binding himself, that he externally manifest the promise, and that the promisee externally manifest his acceptance.

---

110 *De Voto,* lib. VI, c. XV, n. 2.

111 *Theologia Moralis,* tract. XVII, c. III, n. 82.

112 *Theologia Moralis,* lib. III, n. 255.

113 *Theologia Moralis,* I, n. 622.

114 Davis, *Moral and Pastoral Theology* (4 ed., 4 vols., New York: Sheed and Ward, 1943), II, 365; Noldin-Schmitt, *Theologia Moralis,* II, p. 502, n. 546; Aertnys-Damen, *Theologia Moralis,* I, n. 879.

It depends upon the intention of the promisor whether the promise shall bind in virtue of fidelity or of justice. If it is in virtue of fidelity, no right is acquired by the promisee;[115] if it is in virtue of justice, then the third party acquires a right to what is promised, and the act becomes a contract of promise.[116] Ordinarily a promise does not bind in justice, since it is rare that the one who makes a promise intends to bind himself so strictly. An obligation of justice, however, does arise if the promisor expressly or in equivalent terms declares that he is conferring a right on the third party. It also seems to arise if the promisor foresees that the promisee will suffer a great loss from the non-fulfillment of the promise; if the promise is made for services rendered;[117] if the promise is mutual; and, finally, if the promise is made with some solemnity, e.g., if the promise is made under oath[118] or confirmed by a vow.

With this understanding of the nature of a promise, an examination can now be made of the various types of vow favoring third parties as they were described above.

In the first manner of making a vow to favor a third party, the promise was described as made to God alone. Hence, it is obvious that in this type of vow the third party does not acquire a right, since no promise was made to him which he could accept.[119]

---

115 Noldin-Schmitt: ". . . obligatio fidelitatis nullum ius dat promissario in rem promissam, sed ideo solum obligat, quia unusquisque tenetur facto sua conformae promissis."—*Theologia Moralis*, II, n. 547; Vermeersch, *Theologia Moralis*, II, pp. 415-416; Merkelbach, *Theologia Moralis*, II, n. 478.

116 Vermeersch, *loc. cit.*; Noldin-Schmitt, *loc. cit.* A contract obliges in virtue of justice and can be defined as the agreement of two or more to transfer a right (Noldin-Schmitt, *Theologia Moralis*, II, n. 523).

117 Lehmkuhl, *Theologia Moralis*, I, n. 1285.

118 Noldin-Schmitt, *Theologia Moralis*, II, n. 547; Lehmkuhl, *loc. cit.*

119 Suarez, *De Voto*, lib. VI, c. XV, nn. 2, 3; Salmanticenses, *Theologia Moralis*, tract. XVII, c. III, n. 82; St. Alphonsus, *Theologia Moralis*, lib. III, n.

In the second manner of making a vow to favor a third party, this party was described as determined only generically, although later the promise was made known to a particular person of this determined group, who in turn accepted it. Nevertheless, in this type of vow no right is acquired by that particular person, because he was not specified in the promise made to God.[120]

In the third manner of making a vow to favor a third party, the promise was described as made primarily to God and secondarily to a specified third party who accepts it, and thus acquires a right to what was promised. However, it is at least a probable opinion that, since the third party's right is dependent upon the promise made to God, it must necessarily cease to exist when the promise to God ceases, by reason of a dispensation, to be of obligation.[121]

In the fourth manner of making a vow to favor a third party, the promise was described as made to God and to a specified third person, who accepts the promise made with the principal intention of favoring the latter. In this case, the third party is the principal or, at least, the "equally principal" consideration in the vow. From what has been said concerning a promise, it is apparent that the third party in this case acquires a right to what was promised.[122]

255; Lehmkuhl, *Theologia Moralis*, I, n. 622; Ballerini-Palmieri, *Theologia Moralis*, II, 5C1; Noldin-Schmitt, *Theologia Moralis*, II, p. 216, n. 232; Aertnys-Damen, *Theologia Moralis*, I, p. 341, n. 495.

120 St. Alphonsus, *op. cit.*, lib. III, n. 255; Ballerini-Palmieri, *op. cit.*, II, 501; Lehmkuhl, *op. cit.*, I, n. 622.

121 St. Alphonsus, *op. cit.*, lib. III, n. 255; Lehmkuhl, *op. cit*, I, n. 622; Ballerini-Palmieri, *op. cit.*, II, 501; Vermeersch, *Theologia Moralis*, II, p. 196, n. 225; Prümmer, *Theologia Moralis*, II, p. 356, n. 424; Aertnys-Damen, *Theoolgia Moralis*, I, n. 495; Merkelbach, *Theologia Moralis*, II, n. 733.

122 Suarez, *De Voto*, lib. VI, c. XV, n. 7; Salmanticenses, *op. cit.*, tract. XVII, c. III, n. 82; St. Alphonsus, *op. cit.*, lib. III, n. 255; Lehmkuhl, *op. cit.*,

Finally, in the fifth manner of making a vow to favor a third party, the promise was described as made principally to God and secondarily to a specified third party who accepts it; but in addition to accepting it, the latter in turn assumes an obligation in favor of the vowmaker. In this case a right is most certainly acquired by the third party,[123] even though the vow is made primarily in honor of God.[124]

After this examination of the various types of vow that can be made in favor of a third party it is clear that the proviso of canon 1313[125] removes from the dispensing power of the local ordinary, of the clerical exempt superior, and of those who possess delegated power the following vows:

1) the vow which is made primarily for the benefit of a specified person after that party accepts the promise of the prospective benefit;

2) the vow which is made only secondarily in favor of a specified third party who in turn assumes an obligation in favor of the vowmaker, even though God's honor be the principal reason for the vow.

The same proviso leaves to the dispensatory power of the same authors of dispensation the following vows:

1) a vow which is made for the benefit of a third party but not accepted by him;

I, 622; Ballerini, *Theologia Moralis*, II, 501; Wernz-Vidal, *De Rebus*, pars I, n. 557, p. 665; Noldin-Schmitt, *loc. cit.*; Prümmer, *Theologia Moralis*, II, p. 356, n. 423.

123 St. Alphonsus, *op. cit.*, lib. III, n. 255; Ballerini-Palmieri, *op. cit.*, II, 501.

124 Noldin-Schmitt, *op. cit.*, II, p. 216, n. 232.

125 ". . . dummodo dispensatio ne laedat ius aliis quaesitum . . ."

2) a vow made to God for the benefit of a generically determined third party, even though several of this unspecified group later accept the vow;

3) a vow made to God for the benefit of a third party and accepted by that party, when the principal consideration in the vow is God's honor.

While canon 1313 removes the first two types of vow mentioned above from the dispensing power of the local ordinary, of the clerical exempt superior, and of those who have delegated power to dispense from vows, it does not follow as a consequence that the Roman Pontiff can grant a dispensation from these vows. For in these vows a third party acquires a right which ordinarily cannot be jeopardized even by the Roman Pontiff.[126] But at the same time the removal of these two vows from the ordinary dispensing power of the Roman Pontiff does not mean that they are absolutely beyond his supreme power. As a matter of fact, the Roman Pontiff, as well as those who possess either ordinary or delegated power to dispense from private vows, can dispense from the two restricted vows when the third party cedes his right.[127]

When the promise is made in favor of a particular church or ecclesiastical institution, the Roman Pontiff can cede the right and grant a dispensation from the vow.[128] When the promise is made to a particular church over which an ordinary has the right of disposing of its goods, it seems that the same ordinary can cede the right to the

---

126 Suarez, *De Voto*, lib. VI, c. XV, n. 7; St. Alphonsus, *op. cit.*, lib. III, n. 255; Lehmkuhl, *op. cit.*, I, n. 622; Wernz-Vidal, *De Rebus*, pars I, n. 557, p. 665.

127 St. Alphonsus, *loc. cit.*; D'Annibale, *Theologia Moralis*, III, n. 208; Coronata, *Institutiones*, II, n. 897; Prümmer, *Theologia Moralis*, II, p. 356, n. 423.

128 Suarez, *De Voto*, lib. VI, c. XV, n. 7.

benefit promised, and can then grant the dispensation from the vow.[129] Finally, when a private individual has a claim on a vowmaker, it is asserted that the Roman Pontiff can force the promisee to cede his right. If the promisee proved unwilling to do this, his remonstrance is to be considered unreasonable, and therefore devoid of all rightful and juridical effect. In consequence of that fact the Roman Pontiff could deprive him of his alleged right. A proportionate cause, however, must justify such procedure as necessary or useful in the promotion of the common good.[130]

Lastly, it should be noted that those who possess ordinary or delegated power to dispense from private vows can use that power to grant a dispensation from vows favoring a third party when that third party is a member of the Church Triumphant. It was seen above that a promise made to a saint can be a vow or simply a promise.[131] But regardless of whether it is a promise or a vow, the authorities empowered to dispense, as just mentioned, can relax the obligation. The reason for this assertion becomes clear when it is recalled that if these same superiors can dispense from a promise made to God, *a fortiori* they can dispense from promises made to His saints.[132]

---

129 Suarez, *loc. cit.* Canon 1536, § 2, appears to offer support to this opinion in so far as that which is promised to a particular church constitutes a "gift".—"Donatio facta ecclesiae, ab eius rectore seu Superiore repudiari nequit sine licentia Ordinarii."

130 Suarez, *De Voto,* lib. VI, c. XV, n. 7; Schmalzgrueber, *Jus Ecclesiasticum,* lib. III, tit. XXXIV, n. 101; Wernz-Vidal, *De Rebus,* pars I, n. 557, p. 666; Woywood, *Commentary,* I 89-90; Augustine, *Commentary,* VI, 304.

131 *Supra,* p. 8.

132 Suarez, *De Voto,* lib. VI, c. XV, n. 10; Salmanticenses: "Quia ejusdem est auctoritatis commutare aut dispensare, promissiones factas Deo, et factas suae Curiae caelesti, cum non sit minor in Ecclesia auctoritas in concernentibus caelestem Curiam, quam in spectantibus ad ejus Principem."—*Theologia Moralis,* tract. XVII, c. III, n. 82.

B. Private Sworn Vows

Another type of vow which requires, in this chapter, special treatment as an object of dispensation is the sworn vow. A sworn vow is one to which a promissory oath is attached; when the vow to which the oath is added favors a third party, it is called a sworn vow in favor of a third party.[133]

In the matter of dispensation from sworn vows there is presented another instance in which the Code of Canon Law has, by the establishment of definite and precise norms, removed from the field of jurisprudence a much disputed question. Thus canon 1320 states:

> "Qui irritare, dispensare, commutare possunt votum, eandem potestatem eademque ratione habent circa iusiurandum promissorium; sed si iurisiurandi dispensatio vergat in praeiudicium aliorum qui obligationem remittere recusent, una Apostolica Sedes potest iusiurandum dispensare propter necessitatem aut utilitatem Ecclesiae."

Hence, those who possess ordinary or delegated power to dispense from private vows can dispense from sworn vows, without respect to the manner in which the oath stands in relation to the vow, that is, whether the relation be one of subordination to or equality with the vow.[134]

When, however, the dispensation from a sworn vow involves an injury to others who refuse to cede their acquired right, the Holy See alone can grant the dispensation "on account of the necessity or interest of the Church."[135] Merkelbach[136] adds as another ground for

---

133 Cf. Prümmer, *Theologia Moralis*, II, n. 438; Merkelbach, *Theologia Moralis*, II, n. 749; Noldin-Schmitt, *Theologia Moralis*, II, n. 245.

134 Vermeersch-Creusen, *Epitome*, II, p. 455, n. 654; Noldin-Schmitt, *Theologia Moralis*, II, n. 249; Coronata, *Institutiones*, II, n. 905.

135 Woywod, *Commentary*, II, 94; cf. Vermeersch-Creusen, *Epitome*, II, p. 455, n. 654.

136 *Theologia Moralis*, II, n. 757.

such a dispensation the common good. Sworn vows by which a third party acquires a right are fundamentally the same type of vow from which, as we said above, a dispensation is ordinarily impossible without the third party's consent. Otherwise the extraordinary exercise of the Supreme Power of the Roman Pontiff is necessary.[137]

C. *Private Vows of Oriental Catholics*

The Oriental Catholic as a passive subject of dispensation from private vows requires particular attention, especially in view of the great numbers of Orientals who reside within the territories of Latin ordinaries. In treating of them in regard to dispensation from private vows, it is the writer's intention to show to what extent the Latin grantor of a dispensation can dispense from the private vows of Oriental Catholics. For this purpose a distinction will be made between Oriental Catholics who are subject to the Latin ordinaries and those who are not.

1. *Oriental Subjects of Latin Ordinaries*

Members of Oriental rites who leave their own patriarchates and migrate into other parts of the world are under the administration of the Latin clergy.[138] In virtue of this fact[139] the Latin ordinary acquires jurisdiction over

---

137 Cf. *supra*, pp. 157-158.

138 Leo XIII, const. *Orientalium*, 30 nov. 1894, n. 9: "Quicumque orientalis, extra patriarchale territorium commorans, sub administratione sit cleri latini, ritui tamen suo permanebit adscriptus; ita ut, nihil diurnitate aliave causa ulla suffragante, recidat in ditionem Patriarchae, simul ac in eius territorium revenerit." — *Codicis Iuris Cononici Fontes cura Emi Card. Gasparri Editi* (9 vols. Romae [postea Civitate Vaticana]: Typis Polyglottis Vaticanis, 1923-1939, Vols. VII, VIII, et IX cura et studio Emi Card. Serédi), n. 627 (hereafter cited as *Fontes*).

139 Cf. also S.C. de Prop. Fide, 1 maii 1897—*Fontes*, 4935.

the Orientals who have a domicile or quasi-domicile in his territory.[140] This, of course, does not hold for those Orientals who are subject to an Oriental ordinary outside of their patriarchate.[141] Hence, the Latin ordinary can dispense from the vows of all those Orientals who are subject to him. In the case of Oriental Catholics who are travelers outside their patriarchate, the Latin ordinary can likewise grant a dispensation from private vows in virtue of canon 1313, 1°.

When, however, it is a matter of a reserved vow, the Latin ordinary cannot use his quinquennial faculties in favor of his Oriental subjects in the external forum unless these faculties are also granted by the Sacred Congregation for the Oriental Church. Inasmuch as the current faculties of the Latin ordinaries do not contain faculties from the Sacred Oriental Congregation, the Latin ordinary must seek from that Congregation an extension of the faculties granted him by the other Congregations in order that he may dispense his Oriental subjects from reserved private vows in the external forum.[142] In regard to the internal forum, however, the Latin ordinary can use his quinquennial faculties to dispense from the private reserved vows of his Oriental subjects, since these faculties for the internal

140 Duskie, *Canonical Status of Orientals in the United States*; The Catholic University of America Canon Law Studies, n. 48 (Washington, D. C.: The Catholic University of America, 1928), p. 67; Coussa, *Epitome Praelectionum de Iure Ecclesiastico Orientali* (2 vols., Vol. I, Città del Vaticano: Typis Polyglottis Vaticanis, 1940; Vol. II, Venetiis: Typis Polyglottis Insulae S. Lazari, 1941), I, 52.

141 Such are the Ruthenians in the United States.

142 Cf. Plöchl, "Quinquennial Faculties Extended by the S. Congregation for the Oriental Church to Latin Ordinaries"—*The Jurist* (Washington, D. C., 1941—), VI (1946), 73-76.

forum derive from the Sacred Penitentiary, which has competence over all Orientals in the internal forum.[143]

2. *Oriental Catholics Having Their Own Ordinaries*

In the United States and Canada the Greek Ruthenians have their own ordinaries. These ordinaries exercise personal jurisdiction over their subjects. On the other hand, those who are their subjects are in no way under the authority of the Latin ordinary in whose territory they live. Hence the Latin ordinary cannot dispense them from their vows in the external forum either as subjects or as travelers for their relationship to their own ordinary is not founded on a territorial framework but on a personal relationship. The result is that while they are in the United States or in Canada they are always within their diocese, and hence they are never from a canonical viewpoint, travelers within these countries, though they pass from one Latin diocese to another.

In the internal forum, however, the Latin ordinary can dispense from the private vows of Orientals who have their own ordinary. This is due to the superior-subject relationship which arises in the internal forum over those whose confession one can validly hear. Because, however, a person can go to confession to any approved priest even of another rite, all Orientals can go to the Latin ordinary who can thus dispense them from their private vows in both the internal sacramental and the internal extra-sacramental forum.[144] This faculty is also possessed by all Latin

143 S.C. pro Eccl. Orient., resp. 26 iul. 1930—*AAS*. XXII (1930), 394; reported in Bouscaren, *The Canon Law Digest*, I, 174.

144 Canon 905: "Cuivis fideli integrum est confessario legitime approbato etiam alius ritus, cui maluerit, peccata sua confiteri."

priests to whom the Latin ordinary has delegated the power of dispensing from private vows and who are at the same time qualified to hear confessions.

In regard to reserved vows, the Latin ordinary can use his powers as listed in the quinquennial faculties to dispense from the reserved vows of Orientals having their own ordinary. However, it must be remembered that these faculties are being exercised over non-subjects, and hence can be used only when the subject is within the territory of the Latin ordinary. They can, however, be exercised in both the internal extra-sacramental, and the internal sacramental forum.[145]

D. Private Vows of Converts

On the occasion of receiving a person into the Church it is occasionally discovered that the convert made a vow earlier in life. The question then arises whether the vow was valid; in the event that it was valid, whether the vow still binds; and, if so, who can grant a dispensation from its obligation.

In the first place, the validity of the vow of a convert is to be ascertained according to the principles for determining the validity of any vow, whether made by a Catholic or by a non-Catholic. Certainly everyone who enjoys a sufficient use of reason can make a vow.[146] After a vow is made, the same fundamental obligations arise for non-Catholics and Catholics alike, in view of the fact that the obligation of fulfilling a vow arises from the natural law.[147]

145 *Quinquennial Faculties of Ordinaries: Latest Formula for the United States*, VI, official note 1. Text in Bouscaren, *The Canon Law Digest*, II, 41.

146 Canon 1307, § 2.

147 *Supra*, p. 21.

Moreover, when an unbaptized person is received into the Church, a vow made previous to his conversion does not cease to bind. Rather, it then becomes subject not only to the natural law, but in addition, to all the ecclesiastical laws governing vows.

In this regard, a response of the Sacred Penitentiary, issued on November 29, 1842, constitutes a fundamental norm:

> "Protestans votum castitatis nec non paupertatis et obedientiae emisit voce et scripto coram ministro anglicano: quaeritur utrum vim saltem voti simplicis et privati aut irritum omnino sit habendum in casu conversionis ad religionem catholicam."
>
> R. Votum, dé quo in precibus, esse simplex et voventem teneri ad observantiam voti, si veram habuerit intentionem vovendi.[148]

From this it follows that, if a person made a private vow previous to his conversion, it continues to bind after his conversion. In regard to its dispensation, it will be governed by the same rules as a vow made by a Catholic.

If his vow was made in a non-Catholic religious community, a distinction must be made between the religious communities of the Protestant Church and those of the Oriental "Orthodox" Church. In the case of the Protestant communities, since they lack ecclesiastical jurisdiction, vows taken in them are only private vows of obedience, poverty, and chastity. But to establish this, it is necessary to ascertain the presence or absence of a genuine intention to make a vow.[149] Vermeersch, however, without adverting to the response of the Sacred Penitentiary, contends that

---

[148] *Collect. S.C.P.F.*, II, n. 2086.

[149] Mahoney, "Non-Catholic Religious Vows"—*The Clergy Review*, (London, 1931—), XIX (1940), 267.

the vows of converts taken in a Protestant religious community continue to bind only when they were taken absolutely or independently of any relation to the religious association in which they were made. Even in those circumstances he concedes the likely validity of the vow of chastity alone.

In support of the contention just described, Vermeersch points out that formerly the Holy See, in permiting a nun or a lay brother to separate from a religious institute, generally considered the vow of chastity as continuing to bind after the separation, and reserved its future dissolution to itself. This practice was based on the presumption that the vow of chastity was made as an absolute promise to God, whereas the vows of obedience and of poverty were made merely in relation to the religious institute.

Today, however, a contrary practice of the Holy See prevails. Now, through secularization, there is granted a dissolution of the three vows of religion.[150] When the religious institute affected is a diocesan community, this secularization can be granted by the local ordinary, so that today a dispensation from a public vow of chastity in such a community is no longer reserved to the Roman Pontiff.

This practice indicates that the Holy See now presumes that vows taken in connection with the religious life are dependent on the religious profession. This in no way prohibits the candidate for religious profession from taking the three vows in an absolute manner and independently of the profession. The practice merely indicates the policy which the Holy See has adopted and on which it acts in the external forum. Accordingly, if the candidate

150 Canon 640, § 1, 2°.

did make these vows in an absolute manner, the vows would continue to be valid even after his separation from the religious institute.

Hence, in each individual instance the person should be asked whether he intended to make his vows independently of the religious institute. If such was not the case, his obligations can be considered as having ceased upon his legitimate separation from the institute. However, if after the completion of his eighteenth year he made the vow of perfect chastity independently of the duration of his religious life, he is then obligated by a vow, the dispensation from which is reserved to the Roman Pontiff.[151]

Although Vermeersch seems to exclude, in the case of a professed member of a non-Catholic religious institute, the likelihood that the vows of obedience and of poverty are taken in an absolute sense, the respone of the Sacred Penitentiary is not so prompt to exclude this likelihood in so far as it affirms the validity of all three vows, provided that a genuine intention of making a vow was had. Hence, on the occasion of receiving into the Church a person who had previously taken vows in a Protestant religious community, inquiry should be made into the manner in which all three vows were taken. If they were taken independently of the religious institute, they continue to bind as private vows, and in their dispensation they are to be governed by all the laws on dispensation from private vows.

On the other hand, however, when a convert prior to his conversion took vows in a religious community of the Oriental "Orthodox" Church, it is quite a different

---

151 Canon 1309; Vermeersch, "Vows of Non-Catholics"—*The Homiletic and Pastoral Review* (New York, 1900—), XXVIII (1928), 1221-1223.

matter. Vermeersch[152] points out that in the Orient "there are subsisting communities or Churches whose existence is recognized as a fact by the Holy See. At the head of those Churches are patriarchs and bishops, who were validly ordained and consecrated; and there has never been any positive act of the Holy Father to suppress the jurisdiction which they possessed over the communities belonging to their respective rites. Gregory XIII, when he reformed the Calendar, wrote to the patriarchs asking them to accept that reformation; they were expressly invited to the Council of Trent and more recently (by the letter *Arcano*, Sept. 8, 1868) to the Vatican Council, in which they were called 'bishops of the Oriental Churches not in Communion with the Holy See'. It is noteworthy that Protestants, on the other hand, received no such *de facto* recognition; to them Pius IX wrote only as individuals, addressing them as 'all Protestants and other non-Catholics'."

Vermeersch then asserts that one may conclude "with Arcadius (*De Poenitentia*, lib. IV, c. 5), Cardinal D'Annibale and other learned authorities, that for the good of souls the Roman Church has allowed ecclesiastical jurisdiction to remain in the schismatic Oriental churches, for the conferring of the Sacraments and the administration of the communities."[153] Furthermore, this seems to be in accord with the present mind of the Church as expressed in the Code of Canon Law. For there canon 2264 allows the validity of all jurisdictional acts of excommunicated persons, unless a declaratory or condemnatory sentence has been inflicted.[154]

---

152 *Loc. cit.*

153 *Loc. cit.*

154 This matter is treated fully by Vermeersch in the article cited.

Hence, in the case of the convert who was previously a member of a religious community in an Oriental "Orthodox" Church, the religious profession must be regarded as valid, and the vows as public. However, as in the case of a convert from Protestantism, an investigation should be made in the individual case to determine if the vows were taken in relation to the religious profession or independently of that profession. In the former case, the vows will be considered to have ceased with the termination of the religious life; in the latter instance, the vows will continue to bind, even though the religious return to the world, unless a dispensation from them is granted in virtue of a faculty delegated by the Holy See.[155]

E. *Community Vows*

It has been seen that a community vow is a vow that is made by a moral person or a community.[156] The doctrine on the dispensation of this type of vow is much the same now as before the Code. Thus the new law states, as a fundamental principle, that a vow as such obligates only the vowmaker.[157] Hence "no one can be bound by and in virtue of the vow of another unless he himself makes the vow; for a vow is a personal act which must be done by the personal will of the one who makes it, and is based proximately and immediately on his free will. The opinion of De Angelis that the vow of a society obliges the future members of the society is contrary to law. Hence, those only are bound by this vow who have the intention to bind themselves by it, or who, with such intention, ratified the

155 Vermeersch, *loc. cit.*

156 *Supra*, pp. 16, 71-72.

157 Canon 1310, § 1: "Votum non obligat, ratione sui, nisi emittentem."

vow made in the name of the society. As regards future members of the society, they can be bound by ecclesiastical law, but not by the vow as such . . ."[158]

Accordingly, since a community vow, as a vow, binds only those who have the intention to bind themselves by it, or who with such intention ratified the vow made in the name of the society, a dispensation from such a vow will be governed by the same laws that govern dispensations from other private vows. Hence, anyone having the faculty to dispense from private vows can grant a dispensation for a just cause to individuals who are bound by a community vow.[159]

---

[158] S.C.C., resol. 18 ian. 1936—*AAS*, XXIX (1937), 344, translation from Bouscaren, *The Canon Law Digest*, II, 391 (under Canon 1310).

[159] Salmanticenses, *Theologia Moralis*, tract. XVII, c. III, n. 87.

CHAPTER VI

CAUSE REQUIRED FOR DISPENSATION FROM PRIVATE VOWS

ARTICLE I. THE NECESSITY OF A CAUSE

A cause for a dispensation can be defined as a fact or motive which *does* prompt or at least *can* prompt the grantor of the dispensation to exercise his dispensing power. By saying that it is a motive or a fact which *can* prompt the granting of a dispensation, one simply means that the cause need not be known by the grantor of the dispensation for the valid exercise of his power. It suffices, rather, that the motive or fact actually exist, even though the author of the dispensation be unaware of this.[1]

The necessity of a cause for granting a dispensation from a vow was the undisputed doctrine before the Code.[2] Canon 1313 reiterates this necessity by stating that the local ordinary, the clerical exempt superior, and those who have delegated power can dispense from private vows for a justifying cause. As will be seen, the nature of this necessity is such that even the Roman Pontiff must be prompted by a justifying cause before he can validly dispense from a vow.

The basis for requiring that a justifying cause prompt the granting of a dispensation from private vows is that the author of such a dispensation is using jurisdictional power which is not proper to the Church, but rather to God. For that reason this power is not to be used arbitrarily, or for trivial reasons. Rather the one who grants a dispensation

1 Rodrigo, *De Legibus*, n. 483.

2 *Supra*, pp. 50-53, 75-77.

from a vow must use his power with reason and justice, not forgetting that a right acquired by God is remitted in this type of dispensation, and that it would be an injustice to remit it except for a reasonable and proportionate cause.[3]

In requiring a cause for a dispensation from a private vow canon 1313 does not state that it is necessary for a valid dispensation. Nevertheless, it is the commonly accepted doctrine that apart from the existence of such a cause a granted dispensation is not only illicit but also invalid. This was the doctrine before the Code, and now, subsequent to the Code, it is in harmony with canon 84, which states that in order to dispense validly from the *ecclesiastical law* of a superior a subordinate needs a justifying and reasonable cause.[4]

This necessity, moreover, of a justifying cause for a dispensation from a private vow is binding not only on the grantor of the dispensation but also on the person who requests the dispensation. Since, however, the grantor of the dispensation acts in God's place in the act of dispensing from a vow, his judgment concerning the sufficiency of the cause should prevail over the petitioner's private judgment.[5]

ARTICLE II. CAUSES SUFFICIENT FOR DISPENSING FROM PRIVATE VOWS

A. Kinds of Causes

For ascertaining the inherent sufficiency of various causes as prompting a dispensation from private vows, one

---

3 Prümmer, *Theologia Moralis,* II, p. 354, n. 421; Coronata, *Institutiones,* II, p. 226, n. 897; Aertnys-Damen, *Theologia Moralis,* I, p. 342, n. 496. Cf. canon 84.

4 Wernz-Vidal, *De Rebus,* pars I, n. 557, p. 667.

5 St. Thomas, *Summa Theologica,* IIa, IIae, q. 88, art. 12, ad 2.

should, for a more accurate understanding of what is a sufficient cause, seek to know substantially how the various kinds of causes are differentiated from one another.

When a cause is itself sufficient to prompt the granting of a dispensation it is said to be a *motivating cause* for the dispensation. When, however, a cause by itself lacks the gravity necessary to prompt the granting of a dispensation, but nevertheless adds to the force of the motivating cause, it is said to be an *impulsive cause.* While one impulsive cause is insufficient for the granting of a dispensation, still a series of impulsive causes can become the equivalent of one motivating cause, and thus may suffice for the granting of a dispensation from private vows.[6]

A cause for the dispensation of a private vow is *public* when the common good is directly intended; *private* when the welfare of a private individual is directly intended. In the earlier centuries of the Church vows were not remitted except for a public cause; in more recent times, however, the private welfare of an individual has been recognized as a sufficient cause for a dispensation.[7] Even when a dispensation is granted for a private cause, this indirectly benefits the public welfare; for there is the greatest advantage to the public good in providing for the private good of the individual members of society.[8]

B. *Proportion Necessary Between Cause and Vow from Which Dispensation is Sought*

A vow is an act of religion most pleasing to God. For that reason persons authorized to remit the obligation of a

---

6 Cf. Rodrigo, *De Legibus*, p. 362, n. 483; Reilly, *Dispensations*, 106.

7 Prümmer, *Theologia Moralis*, II, p. 354, n. 421.

8 St. Thomas, *Summa Theologica*, Ia, IIae, q. 97, art. 4.

vow must do so only for reasons which are proportionate to the excellence and perfection of the vow. Hence, vows which are reserved, or which require unusual sacrifice from the vowmaker, in turn demand a proportionately greater cause than other types of vow for their relaxation.

In order, however, to avoid harassing the vowmaker with possible scruples, a salutary counsel, suggested by most authors and contained in jubilee faculties, advises the use of commutation when the alleged cause for dispensing is considered as possibly insufficient. In this way the deficiency of the cause is supplied by the commutation, and all grounds for scruples are fully allayed.[9] This advice, however, should not exclude a complete dispensation when there is a probably sufficient cause. Incontrovertible certitude in these matters need not be sought with over-anxiety, since in the matter of sufficient cause for a dispensation from a vow, an incontestable certainty is scarcely if ever attainable. If a completely unquestionable certitude were sought every time a dispensation was requested, it is quite likely that a dispensation would never be granted. As a result the power to dispense from vows could prove quite useless. Accordingly, when a cause is certainly or even probably sufficient, the dispensation can be granted absolutely.[10]

C. *Various Causes for Dispensing from Private Vows*

1. *Lack of Perfect Deliberation*

A lack of perfect deliberation in the making of a vow constitutes a cause for dispensing from private vows for

9 Salmanticenses, *op. cit.*, IV, tract. XVII, c. III, n. 120.

10 Salmanticenses, *loc. cit.*

such a lack of deliberation affects the very origin of the obligation. Although the vow is valid, still if it lacked any of the characteristics of a perfect human act it can be remitted through a dispensation.[11] This lack of deliberation is sufficient of itself to prompt the granting of a dispensation from a vow. Even if the person could fulfill the vow, the fact alone that he had made the vow without perfect deliberation would be a sufficient cause for the granting of a dispensation.[12]

This lack of perfect deliberation can arise in three ways. 1) It can arise by reason of the immature age of the vowmaker, as when a vow is made by one who is still below the age of puberty.[13]

2) It can arise from a mental disturbance which harassed the vowmaker at the time the vow was made: thus anger, sorrow, and the fear of death can prompt the imprudent making of a vow. Hence, if a person made a vow on account of a fear of death for himself or for another in time of battle, or on the occasion of a shipwreck, this would ordinarily provide a sufficient cause for dispensing from the vow. There is generally a minimum amount of deliberation which precedes the vow in such cases. Should, however, the facts actually indicate that there was mature deliberation, this circumstance of mental

---

11 Castropalao, *Opus Morale* (7 vols., Vol. I, 3. ed., 1649; Vol. III, 2. ed., 1649, Lugduni, 1631-1651), Tom. III, tract. XV, disp. II, *de voti relaxatione,* pt. 9, n. 7.

12 Castropalao, *Opus Morale,* III, tract. XV, disp. II, *de voti relaxatione,* pt. 9, n. 7; Salmanticenses, *Theologia Moralis,* tract. XVII, c. III, n. 122; St. Alphonsus, *op. cit.,* lib. III, n. 252; Wernz-Vidal, *De Rebus,* pars I, n. 557, p. 667; Coronata, *Institutiones,* II, p. 227, n. 897; Vermeersch-Creusen, *Epitome,* II, p. 449, n. 664; Aertnys-Damen, *Theologia Moralis,* I, p. 342, n. 496.

13 St. Alphonsus, *op. cit.,* lib. III, n. 253.

disturbance would not be a sufficient cause in itself for the dispensation.[14]

3) Finally, a lack of deliberation can arise in consequence of error, or of fraud regarding an accessory cause.[15] Of course if there was error concerning the *motivating* or primary cause, the vow would be invalid.[16]

2. *Notable Difficulty in Keeping the Vow*

Another cause for dispensing from private vows is the notable difficulty which accompanies the fulfilling of the vow, whether this difficulty was or was not foreseen at the time the vow was made; for it is common human experience that the "deed" is always more difficult than the desire to achieve it.[17]

3. *Material or Temporal Loss*

If the vowmaker, his family, or the community to which he belongs would suffer a notable material or temporal loss by the fulfillment of the vow, this impending loss would constitute an ample cause for the granting of a dispensation from a private vow. Thus the fulfillment of a vow to give a large sum of money to a particular church might constitute a notable material loss in view of the change in the vowmaker's financial condition which he

---

14 Canon 103, § 2; Tamburini, *Theologia Moralis*, lib. III, c. XVI, n. 16; Salmanticenses, *loc. cit.*; St. Alphonsus, *op. cit.*, lib. III, n. 252; Wernz-Vidal, *De Rebus*, pars I, n. 557, p. 667.

15 Canons 103, § 2; 104; Castropalao, *Opus Morale*, III, tract. XV, disp. II, *de voti relaxatione*, pt. 9, n. 10; Tamburini, *Theologia Moralis*, lib. III, c. XVI, § 4, n. 17; Salmanticenses, *Theologia Moralis*, tract. XVII, c. III, n. 121.

16 Canon 104.

17 Suarez, *De Voto*, lib. VI, c. XVII, n. 12; Tamburini, *Theologia Moralis*, lib. III, c. XVI, § 4, n. 18; St. Alphonsus, *Theologia Moralis*, lib. III, n. 252; Coronata, *Institutiones*, II, n. 897.

had not contemplated. Likewise a pilgrimage vow, a vow to abstain from certain food, or a vow to fast may easily cause a material loss to the vowmaker. So also, a vow of chastity may entail a notable material loss by reason of the fact that a marriage could not be contracted.

If the substance of this type of cause remains entirely temporal, there should be a commutation added to the dispensation.[18]

4. *Spiritual Loss*

If a vow becomes an occasion for the vowmaker's spiritual ruin, instead of his spiritual advancement, a sufficient cause is had for its dispensation. A vow can become an occasion for the spiritual defection of the vowmaker when, through his particular weakness of character, or through common human frailty, there is a likelihood that he will transgress the vow, e.g., a vow of chastity between married people. The vow can also become the occasion of spiritual loss to the vowmaker, if in the observance of it he becomes disturbed by scruples.[19]

It could occur that a vow will not so much occasion spiritual loss for the vowmaker as impede the attainment of a greater spiritual benefit. A circumstance such as this can be regarded as furnishing a sufficient cause for a dispensation, since a vow is fundamentally intended for the spiritual advancement of the vowmaker.[20]

---

18 Suarez, *De Voto,* lib. VI, c. XVII, n. 14; Tamburini, *op. cit.,* lib. III, c. XVI, § 4, n. 19; Vermeersch-Creusen, *Epitome,* II, p. 443, n. 664.

19 Suarez, *De Voto,* lib. VI, c. XVII, n. 12; Tamburini, *op. cit.,* lib. III, c. XVI, § 4, nn, 21-23; Wernz-Vidal, *De Rebus,* pars I, n. 557, p. 667; Coronata, *Institutiones,* II, p. 227, n. 897.

20 Suarez, *De Voto,* lib. VI, c. XVII, n. 10; Salmanticenses, *op. cit.,* tract. XVII, c. III, n. 125; Vermeersch-Creusen, *Epitome,* II, p. 342, n. 496.

5. *Certain Doubts Which can Constitute Causes for Dispensing from Private Vows*

If a doubt arises concerning certain aspects of a vow, this type of doubt can constitute a cause for a dispensation from the vow. Thus if a person doubts whether he had the intention of making a vow, or whether the vow is an obstacle to a greater good, or whether some evil or harm will derive from the fulfillment of the vow; likewise if a person doubts whether he fulfilled the vow; in all such cases there is cause for the granting of a dispensation from a private vow. As a matter of fact, by the reflex principles of probabilism, these doubts could be said to remove all obligation from such vows. But, as Merkelbach (1871-1942)[21] and Vermeersch (1858-1936),[22] wisely point out, a dispensation would be advisable in practice.

Article III. Particular Questions Concerning the Sufficient Cause for Dispensation from Private Vows

A. *Possible Defects in the Motivating Cause*

The sufficiency of a cause for a dispensation from private vows is not always easy to ascertain. In the first place, canon 84, which admits the validity and the licitness of a dispensation from ecclesiastical law, when given for a doubtfully sufficient cause, cannot be used with the same authority with reference to dispensations from private vows.[23] In canon 84, § 2, the legislator exercises his right

---

21 *Theologia Moralis,* II, n. 725.

22 *Theologia Moralis,* II, p. 192, n. 217.

23 Canon 84, § 1: "A lege ecclesiastica ne dispensetur sine iusta et rationabili causa, habita ratione gravitatis legis a qua dispensatur; alias dispensatio ab inferiore data illicita et invalida est.

§ 2. Dispensatio in dubio de sufficientia causae licite petitur et potest licite et valide concedi."

when he expresses his satisfaction with and binds himself to accept a doubtfully sufficient cause as a reason for a valid and licit dispensation from *his* law. By restricting this concession to ecclesiastical law, the legislator implicitly acknowledges that he cannot declare in law what sufficiency of cause God will definitely be satisfied with in a dispensation from the natural law, e.g., as involved in the obligation of a vow. It is certain that there must be a cause for such a dispensation, even though the Pope be the grantor of the dispensation; but it seems beyond the power of any human legislator to state in law that God is bound to be satisfied with a probably sufficient cause. This is the exclusive right of God, and in ascertaining what God's mind is on the sufficiency of a cause for dispensation from a private vow, one must have recourse to the principles of the natural law.

While, however, the human legislator cannot state that either a doubtfully sufficient or a doubtfully existing cause suffices for the valid and licit granting of a dispensation, still he can determine under what conditions he will not dispense or permit his official grantors of dispensations from private vows to exercise their faculties. This he does when he declares that all rescripts depend for their validity on the truthfulness of the petition,[24] but that the representation of a false plea will not invalidate the granting of a rescript if the one motivating cause is true.[25] Later in canon 62, the legislator states that if the rescript contains a dispensation, the laws of the Code on dispensations are to be followed in addition to those on rescripts in

[24] Canon 40: "In omnibus rescriptis subintelligenda est, etsi non expressa, conditio: *Si preces veritate nitantur,* salvo praescripto can. 45, 1054."

[25] Canon 42, § 2: "Nec obstat expositio falsi, seu obreptio, dummodo vel unica causa proposita vel ex pluribus propositis una saltem vera sit."

general. In other words, dispensations which are granted through a rescript are definitely governed by the laws just explained above. Accordingly, if the cause presented in a petition for a dispensation is objectively false, the dispensation, if granted by way of rescript, will be invalid. By way of analogy it seems that even when the dispensation is given orally it will be invalid if the one motivating cause for the granting of the dispensation is a false one.[26] It is highly improbable that, when a false cause is presented for a dispensation, the legislator would exclude the intention of dispensing if the dispensation is granted in writing, but not exclude it if the dispensation is granted orally.

This conclusion is also the teaching of Beste,[27] of Rodrigo,[28] and of Wernz-Vidal,[29] although these authors do not specifically mention that this doctrine is verified in the matter of dispensing from vows. It is obvious, however, that in canons 40 and 42 the legislator is excluding his intention of granting any dispensation when the conditions stated there are not fulfilled.

In the article which immediately preceded the present one, various causes were presented as being sufficiently grave to prompt the granting of a dispensation from private vows. The concrete application of these is of course a relative matter depending on many contingencies. In granting a dispensation from a private vow, the superior must prudently decide whether a certain cause is sufficient

---

26 Canon 20.

27 "Si intercesserit subreptio vel obreptio, res [dispensatio] erit diiudicanda iuxta regulas . . . in can. 40 et 42 circa rescriptum expositas."—*Introductio*, p. 129.

28 *De Legibus*, n. 492.

29 *Ius Canonicum* (7 tom. in 8 vols., tom. I, *Normae Generales*, Romae: Apud Aedes Universitatis Gregorianae, 1938), I, *Normae Generales*, n. 318, p. 473 (hereafter cited as *Normae Generales*).

for a dispensation from a particular vow in question. It is only natural that doubts will frequently arise and that material mistakes will be made. In the present article these doubts and the problems which derive from them will be examined. The problems or questions are as follows:

1) Whether and to what extent a probably sufficient motivating cause will meet the requirement for the valid and licit granting of a dispensation from a private vow?

2) Whether and to what extent a probably existing cause will warrant the valid and licit granting of a dispensation from a private vow?

3) Whether and to what extent an objectively existing cause which is erroneously thought not to exist will suffice for the valid and licit granting of a dispensation from a private vow?

4) Whether and to what extent a mere putative cause which objectively does not exist suffices for the valid and licit granting of a dispensation from a private vow?

1. *A Probably Sufficient Cause*

All authors agree that a probably sufficient cause is adequate for the licit requesting as well as for the licit and valid granting of a dispensation from a private vow. Likewise they agree on the validity of a dispensation from a private vow when it is granted for a probably sufficient cause, even if it is later discovered that the cause was not sufficient.[30]

---

30 Laymann, *Theologia Moralis*, lib. IV, c. VII, n. 5; Salmanticenses, *Theologia Moralis*, tract. XVII, c. III, n. 117; Lehmkuhl, *Theologia Moralis*, I, n. 623; Noldin-Schmitt, *Theologia Moralis*, II, p. 215, n. 230; Coronata, *Institutiones*, II, p. 227, n. 897; Vermeersch-Creusen, *Epitome*, II, p. 449, n. 644; cf. Rodrigo, *De Legibus*, pp. 336-337, n. 489.

In support of this view it is pointed out that the invalidity of a dispensation from a vow when granted without a cause is based on the presumption that God would not approve the arbitrary use of the power to dispense from vows. Still, God could, if He so desired, remit a vow even though there was no reason for the remission on the part of the vowmaker. In view of this fact it is argued that the validity of a dispensation from a vow when granted for a doubtfully sufficient cause is based on the presumption that, since God can grant a dispensation without a cause inherent in the vowmaker, and in view of the fact that He has not expressly required a certainly sufficient cause for these dispensations in His Church, it can be licitly presumed that God in His infinite wisdom and understanding will be satisfied with a probably sufficient cause for a dispensation from a private vow.[31]

If a probably sufficient cause is not admitted as adequate for both a valid and a licit dispensation from a private vow, the way is then opened for innumerable refusals of dispensations and for an increasing number of disturbed conscience. To assert that God will not be satisfied with a probably sufficient cause seems to deny God's prudence, in view of the undesirable effects which are likely to follow from such a policy.

2. *A Probably Existing Cause*

When the cause for a dispensation is alleged as probably existing, and when in the estimation of the grantor of the dispensation this probability is well founded in reality, the dispensation from a private vow can be licitly requested

---

31 Cf. Rodrigo, *loc. cit.*

as well as validly granted.[32] This opinion, however, is by no means the common opinion today. It is denied by the Salmanticenses,[33] Noldin-Schmitt,[34] Coronata,[35] and Vermeersch-Creusen.[36]

In support of the proposed opinion, the following arguments are presented:

1) St. Thomas teaches that it is the duty of one who wishes to dispense from vows to determine what is more pleasing to God. Accordingly, if the fulfillment of a vow was manifestly more pleasing to God, a superior and the vowmaker would be guilty of sin, if the latter sought and the former granted a dispensation from the vow without any apparent cause for the dispensation. St. Thomas points out, however, that if there exists an apparent cause, which at least makes it doubtful that the observance of the vow is more pleasing to God than a dispensation from the vow would be, then the vowmaker is to follow the judgment of the superior.[37] It seems that the apparent cause of which St. Thomas spoke can be understood as a probably existing cause, and that in such a case a dispensation could be validly granted.

---

32 Cf. Rodrigo, *De Legibus*, p. 367, n. 490; Michiels, *Normae Generales*, II, 511. The writer cites these authors as expressly supporting the expressed opinion in regard to ecclesiastical law only. Rodrigo, however, seems to speak of dispensations in general, and may thus be reasonably understood to include the dispensation from vows.

33 *Theologia Moralis*, tract. XVII, c. III, n. 118.

34 *Theologia Moralis*, II, n. 230.

35 *Institutiones*, II, n. 897.

36 *Epitome*, II, n. 664.

37 ". . . in manifestis dispensatio praelati non excusaret a culpa; puta si praelatus dispensaret cum aliquo super voto de ingressu religionis, nulla apparenti causa obstante. Si autem esset causa apparens, per quam saltem in dubium verteretur, posset stare judicio praelati dispensantis vel commutantis." *Summa Theologica*, IIa, IIae, q. 88, art. 12, ad 2.

2) On reflection, there appears to be no fundamental difference between a probably sufficient and a probably existing cause.

a) A probably sufficient cause which actually is not sufficient is just as powerless to prompt a dispensation from a vow as is a probably existing cause which actually does not exist. On the other hand, a probably existing cause which actually does exist can just as effectively prompt a dispensation as a probably sufficient cause which is actually sufficient. In both cases, the causes presented for the dispensation are equally true in that they are probable; on account of the same factor of probability there is in both cases equal probability of error.

b) From another point of view, it can be added that before a cause for a dispensation from a private vow can be said to exist, the cause must be sufficient; for an insufficient cause is simply not a cause for a dispensation from a private vow. Since, however, a probably sufficient cause may or may not be actually sufficient, it follows that a probably sufficient cause may or may not actually exist. Hence, a probably sufficient cause is reduced to a probably existing cause.

c) Finally, there are many authors who in commenting on canon 84, § 2, regard as having the same canonical force both the doubtfully sufficient cause and the doubtfully existing cause. The writer, however, hesitates to cite these authors as supporting the equal force of these two types of doubt when applied to the matter of dispensing from private vows. Most of them do not discuss the matter in regard to vows. In the case of one author who admits that a probably existing cause can prompt a dispensation from ecclesiastical law,[38] it is found that he denies that a probably existing cause can prompt a dispensation from a private vow.[39]

The writer, however, is of the opinion that, since these authors in speaking of a dispensation from ecclesiastical law attribute to a probably existing cause the same juridical force for prompting a dispensation as they attribute to a probably sufficient cause, it can be maintained that both of these causes have the same force when applied to a dispensation from private vows. Canon 84, § 2, clearly speaks only of a probably sufficient cause. Yet these authors in various ways are able to see also the implied mention of a probably existing cause. Beste,[40] Michiels,[41] as also Rodrigo,[42] Regatillo[43] and Coronata,[44] all profess the same liberal view in this regard.

Now, in the matter of a dispensation from a vow it is clear that a sufficient cause is required. Yet all authors admit that if the cause is only probably sufficient the dispensation may be granted; but they do not go any further.

---

38 "Canon [84] loquitur de dubio sufficientiae causae, non de dubio causae exsistentis; at eadem ratio revera et pro dubio exsistentis causae militare videtur. . ."—Coronata, *Institutiones*, I, p. 128, n. 115.

39 "Dubitans de exsistentia causae nequit dispensare, bene vero dispensat dubitans de causae sufficientia."—Coronata, *Institutiones*, II, p. 227, n. 897.

40 "Canon directe respicit dubium num causa, quae adesse scitur, iusta et sufficiens sit ad dispensationem; idem tamen videtur tenendum, quando dubium versatur circa ipsam exsistentiam causae. Rationes enim eaedem in utroque casu militant: nimirum resecare scrupulos et anxietates tam in oratore quam in dispensante."—*Introductio*, p. 129.

41 ". . . circa ipsam causae justae exsistentiam . . . eadem doctrina videtur omnino tenenda: tum quia in utroque casu eaedem militant rationes: expedit enim, ut claudatur via anxietatibus et scrupulis secus oriundis." *Normae Generales*, II, 511.

42 *De Legibus*, pp. 368-369, n. 490.

43 *Institutiones*, I, n. 178.

44 *Institutiones*, I, n. 115, p. 128.

They are unable to see in this matter of dispensing from a vow the close relationship between a probably existing cause and a probably sufficient cause which so many admit in dispensing from ecclesiastical law. The writer, however, is of the opinion that they can go further, just as they have gone further in the matter of the cause required for a dispensation from ecclesiastical law. In the matter of the cause required for a dispensation from an ecclesiastical law they have clearly gone beyond the strict wording of the law; in the matter of vows they have no express law which states that a dispensation may be granted either for a probably sufficient or for a probably existing cause. Since, practically considered, the probability in either case may be reduced to the same fundamental basis there seems to be no reason for denying that a probably existing cause is less adequate than a probably sufficient cause for prompting the grant of a dispensation from a vow.

3) The same reasons which argue for the acceptance of the validity of a probably sufficient cause argue also for the validity of a probably existing cause. Thus, God has not expressly demanded, for the granting of a dispensation from a vow, a cause concerning whose existence there is absolutely no doubt. Accordingly, it can be presumed that He will be satisfied in His goodness with a probably existing cause. Likewise there are the many dispensations which the contrary policy will cause to be refused; the many anxieties which will be entertained; the many scruples which will be stirred up.

4) *Ex paritate* one may argue as follows: The Church accepts as causes for matrimonial dispensations certain factors whose existence is only probable. As long,

however, as this probability is well founded the Church accepts these causes as sufficient for a dispensation from a matrimonial impediment. Thus the Church accepts the hope of resultant civil peace[45] and the hope of the conversion of the non-Catholic party as sufficient causes for dispensing from certain matrimonial impediments.[46] No one attacks the validity of these dispensations if later the peace that was hoped for is not achieved, or if the conversion that was anticipated does not take place. It is admitted that the dispensation was granted in view of some future beneficial event which did not have to take place, and concerning which there was no complete certitude that it would take place.[47] There was merely a probability that civil peace or a conversion to the faith would result from the marriage. Certainly, God is not to be regarded as being less understanding in His infinite goodness and wisdom than is His Church. Hence it seems that God will also be satisfied with a cause which is truly probable, even from the sole viewpoint of its actual existence, for the granting of a dispensation from private vows.

3. *The Sufficiency of an Objectively Existing Cause*

For a valid dispensation from a private vow it suffices that the cause objectively exist, even though the petitioner or the grantor of the dispensation erroneously thinks that the cause does not exist. Nowhere is it required for the validity of a dispensation from a private vow that the

---

45 O'Mara, *Canonical Causes for Matrimonial Dispensations*, The Catholic University of America Canon Law Studies, n. 96 (Washington, D. C.: The Catholic University of America, 1935), p. 103.

46 O'Mara, *op. cit.*, p. 135.

47 Rodrigo, *De Legibus*, pp. 368-369, n. 490.

petitioner or the grantor of the dispensation possess previous knowledge or verification of the objective existence of a cause. Of course, the dispensation is granted illicitly when the cause is not known as at least probably existing.[48] Since, however, the grantor of the dispensation wills to dispense from the vow, he dispenses validly—not in conscious consequence of, but rather in concurrence with, a motivating cause.[49]

4. *The Sufficiency of a Putative Cause*

The question of whether a dispensation is valid when given for a cause which was erroneously thought to exist depends for its solution on a distinction. If the erroneous judgment was due to the falsity of the one motivating cause given in the petition, it seems that by reason of canon 42, § 2, the dispensation must be considered invalid. In canon 42,. § 2, the legislator expresses his determination not to exercise his proper or vicarious jurisdiction validly, when the one motivating cause in the petition is false. While it could be presumed that God would approve the granting of a dispensation from a private vow when the petition contained a false cause given in good faith, still in canon 42, § 2, the ecclesiastical legislator declares that under such circumstances the dispensation will be invalid, which is the same as saying that the ecclesiastical grantor of a dispensation from private vows will not have the intention of dispensing if the one alleged motivating cause is false. It is self-evident that, if the grantor of the dis-

48 Wernz-Vidal, *Normae Generales*, n. 318, p. 473.

49 Sanchez, *De Matrimonio*, lib. VIII, disp. 17, n. 11; Salmanticenses, *Theologia Moralis*, tract. XVII, c. III, n. 119; St. Alphonsus, *Theologia Moralis*, lib. III, n. 251; Rodrigo, *De Legibus*, n. 491.

pensation does not have the intention of dispensing, the dispensation is null.

On the other hand, if the motivating cause presented in the petition is true, but the erroneous judgment of the existence of a certain cause results from a false evaluation of the petition, the dispensation is valid. Hence, if a cause presented as probably existing is judged as certainly existing by the author of the dispensation, the dispensation is valid, even though later it is discovered that no cause existed in reality. Or perhaps no cause is alleged in the petition. Nevertheless the dispensation is valid if the grantor of the dispensation, on the basis of a probably existing cause known to him personally, judges that there is a cause certainly existing, and dispenses from the vow when in reality no cause exists.

These conclusions follow as logical consequences from the admission that a granted dispensation is valid for a probably existing cause. As soon as a probably existing cause is admitted as sufficient for the granting of a valid dispensation, one must be prepared to admit the validity of that same dispensation when later it is discovered that actually the cause did not exist.[50]

B. The Effect of a Deficient Motivating Cause on a Dispensation

When it is discovered that a defective motivating cause has prompted the granting of a dispensation, there are several possible consequences which may follow from this discovery.

---

50 Cf. Rodrigo, *De Legibus*, p. 370, n. 492; Regatillo, *Institutiones*, I, n. 178.

1) If it is discovered that the one motivating cause was *false*, the dispensation is invalid from the very beginning, even though the presentation of a false cause was not intentional. The dispensation, moreover, does not acquire validity for the future; a new dispensation must be given for a sufficient cause.

2) If it is discovered that the one presented motivating cause was insufficient, though it was orginally evaluated as probably sufficient, the dispensation is to be considered as valid for the past and the future.[51]

3) If there be discovered the non-existence of the one presented motivating cause which erroneously was thought actually to exist then a distincton must be made.

a) If the one motivating cause was evaluated as probably existing, and if in fact the cause did have a probable existence at the time the dispensation was granted, the dispensation from a vow must then be considered valid for the past and the future. In such a case the motivating cause was not presented falsely. Rather, it was alleged to have, and did have, a probable existence, which has already been established as being sufficient for a dispensation.

b) If the one motivating cause was evaluated as certainly existing on the basis of a false allegation in the petition, the dispensation then was never valid in the past, and so cannot become valid in the future. In this case the discovery of the non-existence of the cause reveals the invalidity. If, however, the erroneous judgment was due to a false evaluation of the cause by the grantor of the dispensation, and not to the objective falsity of the petition,

---

[51] Cf. *infra*, pp. 227-229, where it will be shown that a dispensation from a vow does not have a recurrent application (*tractus successivus*).

the dispensation from the vow was valid from the beginning. Since a dispensation from a vow does not have a recurrent application, it is also valid for the future.[52]

C. *Concluding Observations*

The doctrine which has just been presented on the question of the validity of a dispensation from a private vow granted on the basis of a putative cause deviates somewhat from that of the two pre-code schools of thought on the matter, both of which continue to have their adherents even today. The first of these maintains that, when a dispensation is found to have been given for a cause which did not exist, the dispensation is invalid. Among those who hold or held this opinion are to be found Castropalao (1581 - 1633),[53] St. Alphonsus (1696 - 1787),[54] Ballerini (1805 - 1881) - Palmieri (1829 - 1909),[55] Noldin (1838-1922)-Schmitt[56] and Coronata.[57]

The second opinion maintains that even though it be found that a dispensation was granted without a cause, the dispensation was nevertheless valid when it was given in good faith. Those who among others adhered to this opinion were Sanchez (1550-1610),[58] Lessius (1554-1623),[59] Tamburini (1591-1675),[60] and the Salmanticenses (1665-

---

52 Rodrigo, *De Legibus*, pp. 371-372, n. 494; Regatillo, *Institutiones*, I, n. 178.

53 *Opus Morale*, III, tract. XV, disp. II, *de voti relaxatione*, pt. 9, n. 4.

54 *Theologia Moralis*, lib. III, n. 251.

55 *Theologia Moralis*, II, 500.

56 *Theologia Moralis*, II, p. 215, n. 230.

57 *Institutiones*, II, p. 227, n. 897.

58 *De Matrimonio*, lib. VIII, disp. XVII, n. 8.

59 *De Iustitia et Iure*, lib. II, c. 40, n. 119.

60 *Theologia Moralis*, I, lib. III, c. XVI, § 4, n. 3.

1724).[61] Since the Code, Michiels has subscribed to the same doctrine.[62]

The doctrine which has been presented in the present work takes a somewhat middle course. According to this solution of the problem, the truth or falsity of the petition must be taken into consideration. The result is that when a cause for which a dispensation was granted is found not to have existed, the dispensation will be invalid if the cause presented even in good faith was false; it will be valid if the erroneous judgment was due to an incorrect evaluation of a true petition. Among those who hold this opinion on dispensations in general, without affirming or denying that it applies to dispensation from vows, are Beste,[63] Wernz-Vidal,[64] Rodrigo[65] and Regatillo.[66]

---

61 *Theologia Moralis*, IV, tract. XVII, c. III, n. 119.

62 *Normae Generales*, II, 511. Michiels restricts his doctrine to purely ecclesiastical law.

63 *Introductio*, p. 129.

64 *Normae Generales*, n. 318, p. 473.

65 *De Legibus*, p. 370, n. 492.

66 *Institutiones*, I, n. 178.

CHAPTER VII

RESERVED VOWS

Article I. The Nature of Reservation

In speaking of reserved vows canon 1309 merely enumerates the vows reserved to the Holy See; it does not indicate what reservation actually is. From the law in force prior to the Code, however, it is known that the reservation of vows to the Holy See means that their remission through a dispensation is removed completely from the jurisdictional power of persons whose authority is intermediate to that of the Roman Pontiff.[1]

Relative to the power of the local ordinary to dispense from vows it was seen that not all local ordinaries possess this power in the same manner. The residential bishop, it was seen, possesses this power by divine law. The other local ordinaries possess it in virtue of ecclesiastical law. In the case of the latter, it is obvious that the reservation of vows takes from these local ordinaries all their jurisdiction over these particular vows. Thus Sixtus IV[2] warned confessors delegated by the Holy See for the dispensation of vows that a commutation (*a fortiori* a dispensation) of a reserved vow without the proper faculty was invalid.

In the case of residential bishops, although they receive their faculty to dispense from private vows in virtue of the divine law, it was seen that the Roman Pontiff can limit this power.[3] This he does in reserving to the Holy See the two vows mentioned in canon 1309.

---

[1] C. 5, *de poenitentiis et remissionibus*, V, 9, in Extravag. com; Benedictus XIV, const. *Inter praeteritos*, 28 nov. 1749, n. 42—*Bullarium*, VIII, 6.

[2] C. 5, *de poenitentiis et remissionibus*, V, 9, in Extravag. com.

[3] Cf. *supra*, *pp.* 99-102.

The question now is whether this reservation takes away the bishop's power over the two reserved private vows in such a way that a dispensation without the proper faculty would be illicit only or both illicit and invalid. In this writer's opinion, the reservation of the private vows of canon 1309 takes away the bishop's jurisdiction over these two vows, so that a dispensation from these vows without a proper delegation would be invalid. The reasons for this opinion are the following:

1) The idea of reservation in the Code seems always to mean that jurisdiction over the matter reserved is possessed only by him to whom the matter is reserved, or his delegate.[4]

2) In the law before the Code it was plainly stated that neither the residential bishop nor any of those who had quasi-episcopal power could dispense from a reserved vow. No distinction was made between a valid and a licit dispensation; it was simply stated that they could not do it. When it is said that something cannot be done, it means that it cannot be done validly; if a dispensation is not capable of being granted, it is not capable of being granted at all.[5]

Article II. The Vows Which Are Reserved

The number of vows reserved to the Holy See has been reduced by more than half by the Code. Today there

---

[4] Canon 1434; canon 893; Cappello, *Tractatus Canonico-Moralis de Sacramentis* (3 vols. in 6, Vol. II, Pars I, *DePoenitentia*, 4. ed., Romae: Marietti, 1945), *De Poenitentia*, p. 504; canon 2245, § 2; Cappello, *Summa Iuris Canonici*, III, n. 502.

[5] Castropalao, *Opus Morale*, III, tract. XV, disp. II, *de voti relaxatione*, pt. 10, n. 5; Lessius, *De Iustitia et Iure*, lib. II, c. 40, n. 121; Salmanticenses, *Theologia Moralis*, tract. XVII, c. III, n. 99; St. Alphonsus, *Theologia Moralis*, lib. III, n. 258; Lehmkuhl, *Theologia Moralis*, I, n. 627.

are only two private vows reserved to the Roman Pontiff, whereas formerly there were five. The first of these is a vow of perfect and perpetual chastity made unconditionally after the completion of one's eighteenth year. The second is a vow unconditionally made after one's eighteenth year to enter a religious order in which solemn vows are taken.[6]

Article III. The Circumstances Under Which These Vows Are Reserved

A. *General Principles*

Among the fundamental principles for determining when a vow is reserved the most basic to remember is that reservation itself is a discriminatory qualification (*res odiosa*) in law, and is therefore to be interpreted strictly. Through the reservation of vows the ordinary power of the residential bishop and of the others who possess ordinary power is restricted and diminished. Hence, before a vow is said to be reserved, its characteristics must correspond exactly and rigidly to the strict notion of the vow which the legislator has placed under reservation.[7]

Hence, before the two vows mentioned in canon 1309 are said to be reserved they must be: 1) vows in the strict sense; 2) perfect in their species; 3) perfect in regard to the obligation which they impose; 4) absolute; 5) definitely determined; 6) factually certain; 7) properly motivated; and 8) made after the completion of one's eighteenth year. Beyond these requirements pertaining to the substance of the vow, an additional requisite is that the phase of the

---

6 Canon 1309.

7 "Odia restringi et favores convenit ampliari."—Reg. 15, R. J., in VI°; canon 19; Reiffenstuel, *Ius Canonicum*, lib. III, tit. XXXIV, n. 28; Ferraris, *Prompta Bibliotheca*, s. v. "Votum", art. III, n. 79.

vow in issue must pertain to the substance and be more than a mere accidental feature of it. For example, if a person made a vow to enter a *strict* religious order with solemn vows, or if a person vowed to enter a religious community *immediately*, these two features of *strictness* and *immediateness* would not be reserved if the vow was otherwise substantially fulfilled.[8]

1) It is required that the vow which is made be actually a vow. This means that it must be a promise made to God. If the promise is made to a saint or to the Blessed Mother, then it is not to be considered as reserved, since it is not a vow in the strict sense.[9]

2) The vow must be perfect in its species. This means that the object matter of the vow must allow an exact identification with the object matter of the specific kind of vow that is reserved to the Pope.

3) The vow must be perfect in regard to the obligation which it imposes on the vowmaker. This means that the obligation imposed by the vow must be a grave one. A vow which binds only under the pain of venial sin is not regarded as of a perfect character and hence is not reserved.[10]

4) The vow must be absolute. Canon 1309 definitely requires that the vow be absolute. This excludes from the class of reserved vows those whose fulfillment is dependent on some future contingency. A conditional vow of this type suspends the obligation of the vow, so that a person

---

[8] Reiffenstuel, *Ius Canonicum*, lib. III, tit. XXXIV, n. 28; Ferraris, *Prompta Bibliotheca*, s. v. "Votum", art. III, n. 79; Lehmkuhl, *Theologia Moralis*, I, n. 627; Aertnys-Damen, *Theologia Moralis*, I, n. 498.

[9] Reiffenstuel, *op. cit.*, lib. III, tit. XXXIV, n. 29; Ferraris, *ibid.*, n. 80.

[10] Salmanticenses, *op. cit.*, tract. XVII, c. III, n. 103; St. Alphonsus, *op. cit.*, lib. III, n. 258; Noldin-Schmitt, *op. cit.*, II, p. 218, n. 234.

who makes this type of vow cannot be said to have absolutely made a vow until the condition is fulfilled. Even then, after the condition has been fulfilled, it is the common opinion that the vow still remains outside the class of reserved vows.[11]

If, however, the condition upon which the fulfillment of the vow rests is a necessary future event, such a condition is generally regarded as not having been made. Much the same is to be said when the condition is based on a future contingency which is meant only to suspend the time for the fulfillment of the vow, for example, if the vowmaker states, "I promise God that I will enter a religious organization with solemn vows if I live to be twenty-one." Such a vow is understood to indicate not so much a condition, as it indicates the time *when* the vow will be fulfilled. Accordingly it is to be looked on as reserved.[12]

Likewise, if the condition upon which the fulfillment of the vow rests is an event of the past or the present, the vow is reserved. A condition of this type does not suspend the obligation; the obligation is definitely contracted or not contracted at the moment the vow is made, since the condition is not a contingency. Yet, while the obligation is definitely contracted or not contracted, it can happen that knowledge of this fact will not be attainable. Therefore, until definite knowledge of the contracting of the obligation is acquired by the vowmaker, it is the writer's opinion that the vow is not reserved.[13]

---

[11] St. Alphonsus, *Theologia Moralis*, lib. III, n. 261; Ballerini-Palmieri, *Theologia Moralis*, II, p. 505; Aertnys-Damen, *Theologia Moralis*, I, n. 498.

[12] Salmanticenses, *op. cit.*, tract. XVII, c. III, n. 110.

[13] Most of the writers simply state that such a vow is reserved. They do not distinguish between the vows whose binding force is known and the vows whose obligation is unknown. Thus, e.g., the Salmanticenses (*op. cit.*, tract. XVII, c. III, n. 110), Aertnys-Damen (*loc. cit.*), and Noldin-Schmitt, (*loc. cit.*).

5) The vow must be definitely determined. Hence, if the vow is disjunctive, consisting of one part which if vowed alone would be reserved, and another part which if vowed alone would not be reserved, the vow is not reserved, even though there be finally chosen that part which if vowed alone would be reserved.[14] If, however, both parts of the disjunctive vow are reserved, then according to the old authors the vow is reserved.[15] Still it seems that even such a vow is not reserved until one or the other member is specifically selected. Until this is done, the specification as to which vow is binding, is not determined, and certainly not both vows are binding.

6) The vow must be factually certain. Accordingly, if some pertinent factor remained doubtful—for example, the element of full deliberation, or of sufficient intention—the vow would not be reserved.[16]

7) The vow must be properly motivated. This means that the vow must be made directly and primarily out of love for the virtue which one promises to practice. Accordingly a vow made out of motives of unjust and even slight fear,[17] or for some temporal advantage, is not reserved.[18]

---

14 Tamburini, *Theologia Moralis*, lib. III, c. XVI, § 4, n. 31; Salmanticenses, *op. cit.*, tract. XVII, c. III, n. 107; Aertnys-Damen, *op. cit.*, I, n. 498.

15 Suarez, *De Voto*, lib. VI, c. XXIV, nn. 1-4; Sanchez, *De Matrimonio*, lib. VIII, disp. IX, n. 14; Laymann, *Theologia Moralis*, II, lib. IV, tract. IV, c. VIII, n. 12; Ferraris, *Prompta Bibliotheca*, s. v. "Votum", art. III, n. 83; Lehmkuhl, *Theologia Moralis*, I, n. 627.

16 Suarez, *De Voto*, lib. VI, c. XXIV, n. 6; Laymann, *Theologia Moralis*, II, lib. IV, tract. IV, c. VIII, n. 14; Ferraris, *op. cit.*, s. v. "Votum", art. III, n. 82; Noldin-Schmitt, *op. cit.*, II, p. 218, n. 234.

17 Laymann, *op. cit.*, II, lib. IV, c. VIII, n. 11; Reiffenstuel, *Ius Canonicum*, lib. III, tit. XXXIV, n. 30; Aertnys-Damen, *op. cit.*, I, n. 498; Coronata, *op. cit.*, p. 228, n. 897.

18 Noldin-Schmitt: ". . . solum si ex amore virtutis, non ob solum commodum temporale emissum est."—*Theologia Moralis*, II, p. 218, n. 234.

Frequently, conditional vows lack this proper motivation and are thus for a second reason disqualified for classification as reserved vows. For example, a person could promise God that he will keep perfect chastity if he is rescued from a particular danger. Here the rescue from danger is the condition upon which the vow is made. Such a vow is not a promise made to God with the intention purely and simply of honoring Him. Hence it is not reserved.

Likewise, penal vows are not reserved. Such vows inflict an obligation on a person in consequence of the contraction of some guilt. It is obvious, in this case, that the virtue to be practiced by reason of the vow is imposed on rather than embraced by the vowmaker.[19]

8) Finally, the vow must be made after the completion of one's eighteenth year.[20] A vow made before the completion of one's eighteenth year is not reserved; neither is it reserved, if after the completion of one's eighteenth year the same vow is renewed—even though it be renewed with the intention of changing it from a non-reserved to a reserved vow. The reservation of a vow does not depend on the intention of the vowmaker, but rather on the mind of the Church. Therefore, if a vow is to become reserved, a renewal of a non-reserved vow will not suffice. Instead, a new and legitimately made vow is required. All this of course presupposes that a dispensation had not been granted from the vow made prior to the completion of one's eighteenth year.[21]

19 Aertnys-Damen, *loc. cit.*; Noldin-Schmitt, *loc. cit.*

20 Canon 1309.

21 *Jus Pontificium*, I-II (1921-1922), 108-109.

B. The Vows Examined in Particular

In addition to the general principles already given, it will prove helpful to examine the reserved vows individually in order to ascertain when and when not they are reserved. This examination will consist practically in determining when the reserved vow is perfect in its species, that is, when its object matter can be identified with that of the vow which canon 1309 lists as a reserved vow.

1. The Vow of Perfect and Perpetual Chastity

A vow of chastity must first of all be perpetual in order to be reserved. It is perpetual if it is taken for life. A vow, however, taken for a hundred years is regarded as being the equivalent of a vow taken in perpetuity.[22] If, on the other hand, a vow is taken for a limited time, it is not regarded as reserved.[23]

In addition, the vow must be one of *perfect* chastity. This means that it must have as its object the abstention from all sexual pleasure, whether internal or external, licit or illicit.[24] Accordingly the following vows would not be reserved:

1) The vow not to marry.

2) The vow not to ask for the marital right.

3) The vow to receive Sacred Orders; for this is not a vow of chastity, but at most implies the promise to make a vow of chastity.[25]

---

22 Lessius, *De Iustitia et Iure*, lib. II, c. 40, n. 123.

23 Canon 1309.

24 Gasparri, *De Matrimonio*, I, n. 428.

25 Castropalao, *Opus Morale*, III, tract. XV, disp. II, *de voti relaxatione*, pt. 11, n. 1; Salmanticenses, *op. cit.*, tract. XVII, c. III, n. 104; Lehmkuhl, *Theologia Moralis*, I, n. 627; Noldin-Schmitt, *Theologia Moralis*, II, p. 218, n. 234.

4) The vow of virginity, if by it is understood the preservation of that integrity of the body which is lost by the performance of the first conjugal act.[26]

5) The vow of conjugal chastity, even though both concur in the vow; for there still remains the possibility of another marriage after the current one is dissolved by death. Such a vow lacks the necessary note of perpetuity.[27]

2. The Vow to Enter a Religious Institute Where Members Profess Solemn Vows

Before a vow to enter a religious institute whose members take solemn vows can be said to be reserved, it must be established that solemn vows are actually taken in that community. There are certain communities which have solemn vows according to their foundation, but actually take only simple vows. Accordingly, a vow to enter such a community would not be reserved.

At the same time it must be pointed out that, although not all the members of a community take solemn vows, as long as some do take them, a vow to enter such a community is reserved.[28]

C. *The Cessation of the Reservation*

Once a vow is reserved, it ordinarily remains reserved until a dispensation is granted. In case of necessity, however, the reservation ceases, so that one with authority intermediate to that of the Roman Pontiff, if he have ordinary power to dispense from private vows, can grant

26 Salmanticenses, *loc. cit.*

27 Lessius, *loc. cit.*; cf. Aertnys-Damen, *op. cit.*, I, n. 498.

28 Vermeersch-Creusen, *Epitome*, II, p. 446, n. 640.

a dispensation from the two vows reserved in canon 1309. This point will be treated later in this chapter.

But the reservation ceases also when an object matter which is not reserved is substituted for an object matter which is reserved. This occurs when a vow is commuted. Hence, if a reserved vow is commuted, for example, if the vow of perfect chastity is changed into a vow to say the rosary every day, any one with an authority intermediate to that of the Roman Pontiff, if he have also power to dispense from vows, can grant a dispensation from the commuted vow.[29]

When a dispensation from a vow of perfect chastity is granted, it is not infrequently granted only partially for the exclusive purpose and effect of allowing the vowmaker to contract a particular marriage. With such a dispensation the vow continues to bind in part, so that all sinful acts in marriage are at the same time sins against the vow. Moreover, when the marriage for which the dispensation was granted is dissolved by death, or in any other manner, the vow will begin at that very moment to bind with its full original force. Accordingly, if a second marriage is contemplated, another dispensation will be necessary.

The question then arises whether, after there has been granted a dispensation from the vow of perpetual chastity to permit the vowmaker to contract a marriage, the vow is commuted so as to cease to be reserved. That the vow continues to be reserved seems quite certain for the following reasons:

---

[29] Castropalao, *Opus Morale*, III, tract. XV, disp. II, *de voti relaxatione*, pt. 11, n. 5; Salmanticenses, *op. cit.*, tract. XVII, c. III, n. 109; Noldin-Schmitt, *op. cit.*, II, p. 218, n. 235.

1) When a bishop, or anyone else having ordinary power, dispenses from the vow of perfect chastity in a case of urgent necessity, this dispensation is granted for the purpose of allowing a marriage to be contracted. The dispensation does not permit more than the necessity demands. Hence the obligation of the vow ceases with reference to all the legitimate marital acts; it continues to bind and implies an additional guilt for the perpetration of any illegitimate acts in marriage. The same vow regains its original force when the marriage ceases to exist through the intervention of death. Despite all this, no one will say that after the vow has become, through the dispensation, merely one of conjugal chastity, that then the bishop or anyone else having power to dispense from vows could remove the obligation of the vow completely. Yet, if this vow had really been commuted from one of perfect chastity into one of conjugal chastity, anyone having the power to dispense from non-reserved vows should be able to take away its obligation completely.[30]

2) In the appraisal of a dispensation of this kind, even when granted by the Roman Pontiff, attention is not so much to be given to the present status of the vow (conjugal chastity) as to the status which the vow had when it was originally made. For in the granting of the dispensation the mind of the Roman Pontiff is that, except for legitimate marital acts, the vow should remain just as it was in the beginning. This is apparent from the admonition generally given to the confessor who is to grant the dispensation. He is to advise the penitent that the vow will continue to bind: "Quod si iterum contraxerit et

30 De Lugo, *Disputationes Scholasticae et Morales* (2. ed., 8 vols., Parisiis, 1868-1869), VIII, lib. VI, n. 4.

consummaverit matrimonium, aut unquam extra matrimonium fornicatus fuerit, sciat se contra hujusmodi votum facturum." It should be observed that the sin will be committed against *hujusmodi votum,* that is, against the same vow from which the modified dispensation is granted. The sin will be committed against that same vow, and not against a new one, into which one might think the first had been commuted. When a dispensation of the type here being discussed is granted, no commutation takes place, for the first vow continues to bind in virtue of the Roman Pontiff's intention.[31]

It seems, therefore, to be established that vows of perfect and perpetual chastity from which a dispensation has been granted in the manner just described remain reserved. Although this conclusion may seem to be reached in opposition to the general principle stated above—"Odia restringi et favores convenit ampliari"—[32] such opposition does not really exist. There is no room for the restriction of a burden whose continued existence can not be called into question, and similarly there can be no thought to warrant the amplifying of a favor to which the modified dispensation never gave actual existence.

Article IV. Dispensation from Reserved Vows

A. *By the Roman Pontiff*

Naturally, the Roman Pontiff can dispense from the vows reserved to the Holy See. Likewise, the various Roman Congregations can grant dispensations from reserved vows within the sphere of their own competence.

---

[31] De Lugo, *ibid.*, n. 7; Teodori, "Altera voti Dispensatio"—*Apollinaris* (Romae, 1928—) VI (1933), 505-506.

[32] Reg. 15, R. J., in VI°.

From the Holy See this power to dispense from reserved vows is communicated to others throughout the world through delegated power. It must be noted, however, that this power to dispense from reserved vows is not contained in the faculty which authorizes one through a grant from the Holy See to dispense from private vows in general. In order to vindicate one's claim to the faculty of dispensing from reserved vows, one must establish receipt of either a special concession made to dispense from a particular reserved vow, or of a general concession to dispense from all reserved vows.[33]

B. By the Local Ordinary

1. With Delegated Faculties

Delegation is the normal way in which subordinates of the Roman Pontiff obtain the faculty to dispense from reserved private vows. Ordinarily the recipients of this faculty exercise it as delegates of the Roman Pontiff. When, however, the person who obtains the faculty is a residential bishop, there is some question whether, in thus regaining a power which belongs to his native competence, he regains it and exercises it as an ordinary or as a delegated power.

Suarez[34] asserted that the bishop possessed this faculty as delegated power. Triebs († 1942),[35] writing in the present time, maintains that the residential bishop in this case exercises ordinary power. His doctrine, however, be-

---

33 ". . . nisi ex speciali licentia, et certa scientia nostra. . ." — c. 5, *de poenitentiis et remissionibus*, V, 9, in Extravag. com.; Salmanticenses, *Theologia Moralis*, tract. XVII, c. III, n. 116; St. Alphonsus, *Theologia Moralis*, lib. III, n. 258.

34 *De Voto*, lib. VI, c. XXV, n. 1.

35 *Handbuch des kanonischen Eherechts* (Breslau: Ostdeutsche Verlaganstalt, 1933), p. 214.

comes inconsistent when he asserts that the power to dispense from an unconsummated marriage, though belonging to the native competence of the bishop, is exercised by him as a delegated power when he is authorized by the Holy See to conduct an informative process for the granting of such a dispensation. Triebs does not state this expressly, but he does seem to imply the same, for he speaks not of the bishop *delegating* this faculty of conducting the informative process, but rather of subdelegating it. Subdelegation of a faculty, however, is not an act of one who possesses that faculty in virtue of ordinary power. It is rather an act of one who possesses a delegated power.[36]

Furthermore, as Suarez[37] points out, even though it be true that the residential bishop obtains ordinary power over reserved vows when the reservation is removed or when he is granted a privilege of dispensing from reserved vows, still he cannot be said to obtain this power when he is simply delegated for a particular case or for a certain length of time through the Quinquennial Faculties. Such a communication of power is temporary; the reservation is not removed; there is simply a grant of jurisdiction for dispensing from *reserved* vows. Accordingly, the residential bishop is to be considered as receiving and exercising this power in the same manner as any one else who is delegated by the Holy See to dispense from private vows.

2. *In Urgent Necessity*

Although the normal procedure for obtaining the faculty of dispensing from a reserved vow is to have recourse to the Holy See, this is not always feasible. Further-

36 Canon 199.

37 *Loc. cit.*

more, the law of the Code on granting dispensations in urgent necessity seems inapplicable in view of the fact that the legislator speaks there exclusively of ecclesiastical law. Thus canon 81 states:

> "A generalibus Ecclesiae legibus Ordinarii infra Romanum Pontificem dispensare nequeunt, ne in casu quidem peculiari, nisi haec potestas eisdem fuerit explicite vel implicite concessa, aut nisi difficilis sit recursus ad Sanctam Sedem et simul in mora sit periculum gravis damni, et de dispensatione agatur quae a Sede Apostolica concedi solet."

Accordingly, the granting of a dispensation from a vow does not seem to come within the preview of this canon, since a vow does not bind by ecclesiastical law. Consequently the authors have recourse to *epikeia*.[38]

Nevertheless, there are some authors who seem to use canon 81 to authorize an ordinary (hence not the minor clerical exempt superior) to dispense from a reserved vow when recourse to the Holy See is difficult and there is serious danger in delay.[39] This theory is not without foundation, especially when one considers that, though the vow does not bind by ecclesiastical law, still the reservation does. Hence the ordinary can lawfully employ the approved principle of canon 81 to dispense from the reservation, and with the reservation removed he can then dispense from the vow.

But even if canon 81 is not accepted as applying theoretically to the dispensation from reserved vows in an urgent necessity, it will be seen that in practice the other explanation based on *epikeia* is almost identical with the

---

[38] Noldin-Schmitt, *Theologia Moralis*, II, p. 218, n. 234, nota 2; Aertnys-Damen, *Theologia Moralis*, I, n. 499.

[39] Regatillo, *Institutiones*, II, n. 157; Cappello, *De Matrimonio*, pars I, n. 305, p. 388.

doctrine which acknowledges the applicability of canon 81. It will also be seen that this doctrine as explained before the Code on the basis of *epikeia* has been somewhat modified since the Code, a modification which Cappello traces to the principle enunciated in canon 81.[40]

According to this doctrine, based on the principle of *epikeia* and drawn from the authors since the Council of Trent, the local ordinary can dispense from reserved vows when there is an urgent necessity attended with the moral impossibility of having recourse to the Holy See in sufficient time to contend with the emergency. An urgent necessity would be present if there was a danger of some grave temporal or spiritual harm coming to the vowmaker or a third party.[41]

This concession, however, of dispensing from reserved vows in an urgent necessity and based on the principle of *epikeia* is not to be used except in so far as it may be imperative. For example, before a marriage there will be need of nothing more than a suspending of the continued obligation of a vow of chastity. In this case the vow will continue to bind in relation to all illicit acts in marriage; after the marriage has been dissolved by death, if the surviving party is the vowmaker, the vow will once more bind with its original force.[42]

---

40 *Loc. cit.* Cf. *infra,* pp. 211-212, 216.

41 St. Alphonsus, *op. cit.,* lib. III, n. 258; Ballerini-Palmieri, *op. cit.,* II, p. 502.

42 Lehmkuhl, *Theologia Moralis,* I, n. 628; Aertnys-Damen, *Theologia Moralis,* I, n. 499. In virtue of the Quinquennial Faculties, the local ordinaries have received the following faculty: "Dispensandi iusta et rationabili ex causa super matrimonialibus impedimentis minoris gradus quae in can. 1042 recensentur, necnon super impedimentis de quibus in can. 1058 *ad effectum tantum matrimonium contrahendi.*"—*Index Facultatum Quinquennalium,* c. II, n. 1, in

The exact juridical nature of the operation whereby a subordinate of the Holy See dispenses from a reserved vow in an urgent necessity is not certain. One opinion states that the reservation ceases, since the Roman Pontiff does not wish to reserve the vows to himself in a case of urgent necessity. Instead the Pontiff intends that the bishop should use his ordinary power to dispense from the vows.[43] A second opinion, denying that the reservation ceases, affirms that the case remains a "Papal" one; that it is an extraordinary power which the local ordinary or clerical exempt superior uses to dispense from the vow in urgent necessity. Adhering to this opinion are the Salmanticenses,[44] Lehmkuhl,[45] and others.[46]

Of the two opinions, the more probable one seems to be that which maintains that the local ordinary exercises ordinary power when he dispenses from a reserved vow in urgent necessity. In dispensing in such circumstances, the subordinate of the Holy See acts either in virtue of his office, or in consequence of the fact that the reservation ceases, or in view of an approved universal custom. Whichever of these three sources of authorization it may be that

---

Vermeersch-Creusen, *Epitome*, I, p. 537, n. 814. (Italics in text are inserted by the writer.) Through this faculty the local ordinary can suspend the vow of perfect and perpetual chastity to the extent of allowing all acts proper to the marriage state for the duration of that marriage. Should the vowmaker survive the other nuptial partner, the vow then revives with its full obligation. (Müssener, *Das katholische Eherecht in der Seelsorgspraxis* [2. ed., Düsseldorf: L. Schwann, 1933], pp. 110-111.)

43 Lessius, *De Iustitia et Iure*, lib. II, c. XL, n. 127; Reiffenstuel, *Ius Canonicum*, lib. III, tit. XXXIV, n. 42; Ballerini-Palmieri, *Theologia Moralis*, II, 506; D'Annibale, *Theologia Moralis*, III, n. 210; Coronata, *Institutiones*, II, p. 229, n. 897.

44 *Theologia Moralis*, IV, tract. XVII, c. III, n. 96.

45 *Theologia Moralis*, I, n. 628.

46 Cf. *infra*, pp. 219-220.

empowers him to act, each of them empowers him to act with ordinary power.[47]

On the other hand, it seems clear that the subordinate of the Roman Pontiff does not act with delegated power when he dispenses from a reserved vow in urgent necessity. This is true even if it be accepted that he dispenses in virtue of the principle enunciated in canon 81.[48] For nowhere is this power delegated to the local ordinary. The subordinate of the Roman Pontiff, in dispensing from reserved vows in an urgent case, does not exercise an extraordinary power; for the power which he exercises derives either from his office, from custom, or from the fact that the reservation ceases. In each case, it is ordinary power that is utilized.[49]

The question may also be raised whether the difficulty of recourse to the Holy See can be said to be present if there is someone available, for example, the Apostolic Legate, who has the necessary faculty to dispense from the reserved vow in question. It seems, however, that the recourse does remain difficult even though someone be present who has the required faculty. Accordingly, the local ordinary and the clerical exempt superior can dispense from a reserved vow in a case of urgent necessity, even though recourse to the Apostolic Legate be possible. This is based *directly* on canon 81, when this canon is accepted as authorizing the ordinary to grant a dispensation from reserved vows in urgent necessity. Otherwise,

47 Reiffenstuel, *Ius Canonicum*, lib. III, tit. XXXIV, n. 40.

48 Beste (*Introductio*, p. 128) and Michiels (*Normae Generales*, II, 486) consider the faculty granted in canon 81 as implying an exercise of ordinary power.

49 Reiffenstuel, *Ius Canonicum*, lib. III, tit. XXXIV, n. 41.

the doctrine here asserted rests on canon 81 through a legal analogy.[50]

Canon 81 states that though the faculty to dispense from general ecclesiastical law must be obtained from the competent ecclesiastical authority, still if recourse to the Holy See is difficult and there is danger of great harm in delay, the ordinary can dispense from those laws, from which the Holy See usually dispenses even though someone be present who is competent to grant the dispensation. So, too, in the case of reserved vows. They are reserved to the Holy See from whom there must be obtained the faculty for relaxing the vow by means of a dispensation. But in the light of canon 81, and because of the strict interpretation to be adopted in the matter of the reservation of vows, if recourse to the Holy See is morally impossible and there is serious danger in delay, the reservation is thought to cease and the ordinary can dispense without recourse to any other competent superior.

C. *By the Application of the Principle of Canon 1111*

Prior to the Code the circumstance of urgent necessity for dispensing from the vow of perfect and perpetual chastity in relation to marriage was required only before the marriage. After the marriage had already been contracted, the local ordinary and regular confessors could dispense from the vow of chastity for the purpose of allowing the vowmaker to seek the marriage right, even when there was no urgent necessity arising from a danger of spiritual or temporal loss.[51]

---

50 Canon 20.

51 Lessius, *De Iustitia et Iure,* lib. III, c. LX, n. 125; Castropalao, *Opus Morale,* Tom. III, tract. XV, disp. II, *de voti relaxatione,* pt. 12, n. 9; Tamburini, *Theologia Moralis,* lib. II, c. XVI, § 4, n. 42; St. Alphonsus, *op. cit.,* lib. III, n. 258; Lehmkuhl, *op. cit.,* I, n. 628.

Since the Code, authors do not attribute this latter power to the local ordinary.[52] Instead, the Quinquennial Faculties give to all local ordinaries (thus excluding clerical exempt superiors who are not local ordinaries) the following faculty:

> "Dispensandi ad petendum debitum coniugale cum transgressore voti castitatis perfectae et perpetuae, privatim post completum XVIII aetatis annum emissi, qui matrimonium cum dicto voto contraxerit, huiusmodi poenitentem monendo ipsum ad idem votum servandum teneri tam extra licitum matrimonii usum quam si coniugi supervixerit."[53]

But in regard to this matter Cardinal Gasparri in 1932 presented a more complete understanding of canon 1111, from which, if accepted, radical changes must necessarily follow in the matter of dispensing from reserved and non-reserved vows after the vowmaker has entered marriage.[54] According to this new interpretation, canon 1111 implies a limited dispensation for the person who violates a vow of chastity by illicitly contracting marriage. Through this limited dispensation from the vow of chastity, the vowmaker is permitted to seek and to render the conjugal rights and to exercise all licit acts of married life.[55] If, however, the vowmaker sins against chastity during married life, he also sins against the vow. Likewise, when the marriage is dissolved by death, if the surviving party is the

---

[52] This limitation seems to be based on the principle enunciated in canon 81. Thus Cappello, *De Matrimonio,* pars I, n. 305, pp. 387-388. Cf. also Cappello, *Summa Iuris Canonici,* I, n. 127, p. 140; Michiels, *Normae Generales,* II, 487; Vermeersch-Creusen, *Epitome,* I, n. 161, ad 11.

[53] *Index Facultatum Quinquennalium,* VI, n. 7—in Vermeersch-Creusen, *Epitome,* I, p. 541, n. 814; also in Bouscaren, *The Canon Law Digest,* II, 40.

[54] *De Matrimonio,* I, nn. 428-431.

[55] Canon 1111: "Utrique coniugi ab ipso matrimonii initio aequum ius et officium est quod attinet ad actus proprios coniugalis vitae."

vowmaker, he or she will be bound by the vow with its complete and original force.[56]

Cappello[57] calls this operation of canon 1111 a suspension. Gasparri calls it a limited dispensation. To call it a limited, tacit[58] suspension, however, seems even more accurate, for although a dispensation in the strict sense has not been granted, neither has a complete suspension of the vow been given. Part of it continues to bind; part of it is suspended. The difference is one of terminology. The use of the designation "dispensation in a limited sense" is in complete harmony with the vocabulary on this matter as found before the Code. But as Cappello rightly points out, the term "dispensatio limitata" is not found in the Code. In treating of the force of canon 1111 at the present time, the writer does not intend to confine himself to either of these particular terms. The term dispensation will be most frequently used, its meaning being clear from the context.

In support of this new interpretation of canon 1111 the following arguments can be adduced:

1) As Gasparri shows, in the preparation of the text of canon 1111 the consultors were first presented with the following proposed schema for the canon:

> § 1. Utrique coniugi ab ipso matrimonii initio aequm ius et officium est in ordine ad actus per se aptos ad prolis generationem;
>
> § 2. Coniux solum in casu quo castitatis voto teneatur nequit petere debitum coniugale, licet reddere et possit et debeat.

Two months were spent in deliberation on it, and as the result of this deliberation the present canon 1111 was

56 Gasparri, *ibid.*, n. 430.

57 *De Matrimonio,* Pars II, p. 220, n. 737.

58 Oesterle, "Keuschheitsgelübde und Ehe." — *Theologischpraktische Quartalschrift,* LXXXIX (1936), 573-580.

placed in the Code. After comparing the original schema and the present canon, it can be seen that the second paragraph has been removed entierly. In addition, the words of the original first paragraph have been changed from *in ordine ad actus per se aptos ad prolis generationem* to *quod attinet ad actus proprios vitae coniugalis.*

Because of this Gasparri concludes: "Igitur hac duplici mutatione Codex per cit. can. 1111 edixit, inito matrimonio utrique coniugi aequum ius et officium esse non solum ad copulam, sed ad omnes actus proprios vitae coniugalis, suppressa exceptione pro parte quae votum castitatis emiserat."[59]

2) Furthermore, the text of the law demands this interpretation. Cap. III, tit. VII, lib. III, of the Code speaks of the prohibitive impediments to marriage of which perfect chastity is one.[60] The effects of a marriage entered into contrary to a vow of perfect chastity are not stated in canon 1058. Later, however, in Cap. IX, tit. VII, lib. III, can. 1110-1117, the effects of marriage are stated. Applying here the rule "a rubro valet illatio ad nigrum,"[61] one sees immediately in canon 1111 the effect of a marriage entered into contrary to a vow of chastity. If the vow of perfect chastity continued to bind subsequent to the contraction of marriage, then it would have been indicated for the legislator to say "salvo voto castitatis," as he did with

---

59 *De Matrimonio,* I, n. 429.

60 Canon 1058.

61 This rule is found in the Glossators (Cappello, *Summa Iuris Canonici,* I, n. 85, p. 92, nota 3.) and is certainly to be followed in interpreting the Code, since the rubrics derive from the legislator himself. The text of the law, however, can derogate or contradict the rubric, in which case the meaning of the rubric will be determined by the text. Most frequently, however, the text will be determined by the rubric. (Van Hove, *De Legibus Ecclesiasticis* [Mechliniae-Romae: 1930], n. 255; Michiels, *Normae Generales,* I, 4C8, nota 5.)

equivalent terms in the preparatory schema. The fact that this conditional limitation was not included in canon 1111 after it had been in the original schema is very significant, especially when one compares canon 1111 with subsequent canons of the same chapter on the effects of marriage. In canons 1112; 1114; 1115; § 1; 1116 and 1117, the legislator has expressly included a limitation on the usual effects of matrimony. The fact that he did not indicate any limitation regarding the matrimonial effects mentioned in canon 1111, can, therefore, indicate only that he did not intend to limit them.[62]

Hence canon 1111 must be regarded as pointing to an implicit suspension of the vow granted by the legislator in regard to the acts proper to conjugal life.[63] Implicit dispensations such as this are not alien to the Code. Thus an explicit dispensation from an unconsummated marriage always contains an implicit dispensation from the impediment of crime arising from adultery committed with a promise or an attempt to contract marriage.[64] As Michiels states, "Certe adest dispensatio tacita, quando superior ex certa scientia aliquid positive praecipit vel concedit subdito, quod sine dispensatione fieri aut valere non potest; puta, si Episcopus ordines conferat alicui, quem scit esse irregularem, vel si subdito praecipiat comedere carnes, die prohibito."[65]

---

62 Oesterle has treated this matter thoroughly and accurately in *art. cit.*—*TPQ*, LXXXIX (1936), 576.

63 Compare canon 1315: "Vota ante professionem religiosam emissa suspenduntur donec vovens in religione permanserit."

64 Canon 1053. Cf. also canons 1047; 1049; 1052; 991, § 1; Oesterle, *ibid.*, p. 577.

65 *Normae Generales*, II, p. 459. As is evident from the context, Michiels here designates as a tacit dispensation what the writer considers an implicit dispensation.

In the matter at hand the legislator gravely prohibits[66] marriage on the part of persons who have made a vow of perfect chastity.[67] Yet, if they marry in violation of the vow, he attributes to both of them equal rights to all acts proper to the conjugal life. It seems quite impossible for him to do this unless he also suspends the vow; otherwise he would have to add to the text of canon 1111 some such phrase as *salvo voto castitatis.*

3) Furthermore, such a suspension is not given without a proper cause, for it has always been recognized that by the very contract of marriage there exists a sufficient cause for dispensing from or suspending a vow of chastity.[68]

4) This interpretation provides in addition a satisfactory substitute for the custom which existed before the Code. This custom permitted those who had ordinary power to dispense from vows, and regular confessors to dispense from a vow of perfect and perpetual chastity for the purpose of permitting a person to seek the marriage right, even when there was no danger in any delay relative to the grant of the dispensation. Since the Code, the authors have not spoken of this. With the more complete explanation of canon 1111 as offered by Gasparri, a satisfactory remedy is presented which more than compensates the beneficent effects of the former custom.

5) Finally, the usual procedure of the Sacred Penitentiary confirms this interpretation. When petitioned after marriage for a dispensation from the vow of perfect and perpetual chastity, the Sacred Tribunal has two courses of action from which it selects its manner of responding.

---

66 Canon 1036.

67 Canon 1058.

68 The danger of violating the vow is self-evident.

Either it grants the dispensation absolutely, or it declares that in view of the peculiar circumstances of the case a dispensation is not necessary.[69]

As a result of this interpretation, the faculty given to ordinaries by the Sacred Penitentiary can be considered superfluous. The fact that it has been given is not an argument against Gasparri's opinion. The Tribunals and Congregations of Rome retained after the Code the formularies which were used prior to 1918. After 1918 the Congregation of the Sacraments gave the faculty to dispense from certain impediments of the major degree. Among these it enumerated the impediment of consanguinity in the third degree touching on the first. When the attention of the Congregation was called to the fact that consanguinity in the third degree touching on the first was no longer an impediment of major degree,[70] it changed the wording of the faculty by omitting the words *maioris gradus.*[71]

Since Gasparri[72] proposed his opinion in 1932, it has gradually gained new adherents. At present the following are known to the writer to have assented to this more complete interpretation of canon 1111: Oesterle,[73] Cappello[74] and Donovan.[75]

Coronata, while not admitting this to be the common opinion, nevertheless proposes it, and does not reject it.[76]

---

69 Cappello, *De Matrimonio,* Pars II, p. 220, n. 737.

70 Canons 96, § 3; 1042.

71 Oesterle, *ibid.,* p. 579.

72 *De Matrimonio,* I, nn. 428-431.

73 "Keuschheitsgelübde und Ehe."—*TPQ,* LXXXIX (1936), 573-580.

74 *De Matrimonio,* pars II, p. 220, n. 737.

75 "An Outdated Interpretation of Canon 1111."—*Homiletic and Pastoral Review,* XLI (1941), 1169-1173.

76 *De Sacramentis Tractatus Canonicus* (3 vols., Taurini-Romae: Marietti, 1943-1946. Vol. III, *De Matrimonio,* 1946), *De Matrimonio,* n. 249, pp. 304-305.

This opinion, however, does have its opponents. Thus Payen[77] rejects it completely and maintains that the common and accepted interpretation of canon 1111 is to be retained. Wernz-Vidal[78] do not treat of this interpretation of canon 1111. Nevertheless, they implicitly reject it in a rather forceful manner when they declare that the exercise of the right to the marital debt can cease or be temporarily suspended. They further point out that the right to ask for the marital debt can be so removed from one partner to the marriage that until this right is restored this partner remains obligated to render the debt, and the other partner retains a strict right to request the debt. As an example of this type of case they cite the instance of a person who had made a vow of chastity. Finally Wernz-Vidal make their stand very clear when, in a footnote,[79] they declare that the marriage partner who is deprived of his right to seek the marital debt because of a vow of chastity which he had made, can regain this right only through a "veram dispensationem legitime obtentam sive a R. Pontifice, v.g. per S. Paenitentiariam, sive ab Episcopis saltem vi facultatum a S. Paenitentiaria ipsis concessarum." In view of the fact that this statement was made by Wernz-Vidal in the third edition of their work, fourteen years after Cardinal Gasparri published his interpretation of canon 1111, it seems obvious that they are definitely, however, tacitly, rejecting his interpretation without caring to mention his name.

---

77 *De Matrimonio* (2. ed., 3 vols., Zi- ka- wei: T'ou-sè-wè, 1935-1936), I, pp. 627-631.

78 *Ius Canonicum ad Codicis Normam Exactum* (7 tomes in 8 vols., Vol. V, *Ius Matrimoniale*, 3. ed. recognita a P. Philippo Aguirre, Romae: Apud Aedes Universitatis Gregorianae, 1946), *Ius Matrimoniale*, n. 559, p. 756.

79 *Ibid.*, nota 9.

The explanation of canon 1111 which has just been completed, though mentioning only the vow of chastity and its suspension, is to be understood as applying to both perpetual and temporary vows of chastity as well as to the vow of virginity and its dispensation.[80] Accordingly, a person who, when bound by a vow of virginity, illicitly contracts marriage, may in virtue of canon 1111 petition for the first marital act by which virginity is lost.

D. By Regular Confessors

The privilege of the regular confessor to dispense from private vows has already been investigated. Since the regular confessor is said to be able by reason of this privilege to dispense from all vows from which the bishop can dispense in virtue of his ordinary power, it seems that the power of the regular confessor is co-extensive with that of the local ordinary in regard to dispensing from private vows.[81]

But then the question arises, "Can the regular confessor dispense from a reserved vow in urgent necessity?" It has been seen that the bishop can do this, but in reference to the regular confessor's power to do it there is not complete agreement. It is denied by a respectable group of authors, among who are Laymann (1574-1635),[82] Castropalao (1581-1633),[83] Tamburini (1591-1675),[84] La Croix (1652-1714),[85] the Salmanticenses (1665-1724),[86] and

80 Gasparri, *op. cit.*, I, n. 427.

81 Shuhler, *Privileges of Regulars to Absolve and Dispense*, p. 141. Cf. *supra*, pp. 62-63.

82 *Theologia Moralis*, lib. IV, tract. IV, c. VIII, n. 17.

83 *Opus Morale*, III, tract. XV, disp. *de voti relaxatione*, pt. 12, n. 7.

84 *Theologia Moralis*, lib. III, c. XVI, § 4, n. 49.

85 *Theologia Moralis*, lib. III, pars I, n. 554.

86 *Theologia Moralis*, tract. XVII, c. III, n. 96.

Lehmkuhl (1834-1918).[87] St. Alphonsus (1696-1787)[88] acknowledged that this opinion was the more common one, but at the same time he also acknowledged the probability of the opposite opinion. Prümmer (1866-1931)[89] also seems to reject the idea that the regular confessor can dispense from reserved vows in urgent necessity.

The basis for the viewpoint of these authors is that the bishop does not exercise ordinary power in dispensing in urgent necessity from a reserved vow. Since, however, the regular confessor can dispense only from those vows from which the bishop dispenses with ordinary power, it is obvious that he cannot in urgent necessity dispense from a reserved vow. In the opinion of the proponents of this explanation the vow remains reserved to the Holy See even in urgent necessity; it is only accidentally that the bishop can dispense from it, viz., in virtue of an extraordinary power.[90]

As favoring the extension of the regular confessor's faculty to include the power of dispensing from reserved vows in urgent necessity, the following may be cited: Reiffenstuel (1642-1703),[91] D'Annibale (1815-1892),[92] Ballerini (1805-1881)-Palmieri (1829-1909),[93] Aertnys (1828-1915)-Damen,[94] and Shuhler.[95] Their opinion is based on

87 *Theologia Moralis,* I, n. 478.

88 *Theologia Moralis,* lib. III, n. 258.

89 *Theologia Moralis,* II, n. 427.

90 Castropalao, *loc. cit.*; Salmanticenses, *loc. cit.*; Tamburini: "Ratio differentiae est quia potestas dispensandi ex vi urgentis necessitatis fundatur in jurisdictione extraordinaria quam habent Episcopi: at quoad Saeculares hac non fruuntur Religiose."—*loc. cit.*

91 *Ius Canonicum,* lib. III, tit. XXXIV, n. 42.

92 *Theologia Moralis,* III, n. 210.

93 *Theologia Moralis,* II, p. 506.

94 *Theologia Moralis,* I, n. 499.

95 *Op. cit.,* p. 141.

the belief that the bishop exercises an ordinary power in dispensing from a reserved vow in urgent necessity. For since the regular confessor can dispense from these vows from which the bishop dispenses with ordinary power, he can, accordingly, dispense from reserved vows in urgent necessity. Inasmuch as it seems unsatisfactory to explain the bishop's power of dispensing from reserved vows in urgent necessity as anything else than ordinary,[96] this opinion which favors the regular confessor's power to dispense from reserved vows in urgent necessity appears to be the more probable of the two offered opinions.

---

96 Cf. *supra*, pp. 209-210.

CHAPTER VIII

ULTIMATE DISPOSITIONS ON DISPENSATION FROM PRIVATE VOWS

ARTICLE I. THE FORM OF THE DISPENSATION

The proper form for the granting of a dispensation from private vows requires first of all that the grantor of the dispensation have the intention of dispensing and that he do it freely.[1] It is not necessary that fear be entirely excluded, provided that true consent is given. When true consent is given, though there be coercion, the person nevertheless acts freely, and no law invalidating the dispensation is to be found.[2]

Secondly, there must be no concealment of the truth (*subreptio*) or expression of falsehood (*obreptio*) in the petition which would invalidate the dispensation according to canon 42, §§ 1, 2. Thus, if the substance or object of the vow is not fully explained in the petition, the dispensation can be invalid, for example, if a person with a vow of perfect and perpetual chastity asks for a dispensation from the vow of not marrying. This petition does not express the complete substance or object of the vow. The dispensation granted in response to such a petition could be invalid on two points, but certainly on one. First of all, the vow from which the dispensation is actually granted does not correspond to the vow by which the petitioner is bound. Hence the dispensation does not touch the objective vow but rather the vow mentioned in the petition. Secondly, the one granting the dispensation may

[1] Wernz-Vidal, *De Rebus*, pars I, n. 557, p. 668.

[2] Canon 103, § 2; Suarez, *De Voto*, lib. VI, c. XXVI, n. 17.

perhaps not possess the faculty to dispense from the vow of perfect and perpetual chastity. As a result, his dispensation from the vow of not marrying is entirely without value, since the vow not to marry does not exist in the case at hand, and at the same time he lacks the faculty to dispense from the vow which does exist.[3]

The expression of falsehood in the petition can also invalidate a dispensation from a private vow. It is true that canon 42, § 2, considers a dispensation valid as long as the one motivating cause is true. Still, the canon does not intend thereby to permit the falsity of the rest of the petition. Paragraph two of this canon rather presupposes the fulfillment of the first paragraph of the same canon. If, however, the first paragraph prohibits the concealment of the truth, and the expression of the truth is necessary for the validity of a dispensation from private vows, *a fortiori*, or at least *aequo iure*, it prohibits a false explanation of the necessary facts.[4]

Speaking of the external formalities to be used in the granting of a dispensation from a private vow, Suarez says that sufficient indication must be given by external signs that a dispensation is being granted.[5] In the external forum the licit granting of a dispensation from vows requires that this external sign be in writing.[6] The purpose of this is to provide a means of proving that the dispensation was granted. Hence in a case of necessity this external sign may be given orally, or even by telephone or

[3] Suarez, *De Voto*, lib. VI, c. XXVII, n. 6; Wernz-Vidal, *loc. cit.*

[4] Suarez, *De Voto*, lib. VI, c. XXVII, n. 8; Rodrigo, *De Legibus*, nn. 789, 790.

[5] *De Voto*, lib. VI, c. XXVII, n. 19.

[6] Cf. canon 56: "Executio rescriptorum quae forum externum respiciunt, scripto facienda est."

telegraph.[7] In the internal sacramental forum, on the other hand, the dispensation is to be given orally. In the internal extra-sacramental forum the dispensation in the majority of cases should be given orally. However, where circumstances permit, it should be given in writing or at least note made of it in the secret archives.[8] The obligation to make note in the secret archives of the granting of the dispensation appears to bind gravely, if the vow from which the dispensation is granted happens to be a matrimonial impediment.[9]

Beyond the requirement of an external sign there is no other determination of the form for dispensing from a private vow. There is no formula prescribed upon which the effect of the dispensation depends. Accordingly, it will be sufficient if words are used which signify what is being done.[10]

Article II. The Effects of a Dispensation

When a dispensation strictly so called is granted from a private vow in an absolute manner, it immediately and completely removes the obligation of the vow.[11] Frequent indication has already been given, however, that the term "dispensation" does not always signify a total removal of the obligation of the vow. On occasion, only a limited or partial effect follows from the granting of the dispensation. The limitation of the effect, however, is not a limitation which touches the grantor of the dispensation. He who can grant a dispensation from a vow with a complete and

---

[7] Rodrigo, *De Legibus*, n. 824; Beste, *Introductio*, p. 115.
[8] Rodrigo, *loc. cit.*
[9] Canon 1047. Cf. Gasparri, *De Matrimonio*, I, n. 406.
[10] Suarez, *loc. cit.*; Beste, *loc. cit.*
[11] Suarez, *De Voto*, lib. VI, c. IX, nn. 2, 16; Wernz-Vidal, *loc. cit.*

total removal of the obligation of the vow can grant also a dispensation from a vow in any of the limited ways in which this is possible.[12]

Sometimes, instead of granting a complete dispensation, the superior commutes the vow into a work that is less good than the work proposed and promised in the original vow. This takes place in the following manner: a dispensation is granted from the original vow with the total removal of its obligation, but under the set condition that the dispensed person make another vow.[13] This can be done in regard to non-reserved vows by all those who have the power to dispense from such vows; in regard to reserved vows it can be done by those who possess the proper faculty to dispense or *to commute by dispensing* from reserved vows. Those who have the power to dispense can remove the obligation fully or partially; those who have the power *to commute by dispensing* can remove the obligation of the vow only partially.[14]

On occasion, too, there may be a suspension of the obligatory force of the vow. Then the obligation of the vow ceases wholly or partially for the present, but revives at a later date. Thus, in virtue of canon 1315, all vows

---

12 Cf. Reg. 35, 53, R.J., in VI°: "Plus semper in se continet quod est minus," and "Cui licet quod est plus, licet utique quod est minus."; canon 1314.

13 Lessius: "Commutare vero est condonare cum onere, nempe ut loco prioris obligationis suscipias aliam: secunda enim obligatio in quam fit commutatio, non tam nascitur ex auctoritate praelati commutantis (quod valde notandum est) quam ex consensu acceptantis, in quo consensu implicite continetur votum alterius boni. Itaque in dispensatione Praelatus condonat absolute; in commutatione condonat solum sub conditione nempe si voveas aliud."—*De Iustitia et Iure,* lib. II, c. 40, n. 108.

14 Cf. canon 1314: "Opus voto non reservato promissum potest . . . commutari in minus vero bonum ab illo cui potestas est dispensandi ad normam can. 1313."

made before religious profession are suspended as long as the vowmaker remains bound by that religious profession.[15]

Since in virtue of canon 1315 religious profession suspends all vows made prior to the profession, the question arises whether this canon prohibits the making of a private vow after religious profession. If a religious does make a vow, does it lack all validity, then and also later? Or is the vow thus made a valid vow, the operativeness of which is suspended only for the duration of the profession but later is revived upon departure from the community on the part of the person who has been freed of his vows of religion? Or is the vow a valid vow which has immediate operative force? It is quite certain that a professed religious can make a private vow. Canon 1315 treats of suspending only those vows made prior to the religious profession. It does not mention those which are made subsequent to the profession. Hence it seems that the legislator did not intend in this canon to touch in any way private vows made following religious profession.

Instead, it seems to be the purpose of canon 1315 to suspend all those obligations arising from vows which a person might have incurred at a time when he did not foresee his becoming a religious. In this way, canon 1315 removes all unforeseen hindrances to the fulfillment of the vows of religion. Vows made subsequent to profession, however, are made with ample awareness of their compatibility with the religious life. Hence it appears not to be the purpose of canon 1315, in any manner, to touch on the subject of vows made after profession.

---

15 "Vota ante professionem religiosam emissa suspenduntur, donec vovens in religione permanserit."

In view of what has been said, it is obvious that professed religious can validly make private vows subsequent to their profession.[16] Thus, while the religious profession itself would suspend only those vows whose fulfillment would be harmful to the religious life, canon 1315 effects the suspension of the operative force of even those private vows whose fulfillment would not be out of harmony with the religious life.[17]

Finally, on occasion, the obligation of fulfilling a vow is only deferred. When this is done, the vow has not begun to bind, and the inception of its binding force is postponed still further by the deferment. For example, a person may make a vow to enter the religious life when he has reached the age of twenty-one; a dispensation for the purpose of deferring the fulfillment of the vow could postpone the date for the entrance.[18]

Article III. The Cessation of Dispensations from Private Vows

Canon 86[19] of the Code states that a dispensation which has a recurrent application ceases not only in the same manner as does a privilege, but also with the total and certain cessation of the one motivating cause which prompted the granting of the dispensation. A dispensation which has a recurrent application is distinguished from a dispensation which has only a single application.

---

16 *Review for Religious* (1941—), I (1941), 70; cf. Coronata, *Institutiones*, II, n. 891.

17 Vermeersch-Creusen, *Epitome*, II, n. 646.

18 C. 8, X, *de voto et voti redemptione*, III, 34; Potthast, n. 1137; Wernz-Vidal, *De Rebus*, pars I, n. 557, p. 668.

19 "Dispensatio quae tractum habet successivum, cessat iisdem modis quibus privilegium, nec non certa ac totali cessatione causae motivae."

Thus a dispensation from the Lenten fast, granted to a person in failing health, is repeatedly applied on each successive day of Lent, since the obligation of fasting arises anew each day. A dispensation which has only a single application relaxes a law having a single obligation which, once removed, does not revive of itself. For example, if there be granted a dispensation from the impediment of mixed religion in order to allow a particular couple to marry, that dispensation continues of itself, and never needs to be reapplied in relation to that couple. For the bond of law forbidding that marriage is removed by the dispensation, and it does not recur of itself, unless some external circumstance intervenes.[20]

It is the commonly accepted doctrine that a dispensation from a vow does not have a recurrent application. A vow originates in the free will of the vowmaker, and not in the will of one distinct from the vowmaker. Hence, once the obligation of the vow is removed through a dispensation, that obligation does not revive, unless the person receiving the dispensation makes another vow. Obviously, then, the dispensation cannot be recurrently applied, if with reference to the vow there exists no obligation which is susceptible of being recurrently relaxed.[21]

Canon 86 states how dispensations cease when they have a recurrent application. Does this indicate that dispensations which do not have a recurrent application do not cease? The silence of the Code on this matter is not to be understood as affirming the unlimited continued existence of the effect attaching to such dispensations. The

---

20 Reilly, *Dispensations*, p. 124.

21 Van Hove, *De Dispensationibus*, n. 494; Cappello, *Summa, Iuris Canonici*, I, n. 137; Woywod, *Commentary*, I, 36.

Code's silence rather emphasizes the continued existence of this type of dispensation, and excludes every form of cessation as being inapplicable to such a dispensation, unless that form arise from the very nature of the dispensation itself (a temporary dispensation) or from the object matter of the dispensation (e.g., object matter which becomes noxious).

Here it becomes necessary to determine and to ascertain the circumstances under which a dispensation from a private vow ceases in consequence of its very nature. To accomplish this, the writer will first appraise the influence, if any, which the cessation of the one motivating cause may have on a dispensation from private vows. Thereupon, he will examine the various ways in which a privilege ceases, and then will determine their influence on the cessation of a dispensation from private vows. For in view of the fact that a dispensation is a privilege, it will cease in the same manner as does a privilege.

A. *The Cessation of the One Motivating Cause in Relation to the Cessation of a Dispensation from Private Vows*

1) A dispensation from a vow which has been granted and used does not cease if the original motivating cause eventually ceases. This is obvious in the light of what has been said, for in the case as considered the dispensation is applied only once. The continued existence of the cause is not necessary for a dispensation which does nōt have a recurrent application.[22]

2) When the one motivating cause which prompted the granting of the dispensation from a vow ceases before

22 "Factum legitime retractari non debet, licet casus postea eveniat, a quo non potuit inchoari."—Reg. 73, R. J., in VI°; Regatillo, *Institutiones*, I, n. 180.

the dispensation has been used, the matter is less obvious. Thus, a dispensation may be granted from a vow of chastity in order to allow a person to contract marriage, the motivating cause being the legitimation of a child. If the child dies before the marriage takes place, does the dispensation cease? It seems quite certain that the dispensation does not cease, since a cause is necessary only at the time at which the dispensation is granted. A dispensation from vows is not granted with a limitation that the cause will exist in the future or will continue to exist. It is granted for a cause which does exist, and which may or may not continue to exist.[23] This is confirmed by canon 41,[24] which determines the time at which the petition for a rescript must be verified — namely, when the rescript is issued, for those rescripts in which no executor is required; for the others, at the time of their execution.

Furthermore, when a dispensation is granted validly, he to whom it is granted has the right to use it. Once, however, a right is acquired it cannot be revoked by the cessation of the cause on account of which it was granted.[25]

3) When the one motivating cause ceases before the execution of a dispensation from a vow, even though it has already been granted in *forma commissoria*, the dispensation ceases inasmuch as it has not yet been applied to the vowmaker, and the bond of the vow has not yet been broken. This is, likewise, confirmed by canon 41.

---

23 Van Hove, *loc. cit.*; Cappello, *loc. cit.*; Woywod, *loc. cit.* contra Lehmkuhl, *Theologia Moralis*, I, n. 269.

24 "In rescriptis quorum nullus est exsecutor, preces veritate nitantur oportet tempore quo rescriptum datum est; in ceteris tempore exsecutionis."

25 Castropalao, *Opus Morale*, tract. III, *de legibus*, disp. IV, pt. 15, n. 7. Cf. also Reg. 73, R. J., in VI°, *supra*, p. 229.

B. Forms of the Cessation of Privileges Applied to Dispensation from Private Vows

The influence of the cessation of the one motivating cause on a dispensation from private vows has been examined. It remains now to determine which forms of the cessation of a privilege apply to a dispensation from vows. The various ways in which a privilege ceases are indicated in canons 71-78. Thus a privilege ceases when it is revoked or renounced, when the superior who granted it goes out of office, or when the person who received it dies, when the privilege is no longer used, or when a contrary usage has supplanted the use of the privilege,[26] when the privilege becomes harmful or illicit through a change of circumstances, when the definite period of time or the definite number of cases for which the privilege was granted expires or is exhausted respectively, and, finally, when a suspensive condition is not fulfilled or a resolutive condition is verified.[27]

When the various modes of the cessation of a privilege stated above are applied to a dispensation from vows, the following conclusions seem deducible.

1) A dispensation from a vow cannot be revoked, since the obligation of a vow arises from the free will of the vowmaker and not from the will of a superior. Once this obligation is totally removed through a dispensation, it cannot be reimposed by means of an act which revokes the grant of the dispensation. The obligation of a vow once relaxed through a dispensation revives only if the vow-

26 Only privileges which are burdensome to others cease by non-use or contrary usage, and then only if there enters legitimate prescription, or if the non-use is equivalent to a tacit renunciation. Cf. canon 76.

27 Castropalao, *Opus Morale*, Tom. III, tract. III, *de privilegiis*, disp. IV, pt. 14, n. 2; Regatillo, *Institutiones*, I, n. 167; Rodrigo, *De Legibus*, n. 951.

maker himself makes a new vow. If a dispensation was granted with certain limitations, it would cease when these limitations were reached. Yet, its cessation then would not be due to a subsequent decision of the author of the dispensation to recall it, but rather to the limitation which was purposely included in the original act of the granting of the dispensation.[28]

2) A dispensation from a private vow can be renounced with the resultant cessation of its effects at least in the internal forum. The dispensation, however, does not cease for the reason that the former vow begins to bind once more, but in view rather of the fact that the renunciation of the dispensation is equivalent to the taking of a new vow. Strictly considered, however, the renunciation of a dispensation from a vow is impossible. Renunciation seeks to restore the numerically identical obligation which existed before the dispensation was granted. In ordinary law this is possible, for although a dispensation is granted, the law still continues to bind the other members of the community. With the cessation of the dispensation that same bond begins once more to bind the person previously free from the obligation of that bond. In regard to vows it is somewhat different. A complete dispensation takes away the total obligation of the vow; it does not merely suspend it. Thereafter, the obligation can never be reimposed or restored as the numerically identical obligation. But if the former vowmaker freely makes the same vow once more, the obligation can be restored in kind.[29]

---

28 Suarez, *De Legibus*, lib. VIII, c. 37, n. 10; Cappello, *Summa Iuris Canonici*, I, n. 136; Rodrigo, *De Legibus*, n. 508.

29 Castropalao, *Opus Morale*, III, tract. III, *de legibus*, disp. IV, pt. 17, n. 6; Rodrigo, *De Legibus*, n. 513; Cappello, *Summa Iuris Canonici*, I, n. 138.

3) A dispensation from vows is never granted under such a phase as "*ad beneplacitum nostrum*" or its equivalent. Hence, when the superior who grants the dispensation goes out of office, the dispensation continues.[30]

4) A dispensation from a vow ceases with the death of the vowmaker, but the obligation of the vow ceases also. Yet in a certain sense, a dispensation can be said to continue after the death of the vowmaker. Canon 1310, § 2, states that the obligation of a *real* vow, and of a *mixed* vow for that part which is *real*, passes on to the heirs of the vowmaker.[31] If, however, the vowmaker obtained a dispensation from the real or mixed vow prior to his death, that dispensation may be said to continue even after the death of the vowmaker, in the sense that it continues to be the radical source of the heir's release from the obligations assumed through the testator's vow.

5) As to whether the non-use or the contrary use of a dispensation from a private vow can bring about the cessation of the dispensation, the following can be stated. The obligation of a former vow cannot be said to revive simply in view of the consideration that the vowmaker omits those actions which the dispensation from the vow would permit him to perform (non-use); neither can that obligation be said to revive when the vowmaker performs those works which the dispensation would permit him to omit (contrary use). Hence the continued non-use or contrary use of a dispensation from a vow can never bring about a cessation of the dispensation and the consequent revival of the erstwhile obligation attending the vow. This is true,

---

30 Rodrigo, *De Legibus*, n. 519.

31 "Voti realis obligatio transit ad heredes; item obligatio voti mixti pro parte qua reale est."

whether sufficient time passes for legitimate prescription to set in, or whether sufficient indications are offered by the non-use of the dispensation that a tacit renunciation is present. Factors such as these can cause the dispensation from the vow to cease only if the vowmaker wills to make another vow.

6) In regard to a change of circumstances, and the influence of that change on a dispensation from a vow, it appears obvious that a dispensation does not cease in this manner. No external influence can create a votive obligation for another. Such a transformation of conditions can once more place a person under the obligation of a law from the observance of which he had been dispensed. This is possible because the obligation of law continues to exist for others even after the dispensation is granted to an individual. But after a dispensation is granted from a vow, the obligation of that vow ceases, and it cannot be revived except by the vowmaker himself.

7) If a dispensation from a vow is granted for a specified period of time (the vow is suspended either fully or partially), the dispensation ceases when that time has elapsed. Likewise, if a dispensation is granted for the licit or valid performance of some act, the dispensation in regard to future acts ceases after that act has been fully completed, e.g., a dispensation from the vow of chastity which is granted for the contracting of one marriage ceases after that marriage is dissolved.

8) Likewise, a vow ceases upon the verification of a resolutive condition, e.g., if a dispensation from a vow to say the Rosary every day is granted under the condition that the vow will revive if the dispensed person ever again

becomes intoxicated.[32] Finally, a dispensation from a vow ceases if the suspensive condition under which it was granted is not fulfilled, or if the one motivating cause on account of which the dispensation was granted ceases before the condition is fulfilled.[33]

Article IV. Actual Practice Attending Dispensation From Private Vows

In the actual practice of the granting of a dispensation from a private vow two factors must be kept in mind. First, the dispensation should ordinarily be given in the internal forum, preferably the internal sacramental forum.[34] A private vow is a matter between the individual and God. Its relaxation is ordinarily of interest and advantage only to the vowmaker. Hence, whether the vow be public or secret, its remission should be granted in the internal forum.[35] If, however, a private vow which is at the same time a matrimonial impediment becomes publicly known, it then falls under the authority of the Church as a society, and should be relaxed in the external forum.[36] Likewise, if scandal is caused by the violation of a private vow that is publicly known, or if the rights of a third party are involved, the dispensation should be granted in the external forum.[37]

---

32 Cf. Rodrigo, *De Legibus*, n. 951; Regatillo, *Institutiones*, I, n. 167.

33 Cf. canons 42; 45. Michiels: ". . . ad validitatem et legitimationem dispensationis requiritur, ut preces (ad quas essentialiter pertinet existentia causae motivae. . .) veritate nitantur momento, quo dispensatio revera, in actu secundo, conceditur."—*Normae Generales*, II, 517.

34 Prümmer, *Theologia Moralis*, II, n. 428.

35 Cf. Maroto, *Institutiones*, I, 857.

36 Cf. Maroto, *Institutiones*, I, n. 860.

37 Cf. Maroto, *loc. cit.*

In the second place, care should be taken lest through a complete dispensation there be occasioned the complete loss of the merit which derives from the vow. In the internal forum, therefore, the vowmaker should be encouraged, whenever this is expedient, to accept a commutation of the object matter of the vow into something of a similar character.[38]

Prümmer[39] points out that the author of a dispensation from vows should not be too scrupulous about the sufficiency of a cause for a dispensation. If the subject insists on obtaining a dispensation, he is already in a danger of violating the vow and therefore a sufficient cause is present. This is also the policy of the Sacred Congregation for Religious today.

With this in mind, the writer suggests that the grantor of a dispensation from a private vow be not too anxious about seeking rather the commutation of every vow presented to him for dispensation. He should first ascertain the petitioner's degree of readiness to substitute another vow, and then proceed accordingly. When a dispensation is sought from a private vow, it is frequently done in view of the fact that the vow was made rashly. The petition for the dispensation is an attempt to correct a mistake. An unwarranted commutation of such a vow would be a mere repetition of the original imprudence.

---

38 Vermeersch, *Theologia Moralis,* II, n. 225; Prümmer, *Theologia Moralis,* II, n. 428.

39 *Ibid.*, n. 421.

CONCLUSIONS

As a result of this study the following conclusions are offered:

1). The faculty to dispense from private vows belong to the radical jurisdiction of the residential bishop.[1]

2). The limitation of the radical jurisdiction of the bishop in the matter of dispensing from vows takes away his jurisdiction completely, so that a dispensation from reserved vows without proper delegation is invalid.[2]

3). The influence of light fear cannot be said to annul the making of a vow.[3]

4). Exempt professed religious and exempt novices have the right to seek, and the local ordinary has the power to grant to them, a dispensation from a private vow.[4] Postulants in exempt religious institutes can be dispensed from private vows by their proper ordinary or by the local ordinary.[5]

5). The clerical exempt superior can dispense anywhere in the world from the private vows of professed religious and novices who are subject to him; from the private vows of postulants and others mentioned in canon 514, § 1, he can dispense only while these persons are within the religious house though he, himself, be outside the religious house.[6]

6). The following vows made in favor of a third party are removed from the authority of all those whose

---

1 Cf. *supra*, pp. 100-102.

2 Cf. *supra*, pp. 193-194.

3 Cf. *supra*, pp. 5-7.

4 Cf. *supra*, pp. 127-136.

5 Cf. *supra*, pp. 136-137.

6 Cf. *supra*, pp, 145-148.

authority is intermediate to that of the Holy See: a) the vow which is made primarily for the benefit of a specified person after that person accepts the promise; b) the vow which is made in favor of a specified third party who in turn obligates himself to the vowmaker, even though God's honor be the principal reason for the vow.[7]

7). The private vows of converts are governed by the laws on dispensation from private vows as contained in the Code.[8]

8). A probably existing cause suffices for the granting of a dispensation from a private vow.[9]

9). A dispensation from a vow granted for a cause which is later discovered not to have existed is invalid if the erroneous judgment is due to the falsity of the motivating cause presented in the petition, even though the seeking and the granting of the dispensation were undertaken in good faith.[10]

10. When the residential bishop dispenses from a reserved vow in virtue of a special faculty from the Holy See he exercises delegated power;[11] when he dispenses from a reserved vow in the case of an urgent necessity he exercises ordinary power. In consequence of the doctrine inherent in the latter statement the regular confessor can also dispense from a reserved vow in the case of an urgent necessity.[12]

---

7 Cf. *supra*, pp. 152-159.
8 Cf. *supra*, pp. 164-169.
9 Cf. *supra*, pp. 182-187.
10 Cf. *supra*, pp. 189-191.
11 Cf. *supra*, pp. 205-206.
12 Cf. *supra*, pp. 206-210.

BIBLIOGRAPHY

Sources

Acta Apostolicae Sedis, Romae, 1909—

Augustinus a Virgine Marie, *Compendium Privilegiorum Omnium Religionum*, Lugduni, 1661.

Bullarium Ssmi Domini nostri Benedicti XIV, ed. nova, 13 vols., Mechlinae, 1826-1827.

Bullarum Diplomatum et Privilegiorum Sanctorum Pontificum Taurinensis Editio, 25 vols., Augustae Taurinorum, 1857-1872.

Codex Iuris Canonici Pii X Pontificis Maximi iussu digestus, Benedicti Papae XV auctoritate promulgatus, Romae: Typis Polyglottis Vaticanis, 1917. Reimpressio, 1933.

Codicis Iuris Canonici Fontes cura Emi Card. Gasparri Editi, 9 vols., Romae (postea Civitate Vaticana): Typis Polyglottis Vaticanis, 1923-1939. (Vols. VII, VIII, et IX cura et studio Emi Card. Serèdi.)

Collectanea S. Congregationis de Propaganda Fide, 2 vols., Romae, 1907.

Corpus Iuris Canonici, ed. Lipsiensis 2. post Aemilii Ludovici Richteri curas . . . instruxit Aemilius Friedberg, Lipsiae: Ex Officina Bernhardi Tauchnitz, 1879-1881. Editio anastatice repetita, Lipsiae: Tauchnitz, 1922.

Corpus Iuris Civilis, Vol. II, ed. stereotypa nona, *Codex Iustinianus*, quem recognovit et retractavit Paulus Krueger, Berolini: Apud Weidmannos, 1915.

Decretales D. Gregorii IX una cum Glossis Restitutae, Romae, 1582.

Decretum Gratiani Emendatum et Notationibus Illustratum una cum Glossis, Gregorii XIII, Pont. Max. iussu editum, 2 vols., Romae, 1582.

Denzinger, H., Bannwart, C., Umberg, J.B., *Enchiridion Symbolorum, Definitionum, et Declarationum de Rebus Fidei et Morum*, 21-23 ed., Friburgi Brisgoviae: Herder & Co., 1937.

Jaffè, Philippus, *Regesta Pontificum Romanorum ab condita Ecclesia ad annum post Christum natum MCXCVIII*, ed. 2. correctam et auctam auspiciis Gulielmi Wattenbach curaverunt F. Kaltenbrunner, P. Ewald, S. Loewenfeld, 2 vols. in 1, Lipsiae: 1885-1888.

Liber Sextus Decretalium D. Bonifacii Papae VIII suae integritati una cum Clementinis et Extravagantibus earumque Glossis restitutus, Romae, 1582.

Mansi, J. D., *Sacrorum Conciliorum Nova et Amplissima Collectio*, 53 vols. in 60, Paris-Leipzig-Arnhem, 1901-1927.

Potthast, A., *Regesta Pontificum Romanorum inde ab anno post Christum natum MCXCVIII ad annum MCCCIV*, 2 vols., Berolini, 1874-1875.

Reference Works

Aertnys, J.-Damen, C., *Theologia Moralis*, 11. ed., 2 vols., Taurini-Romae: Marietti, 1928.

Alphonsus de Liguori, St., *Theologia Moralis*, ed. L. Gaudé, 4 vols., Romae, 1905-1912.

Augustine, Charles, *A Commentary on the New Code of Canon Law,* 8 vols. Vol. VI, *Administrative Law,* 2. ed., St. Louis: B. Herder Co., 1923.

Ayrinhac, H. A., *Constitution of the Church,* New York: Benziger, 1924.

Ballerini, A.-Palmieri, P., *Opus Theologicum Morale,* 7 vols., Prati, 1889-1893.

Bargilliat, M., *Praelectiones Juris Canonici,* 37 ed., 2 vols., Parisiis: Basten, Berche, et Pagis, 1923.

Benko, M., *The Abbott Nullius,* The Catholic University of America Canon Law Studies, n. 173, Washington, D. C.: The Catholic University of America Press, 1943.

Bernardus Papiensis, *Summa Decretalium,* ed. E. A. T. Laspeyres, Ratisbonae, 1861.

Berutti, C., *Institutiones Iuris Canonici,* 6 vols., Vol. III, Taurini-Romae: Marietti, 1936.

Beste, U., *Introductio in Codicem,* 2. ed., Collegeville, Minn.: St. John's Abbey Press, 1944.

Billot, L., *Tractatus de Ecclesia,* 4. ed., 2 vols., Romae: Apud Aedes Universitatis Gregorianae, 1921.

Blat, A., *Commentarium Textus Codicis Iuris Canonici,* 5 vols. in 6, Romae: Libreria del Collegio "Angelico", 1919-1927.

Bouix, D., *Tractatus de Episcopo,* 2. ed., 2 vols. in 1, Parisiis, 1873.

Bouscaren, T.L., *The Canon Law Digest,* 2 vols., Milwaukee: Bruce, 1934, 1943.

Brys, J., *De Dispensatione in Iure Canonico praesertim apud Decretistas et Decretalistas usque ad Medium Saeculum Decimum Quartum,* Brugis: Car. Beyaert, 1925.

Cappello, F., *Summa Iuris Canonici,* 3 vols., Vols. I-II, 3. ed., Vol. III, 2. ed. Romae: Apud Aedes Universitatis Gregorianae, 1938-1940.

——— *Tractatus Canonico-Moralis de Sacramentis,* 3 vols. in 6, Romae: Marietti, 1932-1939. Vol. III, Partes I et II, *De Matrimonio,* 4. ed., 1939; Vol. II, Pars I, *De Poenitentia,* 4. ed., 1945.

Cavagnis, *Institutiones Iuris Publici Ecclesiastici,* 2 vols., Romae, 1882-1883.

Castropalao, F., *Opus Morale,* 7 vols., Vol. I, 3. ed., 1649, Vol. III, 2. ed., 1649, Lugduni, 1631-1651.

Clancy, P., *The Local Religious Superior,* The Catholic University of America Canon Law Studies, n. 175, Washington, D. C.: The Catholic University of America Press, 1943.

Coronata, Matthaeus Conte a, *Institutiones Iuris Canonici,* 5 vols., Vols. I-IV, 2. ed., 1939-1945; Vol. V, 1936, Taurini-Romae: Marietti, 1936-1945.

——— *De Sacramentis Tractatus Canonicus,* 3 vols., Taurini-Romae: Marietti, 1943-1946. Vol. III, *De Matrimonio,* 1946.

Costello, J., *Domicile and Quasi-Domicile,* The Catholic University of America Canon Law Studies, n. 60, Washington, D. C.: The Catholic University of America, 1930.

Coussa, A., *Epitome Praelectionum de Iure Ecclesiastico Orientali,* Vol. I, Città del Vaticano: Typis Polyglottis Vaticanis, 194C; Vol. II, Venetiis; Typis Polyglottis Insulae S. Lazari, 1941.

D'Annibale, J., *Summula Theologiae Moralis*, 5. ed., 4 vols., Romae, 1908-1909.

Davis, H., *Moral and Pastoral Theology*, 4. ed., 4 vols., New York: Sheed and Ward, 1943.

De Angelis, P., *Praelectiones Juris Canonici*, 5 vols. in 9, Romae, 1877-1891.

De Lugo, I., *Disputationes Scholasticae et Morales*, 2. ed., 8 vols., Parisiis, 1868-1869.

Duskie, J., *The Canonical Status of the Orientals in the United States*, The Catholic University of America Canon Law Studies, n. 48, Washington, D. C.: The Catholic University of America, 1928.

Fagnanus, P., *Commentaria in Quinque Libros Decretalium*, 4 vols., Venetiis, 1709.

Ferraris, L., *Prompta Bibliotheca Canonica, Iuridica, Moralis, Theologica, nec non Ascetica, Polemica, Rubricistica, Historica*, 8 vols., Parisiis, 1852-1857.

Freisen, J., *Geschichte des kanonischen Eherechts bis zum Verfall der Glossenliteratur*, 2. ed., Paderborn, 1893.

Gasparri, Petrus, *Tractatus Canonicus de Matrimonio*, editio nova ad mentem Codicis I. C., Romae: Typis Polyglottis Vaticanis, 1932.

Genicot, E.-Salsman, I., *Institutiones Theologiae Moralis*, 13. ed., 2 vols., Bruxellis: L'Edition Universelle, S. A., 1936.

Hostiensis, Cardinalis (Henricus de Segusia), *Commentaria in Quinque Decretalium Libros*, 5 vols. in 3, Venetiis, 1581.

——— *Summa Aurea*, Venetiis, 1570.

Kuttner, S., *Repertorium der Kanonistik* (1140-1234), Città del Vaticano: Bibliotheca Apostolica Vaticana, 1937.

La Croix, C., *Commentaria in Universam Theologiam Moralem*, 3 vols., Venetiis, 1756.

La Grange, J. M., *Évangile selon Saint Matthieu*, 3. ed., Libraire Victor Lecoffre, 1927.

Laymann, P., *Theologia Moralis*, 6. ed., 5 vols. in 2, Bambergae, 1569.

Lehmkuhl, *Theologia Moralis*, 11. ed., 2 vols., Friburgi, 1910.

Lercher, L., *Institutiones Theologiae Dogmaticae*, 4 vols., Oeniponte: Fel. Rauch, 1927-1930.

Lessius, L., *De Iustitia et Iure Ceterisque Virtutibus Cardinalibus*, 4 vols. in 1, Antverpiae, 1617.

——— *De Iure et Iustitia Compendium*, Duaci, 1634.

Leurenius, P., *Forum Ecclesiasticum in quo Jus Ecclesiasticum Universum Explanatur*, 5 vols. in 3, Venetiis, 1729.

McDonough, T., *Apostolic Administrators*, The Catholic University of America Canon Law Studies, n. 139, Washington, D. C.: The Catholic University of America Press, 1941.

Marc, C.-Gestermann, F.X.-Raus, J. B., *Institutiones Morales Alphonsianae*, 18. ed., 2 vols., Lugduni: Vitte, 1927-1928.

Maroto, P., *Institutiones Iuris Canonici*, 2 vols., Romae, 1919-1921. Vol. I, 3. ed., Romae: Apud Commentarium pro Religiosis, 1921.

Merkelbach, B., *Summa Theologiae Moralis ad Mentem D. Thomae et ad Norman Iuris Novi*, 2. ed., 3 vols., Parisiis: Desclée, de Brouwer, 1935-1936.

Michiels, G., *Normae Generales Juris Canonici*, 2 vols., Lublin-Polonia: Universitas Catholica, 1929.

Monin, *De Curia Romana*, Lovanii: Van Linthout, 1912.

Müssener, H., *Das katholische Eherecht in der Seelsorgspraxis*, 2. ed. Düsseldorf: L. Schwann, 1933.

Navarrus (Martinus de Azpilcueta) *Opera Omnia*, 6 vols., Venetiis, 1618-1621.

Noldin, H. - Schmitt, A., *Summa Theologiae Moralis iuxta Codicem Iuris Canonici*, 25. ed., 3 vols., Oeniponte: Rauch, 1938.

O'Mara, W., *Canonical Causes for Matrimonial Dispensations*, The Catholic University of America Canon Law Studies, n. 96, Washington, D. C.: The Catholic University of America, 1935.

Ottaviani, A., *Institutiones Iuris Publici Ecclesiastici*, 2. ed., 2 vols., Romae: Typis Polyglottis Vaticanis, 1935-1936.

Panormitanus, Abbas (Nicolaus de Tudeschis), *Commentaria in Quinque Libros Decretalium*, 5 vols. in 7, Venetiis, 1588.

Payen, *De Matrimonio*, 2. ed., 3 vols., Zi- ka- wei: T'ou- sè- wè, 1935-1936.

Pirhing, E., *Jus Canonicum Universum secundum Titulos Decretalium Distributum, Novo Methodo Explicatum*, 5 vols. in 4, Dilingae, 1674-1678.

Prümmer, D., *Manuale Theologiae Moralis secundum Principia S. Thomae Aquinatis*, 8. ed., recognita a P. Dr. Engelberto M. Münch, 3 vols., Friburgi Brisgoviae: Herder, 1935-1936.

Raymundus de Pennafort, *Summa*, Veronae, 1744.

Regatillo, E., *Institutiones Iuris Canonici*, 2 vols., Santander: Sal Terrae, 1941-1942.

Reiffenstuel, A., *Ius Canonicum Universum*, 7 vols., Parisiis, 1864-1870.

——— *Theologia Moralis*, 2 vols., Mutinae, 1758.

Reilly, *The General Norms of Dispensation*, The Catholic University of America Canon Law Studies, n. 119, Washington, D. C.: The Catholic University of America Press, 1939.

Rodrigo, L., *Praelectiones Theologico-Morales Comillenses*, tom. II, tract. *De Legibus*, Santander: Sal Terrae, 1944.

Roberti, F., *De Processibus*, 2 vols., Romae: Apud Aedes Facultatis Iuridicae ad S. Apollinaris, 1926.

Refinus, *Die Summa Decretorum des Magister Rufinus*, hrsg. von D. Heinrich Singer, Paderborn, 1902.

Ryan, G., *Principles of Episcopal Jurisdiction*, The Catholic University of America Canon Law Studies, n. 120, Washington, D. C.: The Catholic University of America Press, 1939.

Sägmüller, J. B., *Lehrbuch des katholischen Kirchenrechts*, 2 vols., Freiburg in Breisgau: Herdische Verlag, 1904.

Salmanticenses, *Cursus Theologiae Moralis*, 6 vols. in 4, Venetiis, 1714-1728.

Sanchez, T., *Disputationum de Sancto Matrimonii Sacramento Libri Tres*, 3 vols., Venetiis, 1614.

Santi, F., *Praelectiones Iuris Canonici iuxta Ordinem Decretalium Gregorii IX*, 2. ed., 5 vols., Ratisbonae, 1886.

Schaefer, T., *Compendium de Religiosis ad Normam Codicis Iuris Canonici*, 3. ed., Romae: S. A. L. E. R., 1940.

Scherer, Rudolph Ritter von, *Handbuch des Kirchenrechtes*, 2 vols., Graz and Leipzig, 1886-1898.

Schmalzgrueber, F., *Jus Ecclesiasticum Universum*, 5 vols. in 12, Romae, 1843-1845.

Shuhler, R., *Privileges of Regulars to Absolve and Dispense*, The Catholic University of America Canon Law Studies, n. 186, Washington, D. C.: The Catholic University of America Press, 1943.

Soto, D., *De Iure et Iustitia*, 10 vols. in 1, Salmanticae, 1556.

Sporer, Patritius, *Theologia Moralis Decalogalis et Sacramentalis*, 3 vols., Salisburgi, 1711.

Stiegler, M. A., *Dispensation, Dispensationswesen, und Dispensationsrecht im Kirchenrecht*, Mainz, 1901.

Suarez, F., *Opera Omnia*, 26 vols., Parisiis, 1856-1861.

Tamburini, T., *Theologia Moralis*, 3 vols. in 2, Venetiis, 1748.

Thomas Aquinas, St., *Opera Omnia*, 25 vols., Parmae, 1854-1873.

——— *Summa Theologica*, 6 vols., Taurini: Marietti, 1937.

Thomassinus, L., *Vetus et Nova Ecclesiae Disciplina, circa Beneficia et Beneficiarios*, 10 vols., Magontiaci, 1787.

Triebs, F., *Handbuch des kanonischen Eherechts*, Breslau: Ostdeutsche Verlaganstalt, 1933.

Van Hove, A., *De Legibus Ecclesiasticis*, Mechlinae-Romae: H. Dessain, 1930.

——— *De Privilegiis - De Dispensationibus*, Mechlinae-Romae: H. Dessain, 1939.

——— *Prolegomena*, editio altera auctior et emendatior, Mechlinae-Romae: H. Dessain, 1945.

Vermeersch, A.-Creusen, J., *Epitome Iuris Canonici*, 3. ed., 3 vols., Mechlinae et Romae: Dessain, 1927-1928.

Vermeersch, A., *Theologiae Moralis Principia, Responsa, Consilia*, 2. ed., 3 vols., Romae: Università Gregoriana, 1926-1928.

Wernz, F., *Ius Decretalium*, 2. ed., 6 vols., Romae et Prati, 1906-1913.

Wernz, F.-Vidal, P., *Ius Canonicum ad Codicis Normam Exactum*, 7 tomes in 8 vols., Romae: Apud Aedes Universitatis Gregoranae, Tom, I, *Normae Generales*, 1938; Tom. II, *Ius de Personis*, 3. ed., 1943; Tom. III, *De Religiosis*, 1933; Tom. IV, *De Rebus*, pars I, 1934; Tom. V, *Ius Matrimoniale*, 3. ed., a P. Philippo Aguirre, 1946.

Woywod, S., *A Practical Commentary on the Code of Canon Law*, 7. ed., revised by Callistus Smith, 2 vols., New York: Wagner, 1943.

Articles

Donovan, J., "An Outdated Interpretation of Canon 1111"—*Homiletic and Pastoral Review*, XLI (1941), 1169-1173.

Kinane, J., "Legal or Necessary Domicile"—*IER*, XXVII (1926), 647-648.

Kuttner, S., "Pierre de Roissy and Robert of Flamborough"—*Traditio*, II (1944), 492-499.

Mahoney, E., "Non-Catholic Religious Vows"—*The Clergy Review*, XIX (1940), 267.

Meystowicz, J., "Domicilium et Quasi-Domicilium"—*Jus Pontificium*, VI (1926), 34-35.

Oesterle, G., "De Domicilio Religiosorum"—*CpR*, V (1924), 167-178.

——— "Die Dispensgewalt der Regularen bei einfachen Gelübden der Weltleute"—*Theologie und Glaube*, III (1911), 389-402.

——— "Keuschheitsgelübde und Ehe"—*TPQ*, LXXXIX (1936), 573-580.

——— "Subdelegation einer Dispensvollmacht" — *TPQ*, LXXXVIII (1935), 138-142.

Plöchl, W., "Quinquennial Faculties Extended by the S. Congregation for the Oriental Church to Latin Ordinaries"—*The Jurist*, VI (1946), 73-76.

Teodori, I., "Altera Voti Dispensatio"—*Apollinaris*, VI (1933), 505-506.

Vermeersch, A., "De Facultate Confessariorum Regularium Dispensandi in Saecularium Votis"—*Periodica*, V (1913), 56-59.

——— "Vows of Non-Catholics"—*The Homiletic and Pastoral Review*, XXVIII (1928), 1221-1223.

PERIODICALS

Apollinaris, Romae, 1928—

Clergy Review, The, London, 1931—

Commentarium pro Religiosis, Romae, 1920—; from 1935: *Commentarium pro Religiosis et Missionariis.*

Homiletic and Pastoral Review, The, New York, 1900—

Irish Ecclesiastical Record, The, Dublin, 1864—

Jurist, The, Washington, D. C., 1941—

Jus Pontificium, Romae, 1921—

Periodica de Religiosis et Missionariis, 8 vols., Brugis, 1905-1919 (Vol. I: 1905, 2. ed., 1911; II and III: 1907, 2. ed., 1911; IV: 1909, 2. ed., 1913; V: 1911, 2. ed., 1913; VI: 1912; VII: 1912-1914; VIII: 1919); from 1920: *Periodica de Re Canonica et Morali utili praesertim Religiosis et Missionariis*, 7 vols,, Brugis, 1920-1927 (Vol. IX: 1920; X and XI: 1922-1923; XII: 1923-1924; XIII: 1924-1925; XIV: 1925-1926; XV: 1926-1927); from 1927: *Periodica de Re Morali, Canonica, Liturgica*, Brugis (1927-1936) et Romae (1937—), Vol. XVI, 1937—

Review for Religious, Topeka, 1942—

Theologie und Glaube, Paderborn, 1909—

Theologisch-praktische Quartalschrift, Linz, 1932—

Traditio, Studies in Ancient and Medieval History, Thought, and Religion, New York, 1943—

ABBREVIATIONS

AAS—*Acta Apostolicae Sedis.*

Bull. Rom.—*Bullarum Diplomatum . . . Taurinensis editio.*

Comp. Privil.—Augustinus a Virgine Maria, *Compendium Privilegiorum.*

Collect. S. C. P. F.—*Collectanea S. Congregationis de Propaganda Fide,* ed. 1907.

CpR—*Commentarium pro Religiosis.*

Fontes—*Codicis Iuris Canonici Fontes . . .* Gasparri editi.

IER—*Irish Ecclestiastical Record.*

JK—Jaffé, *Regesta Pontificum Romanorum* (edited by Kaltenbrunner: from 33 to 590).

JE—Jaffé, *op. cit.* (edited by Ewald: from 590 to 882).

JL—Jaffé, *op. cit.* (edited by Loewenfeld: from 882 to 1198).

Mansi—*Sacrorum Conciliorum Nova et Amplissima Collectio.*

Periodica—*Periodica de Re Canonica, Morali,* etc.

PCI—*Pontificia Commissio Interpretationis.*

Potthast—*Regesta Pontificum Romanorum.*

S. C. C.—*Sacra Congregatio Concilii.*

S. C. de Prop. Fide—*Sacra Congregatio de Propaganda Fide.*

S. C. pro Eccl. Orient.—*Sacra Congregatio pro Ecclesia Orientali.*

S. C. pro Rel.—*Sacra Congregatio pro Religiosis.*

TPQ—*Theologish-praktische Quartalschrift.*

ALPHABETICAL INDEX

BIOGRAPHICAL NOTE

JAMES MARTIN LOWRY was born October 31, 1916, in Minooka, Pennsylvania. After completing his elementary training in Woodrow Wilson School, he entered Minooka High School, from which he graduated in 1933. The following September he enrolled in Saint Thomas College, Scranton, Pennsylvania, where he pursued his course of studies for three years. In September of 1936 he entered Saint Bernard's Seminary, Rochester, New York, from which he received the Degree of Bachelor of Arts in 1938. The following September he began his course of theology at the *Collegium Canisianum* in Innsbruck, Austria, and later the same year transferred to Sion, Switzerland, where the courses of the *Collegium Canisianum* were continued in exile. He there continued his studies until May, 1940. The following September he entered Mount Saint Mary's Seminary, Emmitsburg, Maryland, where he completed his theological course. On February 28, 1942, he was ordained to the Sacred Priesthood by the Most Reverend William J. Hafey in Saint Peter's Cathedral, Scranton, Pennsylvania. In September of 1943 he enrolled in the School of Canon Law at the Catholic University of America, where he received the degree of Bachelor in Canon Law in May, 1944, and the degree of Licentiate in Canon Law in May, 1945.

CANON LAW STUDIES*

1. Freriks, Rev. Celestine A., C.PP.S., J.C.D., Religious Congregations in Their External Relations, 121 pp., 1916.
2. Galliher, Rev. Daniel M., O.P., J.C.D., Canonical Elections, 117 pp., 1917.
3. Borkowski, Rev. Aurelius L., O.F.M., J.C.D., De Confraternitatibus Ecclesiasticis, 136 pp., 1918.
4. Castillo, Rev. Cayo, J.C.D., Disertacion Historico - Canonica sobre la Potestad del Cabildo en Sede Vacante o Impedida del Vicario Capitular, 99 pp., 1919 (1918).
5. Kubelbeck, Rev. William J., S.T.B., J.C.D., The Sacred Penitentiaria and Its Relation to Faculties of Ordinaries and Priests, 129 pp., 1918.
6. Petrovits, Rev. Joseph, J.C., S.T.D., J.C.D., The New Church Law on Matrimony, X-461 pp., 1919.
7. Hickey, Rev. John J., S.T.B., J.C.D., Irregularities and Simple Impediments in the New Code of Canon Law, 100 pp., 1920.
8. Klekotka, Rev. Peter J., S.T.B., J.C.D., Diocesan Consultors, 179 pp., 1920.
9. Wanenmacher, Rev. Francis, J.C.D., The Evidence in Ecclesiastical Procedure Affecting the Marriage Bond, 1920 (Printed 1935).
10. Golden, Rev. Henry Francis, J.C.D., Parochial Benefices in the New Code, IV-119 pp., 1921 (Printed 1925).
11. Koudelka, Rev. Charles J., J.C.D., Pastors, Their Rights and Duties According to the New Code of Canon Law, 211 pp., 1921.
12. Melo, Rev. Antonius, O.F.M., J.C.D., De Exemptione Regularium, X-188 pp., 1921.
13. Schaaf, Rev. Valentine Theodore, O.F.M., S.T.B., J.C.D., The Cloister, X-180 pp., 1921.
14. Burke, Rev. Thomas Jooseph, S.T.D., J.C.D., Competence in Ecclesiastical Tribunals, IV-117 pp., 1922.
15. Leech, Rev. George Leo, J.C.D., A Comparative Study of the Constitution "Apostolicae Sedis" and the "Codex Juris Canonici," 179 pp., 1922.
16. Motry, Rev. Hubert Louis, S.T.D., J.C.D., Diocesan Faculties According to the Code of Canon Law, II-167 pp., 1922.
17. Murphy, Rev. George Lawrence, J.C.D., Delinquencies and Penalties in the Administration and the Reception of the Sacraments, IV-121 pp., 1923.
18. O'Reilly, Rev. John Anthony, S.T.B., J.C.D., Ecclesiastical Sepulture in the New Code of Canon Law, II-129 pp., 1923.

---

* From nn. 1-100 inclusive only nn. 7, 19, 25, 26, 31, 34, and 57 are still obtainable. From n. 101 onward all numbers are available except the following: nn. 101-118 inclusive, and also n. 122.

19. Michalicka, Rev. Wenceslas Cyrill, O.S.B., J.C.D., Judicial Procedure in Dismissal of Clerical Exempt Religious, 107pp., 1923.
20. Dargin, Rev. Edward Vincent, S.T.B., J.C.D., Reserved Cases According to the Code of Canon Law, IV-103 pp., 1924.
21. Godfrey, Rev. John A., S.T.B., J.C.D., The Right of Patronage According to the Code of Canon Law, 153 pp., 1924.
22. Hagedorn, Rev. Francis Edward, J.C.D., General Legislation on Indulgences, II-154 pp., 1924.
23. King, Rev. James Ignatius, J.C.D., The Administration of the Sacraments to Dying Non-Catholics, V-141 pp., 1924.
24. Winslow, Rev. Francis Joseph, O.F.M., J.C.D., Vicars and Prefects Apostolic, IV-149 pp., 1924.
25. Correa, Rev. Jose Servelion, S.T.L., J.C.D., La Potestad Legislativa de la Iglesia Catolica, IV-127 pp., 1925.
26. Dugan, Rev. Henry Francis, A.M., J.C.D., The Judiciary Department of the Diocesan Curia, 87 pp., 1925.
27. Keller, Rev. Charles Frederick, S.T.B., J.C.D., Mass Stipends, 167 pp., 1925.
28. Paschang, Rev. John Linus, J.C.D., The Sacramentals According to the Code of Canon Law, 129 pp., 1925.
29. Piontek, Rev. Cyrillus, O.F.M., S.T.B., J.C.D., De Indulto Exclaustrationis necnon Saecularizationis, XIII-289 pp., 1925.
30. Kearney, Rev. Richard Joseph, S.T.B., J.C.D., Sponsors at Baptism According to the Code of Canon Law, IV-127 pp., 1925.
31. Bartlett, Rev. Chester Joseph, A.M., LL.B., J.C.D., The Tenure of Parochial Property in the United States of America, V-108 pp., 1926.
32. Kilker, Rev. Adrian Jerome, J.C.D., Extreme Unction, V-425 pp., 1926.
33. McCormick, Rev. Robert Emmett, J.C.D., Confessors of Religious, VIII-266 pp., 1926.
34. Miller, Rev. Newton Thomas, J.C.D., Founded Masses According to the Code of Canon Law, VII-93, pp., 1926.
35. Roelker, Rev. Edward G., S.T.D., J.C.D., Principles of Privilege According to the Code of Canon Law, XI-166 pp., 1926.
36. Bakalarczyk, Rev. Richardus, M.I.C., J.U.D., De Novitiatu, VIII-208 pp., 1927.
37. Pizzuti, Rev. Lawrence, O.F.M., J.U.L., De Parochis Religiosis, 1927. (Not Printed).
38. Bliley, Rev. Nicholas Martin, O.S.B., J.C.D., Altars According to the Code of Canon Law, XIX-132 pp., 1927.
39. Brown, Mr. Brendan Francis, A.B., LL.M., J.U.D., The Canonical Juristic Personality with Special Reference to its Status in the United States of America, V-212 pp., 1927.
40. Cavanaugh, Rev. William Thomas, C.P., J.U.D., The Reservation of the Blessed Sacrament, VIII-101 pp., 1927.

41. Doheny, Rev. William J., C.S.C., A.B., J.U.D., Church Property: Modes of Acquisition, X-118 pp., 1927.
42. Feldhaus, Rev. Aloysius H., C.PP.S., J.C.D., Oratories, IX-141 pp., 1927.
43. Kelly, Rev. James Patrick, A.B., J.C.D., The Jurisdiction of the Simple Confessor, X-208 pp., 1927.
44. Neuberger, Rev. Nicholas J., J.C.D., Canon 6 or the Relation of the Codex Juris Canonici to the Preceding Legislation, V-95 pp., 1927.
45. O'Keefe, Rev. Gerald Michael, J.C.D., Matrimonial Dispensations, Powers of Bishops, Priests, and Confessors, VIII-232 pp., 1927.
46. Quigley, Rev. Joseph A. M., A.B., J.C.D., Condemned Societies, 139 pp., 1927.
47. Zaplotnik, Rev. Johannes Leo, J.C.D., De Vicariis Foraneis, X-142 pp., 1927.
48. Duskie, Rev. John Aloysius, A.B., J.C.D., The Canonical Status of the Orientals in the United States, VIII-196 pp., 1928.
49. Hyland, Rev. Francis Edward, J.C.D., Excommunication, Its Nature, Historical Development and Effects, VIII-181 pp., 1928.
50. Reinmann, Rev. Gerald Joseph, O.M.C., J.C.D., The Third Order Secular of Saint Francis, 201 pp., 1928.
51. Schenk, Rev. Francis J., J.C.D., The Matrimonial Impediments of Mixed Religion and Disparity of Cult, XVI-318 pp., 1929.
52. Coady, Rev. John Joseph, S.T.D., J.U.D., A.M., The Appointment of Pastors, VIII-150 pp., 1929.
53. Kay, Rev. Thomas Henry, J.C.D., Competence in Matrimonial Procedure, VIII-164 pp., 1929.
54. Turner, Rev. Sidney Joseph, C.P., J.U.D., The Vow of Poverty, XLIX-217 pp., 1929.
55. Kearney, Rev. Raymond A., A.B., S.T.D., J.C.D., The Principles of Delegation, VII-149 pp., 1929.
56. Conran, Rev. Edward James, A.B., J.C.D., The Interdict, V-163 pp., 1930.
57. O'Neill, Rev. William H., J.C.D., Papal Rescripts of Favor, VII-218 pp., 1930.
58. Bastnagel, Rev. Clement Vincent, J.U.D., The Appointment of Parochial Adjutants and Assistants, XV-257 pp., 1930.
59. Ferry, Rev. William A., A.B., J.C.D., Stole Fees, V-136 pp., 1930.
60. Costello, Rev. John Michael, A.B., J.C.D., Domicile and Quasi-Domicile, VII-201 pp., 1930.
61. Kremer, Rev. Michael Nicholas, A.B., S.T.B., J.C.D., Church Support in the United States, VI-136 pp., 1930.
62. Angulo, Rev. Luis, C.M., J.C.D., Legislation de la Iglesia sobre la intencion en la application de la Santa Misa, VII-104 pp., 1931.
63. Frey, Rev. Wolfgang Norbert, O.S.B., A.B., J.C.D., The Act of Religious Profession, VIII-174 pp., 1931.

64. ROBERTS, REV. JAMES BRENDAN, A.B., J.C.D., The Banns of Marriage XIV-140 pp., 1931.
65. RYDER, REV. RAYMOND ALOYSIUS, A.B., J.C.D., Simony, IX-151 pp., 1931.
66. CAMPAGNA, REV. ANGELO, PH.D., J.U.D., Il Vicario Generale del Vescovo, VII-205 pp., 1931.
67. COX, REV. JOSEPH GODFREY, A.B., J.C.D., The Administration of Seminaries, VI-124 pp., 1931.
68. GREGORY, REV. DONALD J., J.U.D., The Pauline Privilege, XV-165 pp., 1931.
69. DONOHUE, REV. JOHN F., J.C.D., The Impediment of Crime, VII-110 pp., 1931.
70. DOOLEY, REV. EUGENE A., O.M.I., J.C.D., Church Law on Sacred Relics, IX-143 pp., 1931.
71. ORTH, REV. CLEMENT RAYMOND, O.M.C., J.C.D., The Approbation of Religious Institutes, 171 pp., 1931.
72. PERNICONE, REV. JOSEPH M., A.B., J.C.D., The Ecclesiastical Prohibition of Books, XII-267 pp., 1932.
73. CLINTON, REV. CONNELL, A.B., J.C.D., The Paschal Precept, IX-108 pp., 1932.
74. DONNELLY, REV. FRANCIS B., A.M., S.T.L., J.C.D., The Diocesan Synod, VIII-125 pp., 1932.
75. TORRENTE, REV. CAMILO, C.M.F., J.C.D., Las Procesiones Sagradas, V-145 pp., 1932.
76. MURPHY, REV. EDWIN J., C.PP.S., J.C.D., Suspension Ex Informata Conscientia, XI-122 pp., 1932.
77. MACKENZIE, REV. ERIC F., A.M., S.T.L., J.C.D., The Delict of Heresy in its Commission, Penalization, Absolution, VII-124 pp., 1932.
78. LYONS, REV. AVITUS E., S.T.B., J.C.D., The Collegiate Tribunal of First Instance, XI-147 pp., 1932.
79. CONNOLLY, REV. THOMAS A., J.C.D., Appeals, XI-195 pp., 1932.
80. SANGMEISTER, REV. JOSEPH V., A.B., J.C.D., Force and Fear as Precluding Matrimonial Consent, V-211 pp., 1932.
81. JAEGER, REV. LEO A., A.B., J.C.D., The Administration of Vacant and Quasi-Vacant Episcopal Sees in the United States, IX-229 pp., 1932.
82. RIMLINGER, REV. HERBERT T., J.C.D., Error Invalidating Matrimonial Consent, VII-79 pp., 1932.
83. BARRETT, REV. JOHN D. M., SS., J.C.D., A Comparative Study of the Third Plenary Council of Baltimore and the Code, IX-221 pp., 1932.
84. CARBERRY, REV. JOHN J., PH.D., S.T.D., J.C.D., The Juridical Form of Marriage, X-177 pp., 1934.
85. DOLAN, REV. JOHN L., A.B., J.C.D., The Defensor Vinculi, XII-157 pp., 1934.
86. HANNAN, REV. JEROME D., A.M., S.T.D., LL.B., J.C.D., The Canon Law of Wills, IX-517 pp., 1934.

87. Lemieux, Rev. Delise A., A.M., J.C.D., The Sentence in Ecclesiastical Procedure, IX-131 pp., 1934.
88. O'Rourke, Rev. James J., A.B., J.C.D., Parish Registers, VII-109 pp., 1934.
89. Timlin, Rev. Bartholomew, O.F.M., A.M., J.C.D., Conditional Matrimonial Consent, X-381 pp., 1934.
90. Wahl, Rev. Francis X., A.B., J.C.D., The Matrimonial Imepdiments of Consanguinity and Affinity, VI-125 pp., 1934.
91. White, Rev. Robert J., A.B., LL.B., S,T.B., J.C.D., Canonical Ante-Nuptial Promises and the Civil Law, VI-152 pp., 1934.
92. Herrera, Rev. Antonio Parra, O.C.D., J.C.D., Legislacion Ecclesiastica sobra el Ayuno y la Abstinencia, XI-191 pp., 1935.
93. Kennedy, Rev. Edwin J., J.C.D., The Special Matrimonial Process in Cases of Evident Nullity, X-165 pp., 1935.
94. Manning, Rev. John J., A.B., J.C.D., Presumption of Law in Matrimonial Procedure, XI-111 pp., 1935.
95. Moeder, Rev. John M., J.C.D., The Proper Bishop for Ordination and Dismissorial Letters, VII-135 pp., 1935.
96. O'Mara, Rev. William A., A.B., J.C.D., Canonical Causes for Matrimonial Dispensations, IX-155 pp., 1935.
97. Reilly, Rev. Peter, J.C.D., Residence of Pastors, IX-81 pp., 1935.
98. Smith, Rev. Mariner T., O.P., S.T.Lr., J.C.D., The Penal Law for Religious, VIII-169 pp., 1935.
99. Whalen, Rev. Donald W., A.M., J.C.D., The Value of Testimonial Evidence in Matrimonial Procedure, XIII-297 pp., 1935.
100. Cleary, Rev. Joseph F., J.C.D., Canonical Limitations on the Alienation of Church Property, VIII-141 pp., 1936.
101. Glynn, Rev. John C., J.C.D., The Promoter of Justice, XX-337 pp., 1936.
102. Brennan, Rev. James H., S.S., M.A., S.T.B., J.C.D., The Simple Convalidation of Marriage, VI-135 pp., 1937.
103. Brunini, Rev. Joseph Bernard, J.C.D., The Clerical Obligations of Canons 139 and 142, X-121 pp., 1937.
104. Connor, Rev. Maurice, A.B., J.C.D., The Administrative Removal of Pastors, VIII-159 pp., 1937.
105. Guilfoyle, Rev. Merlin Joseph, J.C.D., Custom, XI-144 pp., 1937.
106. Hughes, Rev. James Austin, A.B., A.M., J.C.D., Witnesses in Criminal Trials of Clerics, IX-140 pp., 1937.
107. Jansen, Rev. Raymond J., A.B., S.T.L., J.C.D., Canonical Provisions for Catechetical Instruction, VII-153 pp., 1937.
108. Kealy, Rev. John James, A.B., J.C.D., The Introductory Libellus in Church Court Procedure, XI-121 pp., 1937.
109. McManus, Rev. James Edward, C.SS.R., J.C.D., The Administration of Temporal Goods in Religious Institutes, XVI-196 pp., 1937.

110. Moriarty, Rev. Eugene James, J.C.D., Oaths in Ecclesiastical Courts, X-115 pp., 1937.
111. Rainer, Rev. Eligius George, C.SS.R., J.C.D., Suspension of Clerics, XVII-249 pp., 1937.
112. Reilly, Rev. Thomas F., C.SS.R., J.C.D., Visitation of Religious, VI-195 pp., 1938.
113. Moriarty, Rev. Francis E., C.SS.R., J.C.D., The Extraordinary Absolution from Censures, XV-334 pp., 1938.
114. Connolly, Rev. Nicholas P., J.C.D., The Canonical Erection of Parishes, X-132 pp., 1938.
115. Donovan, Rev. James Joseph, J.C.D., The Pastor's Obligation in Prenuptial Investigation, XII-322 pp., 1938.
116. Harrigan, Rev. Robert J., M.A., S.T.B., J.C.D., The Radical Sanation of Invalid Marriages, VIII-208 pp., 1938.
117. Boffa, Rev. Conrad Humbert, J.C.D., Canonical Provisions for Catholic Schools, VII-211 pp., 1939.
118. Parsons, Rev. Anscar John, O.M.Cap., J.C.D., Canonical Elections, XII-236 pp., 1939.
119. Reilly, Rev. Edward Michael, A.B., J.C.D., The General Norms of Dispensation, XII-156 pp., 1939.
120. Ryan, Rev. Gerald Aloysius, A.B., J.C.D., Principles of Episcopal Jurisdiction, XII-172 pp., 1939.
121. Burton, Rev. Francis James, C.S.C., A.B., J.C.D., A Commentary on Canon 1125, X-222pp., 1940.
122. Miaskiewicz, Rev. Francis Sigismund, J.C.D., Supplied Jurisdiction According to Canon 209, XII-340 pp., 1940.
123. Rice, Rev. Patrick William, A.B., J.C.D., Proof of Death in Prenuptial Investigation, VIII-156 pp., 1940.
124. Anglin, Rev. Thomas Francis, M.S., J.C.D., The Eucharistic Fast, VIII-183 pp., 1941.
125. Coleman, Rev. John Jerome, J.C.D., The Minister of Confirmation, VI-153 pp., 1941.
126. Downs, Rev. John Emmanuel, A.B., J.C.D., The Concept of Clerical Immunity, XI-163 pp., 1941.
127. Esswein, Rev. Anthony Albert, J.C.D., Extrajudicial Penal Powers of Ecclesiastical Superiors, X-144 pp., 1941.
128. Farrell, Rev. Benjamin Francis, M.A., S.T.L., J.C.D., The Rights and Duties of the Local Ordinary Regarding Congregations of Women Religious of Pontifical Approval, V-195 pp., 1941.
129. Feeney, Rev. Thomas John, A.B., S.T.L., J.C.D., Restitutio in Integrum, VI-169 pp., 1941.
130. Findlay, Rev. Stephen William, O.S.B., A.B., J.C.D., Canonical Norms Governing the Deposition and Degradation of Clerics, XVII-279 pp., 1941.

131. Goodwine, Rev. John, A.B., S.T.L., J.C.D., The Right of the Church to Acquire Property, VIII-119 pp., 1941.
132. Heston, Rev. Edward Louis, C.S.C., Ph.D., S.T.D., J.C.D., The Alienation of Church Property in the United States, XII-222 pp., 1941.
133. Hogan, Rev. James John, A.B., S.T.L., J.C.D., Judicial Advocates and Procurators, XIII-200 pp., 1941.
134. Kealy, Rev. Thoomas M., A.B., Litt.B., J.C.D., Dowry of Women Religious, IX-152 pp., 1941.
135. Keene, Rev. Michael James, O.S.B., J.C.D., Religious Ordinaries and Canon 198, V-164 pp., 1942.
136. Kerin, Rev. Charles A., S.S., M.A., S.T.B., J.C.D., The Privation of Christian Burial, XVI-279 pp., 1941.
137. Louis, Rev. William Francis, M.A., J.C.D., Diocesan Archives, X-101 pp., 1941.
138. McDevitt, Rev. Gilbert Joseph, A.B., J.C.D., Legitimacy and Legitimation, X-247 pp., 1941.
139. McDonough, Rev. Thomas Joseph, A.B., J.C.D., Apostolic Administrators, X-217 pp., 1941.
140. Meier, Rev. Carl Anthony, A.B., J.C.D., Penal Administrative Procedure Against Negligent Pastors, XI-240 pp., 1941.
141. Schmidt, Rev. John Rogg, A.B., J.C.D., The Principles of Authentic Interpretation in Canon 17 of the Code of Canon Law, XII-331 pp., 1941.
142. Slafkosky, Rev. Andrew Leonard, A.B., J.C.D., The Canonical Episcopal Visitation of the Diocese, X-197 pp., 1941.
143. Swoboda, Rev. Innocent Robert, O.F.M., J.C.D., Ignorance in Relation to the Imputability of Delicts, IX-271 pp., 1941.
144. Dubé, Rev. Arthur Joseph, A.B., J.C.D., The General Principles for the Reckoning of Time in Canon Law, VIII-299 pp., 1941.
145. McBride, Rev. James T., A.B., J.C.D., Incardination and Excardination of Seculars, XX-585 pp., 1941.
146. Król, Rev. John T., J.C.D., The Defendant in Ecclesiastical Trials, XII-207 pp., 1942.
147. Comyns, Rev. Joseph J., C.SS.R., A.B., J.C.D., Papal and Episcopal Administration of Church Property, XIV-155 pp., 1942.
148. Barry, Rev. Garrett Francis, O.M.I., J.C.D., Violation of the Cloister, XII-260 pp., 1942.
149. Bolduc, Rev. Gatien, C.S.V., A.B., S.T.L., J.C.D., Les Études dans les Religions Cléricales, VIII-155 pp., 1942.
150. Boyle, Rev. David John, M.A., J.C.D., The Juridic Effects of Moral Certitude on Pre-Nuptial Guarantees, XII-188 pp., 1942.
151. Canavan, Rev. Walter Joseph, M.A., Litt.D., J.C.D., The Profession of Faith, XII-143 pp., 1942.
152. Desrochers, Rev. Bruno, A.B., Ph.L., S.T.B., J.C.D., Le Premier Concile Plénier de Québec et le Code de Droit Canonique, XIV-186 pp., 1942.

153. Dillon, Rev. Robert Edward, A.B., J.C.D., Common Law Marriage, X-148 pp., 1942.
154. Dodwell, Rev. Edward John, Ph.D., S.T.B., J.C.D., The Time and Place for the Celebration of Marriage, X-156 pp., 1942.
155. Donnellan, Rev. Thomas Andrew, A.B., J.C.D., The Obligation of the Missa pro Populo, VII-131 pp., 1942.
156. Eltz, Rev. Louis Anthony, A.B., J.C.D., Cooperation in Crime, XII-208 pp., 1942.
157. Gass, Rev. Sylvester Francis, M.A., J.C.D., Ecclesiastical Pensions, XI-206 pp., 1942.
158. Guiniven, Rev. John Joseph, C.SS.R., J.C.D., The Precept of Hearing Mass, XIV-188 pp., 1942.
159. Gulczynski, Rev. John Theophilus, J.C.D., The Desecration and Violation of Churches, X-126 pp., 1942.
160. Hammill, Rev. John Leo, M.A., J.C.D., The Obligations of the Traveler According to Canon 14, VIII-204 pp., 1942.
161. Haydt, Rev. John Joseph, A.B., J.C.D., Reserved Benefices, XI-148 pp., 1942.
162. Huser, Rev. Roger John, O.F.M., A.B., J.C.D., The Crime of Abortion in Canon Law, XII-187 pp., 1942.
163. Kearney, Rev. Francis Patrick, A.B., S.T.L., J.C.D., The Principles of Canon 1127, X-162 pp., 1942.
164. Linahen, Rev. Leo James, S.T.L., J.C.D., De Absolutione Complicis in Peccato Turpi, V-114 pp., 1942.
165. McCloskey, Rev. Joseph Aloysius, A.B., J.C.D., The Subject of Ecclesiastical Law According to Canon 12, XVII-246 pp., 1942.
166. O'Neill, Rev. Francis Joseph, C.SS.R., J.C.D., The Dismissal of Religious in Temporary Vows, XIII-220 pp., 1942.
167. Prince, Rev. John Edward, A.B., S.T.B., J.C.D., The Diocesan Chancellor, X-136 pp., 1942.
168. Riesner, Rev. Albert Joseph, C.SS.R., J.C.D., Apostates and Fugitives from Religious Institutes, IX-168 pp., 1942.
169. Stenger, Rev. Joseph Bernard, J.C.D., The Mortgaging of Church Property, 186 pp., 1942.
170. Waldron, Rev. Joseph Francis, A.B., J.C.D., The Minister of Baptism, XII-197 pp., 1942.
171. Willett, Rev. Robert Albert, J.C.D., The Probative Value of Documents in Ecclesiastical Trials, X-124 pp., 1942.
172. Woeber, Rev. Edward Martin, M.A., J.C.D., The Interpellations, XII-161 pp., 1942.
173. Benko, Rev. Matthew Aloysius, O.S.B., M.A., J.C.D., The Abbot *Nullius*, XVI-148 pp., 1943
174. Christ, Rev. Joseph James, M.A., S.T.L., J.C.D., Dispensation from Vindicative Penalties, XIV-285 pp., 1943.

175. Clancy, Rev. Patrick M. J., O.P., A.B., S.T.Lr., J.C.D., The Local Religious Superior, X-229 pp., 1943.
176. Clarke, Rev. Thomas James, J.C.D., Parish Societies, XII-147 pp., 1943.
177. Connolly, Rev. John Patrick, S.T.L., J.C.D., Synodal Examiners and Parish Priest Consultors, X-223 pp., 1943.
178. Drumm, Rev. William Martin, A.B., J.C.D., Hospital Chaplains, XII-175 pp., 1943.
179. Flanagan, Rev. Bernard Joseph, A.B., S.T.L., J.C.D., The Canonical Erection of Religious Houses, X-147 pp., 1943.
180. Kelleher, Rev. Stephen Joseph, A.B., S.T.B., J.C.D., Discussions with Non-Catholics: Canonical Legislation, X-93 pp., 1943.
181. Lewis, Rev. Gordian, C.P., J.C.D., Chapters in Religious Institutes, XII-169 pp., 1943.
182. Marx, Rev. Adolph, J.C.D., The Declaration of Nullity of Marriages Contracted Outside the Church, X-151 pp., 1943.
183. Matulenas, Rev. Raymond Anthony, O.S.B., A.B., J.C.D., Communication, a Source of Privileges, XII-225 pp., 1943.
184. O'Leary, Rev. Charles Gerard, C.SS.R., J.C.D., Religious Dismissed After Perpetual Profession, X-213 pp., 1943.
185. Power, Rev. Cornelius Michael, J.C.D., The Blessing of Cemeteries, XII-231 pp., 1943.
186. Shuhler, Rev. Ralph Vincent, O.S.A., J.C.D., Privileges of Religious to Absolve and Dispense, XII-195 pp., 1943.
187. Ziolkowski, Rev. Thaddeus Stanislaus, A.B., J.C.D., The Consecration and Blessing of Churches, XII-151 pp., 1943.
188. Heneghan, Rev. John Joseph, S.T.D., J.C.D., The Marriages of Unworthy Catholics: Canons 1065 and 1066, XVI-213 pp., 1944.
189. Carroll, Rev. Coleman Francis, M.A., S.T.L., J.C.L., Charitable Institutions.
190. Ciesluk, Rev. Joseph Edward, Ph.B., S.T.L., J.C.L., National Parishes in the United States.
191. Coburn, Rev. Vincent Paul, A.B., J.C.D., Marriages of Conscience, XII-172 pp., 1944.
192. Connors, Rev. Charles Paul, C.S.Sp., A.B., J.C.D., Extra-Judicial Procurators in the Code of Canon Law, X-94 pp., 1944.
193. Coyle, Rev. Paul Raymond, A.B., J.C.D., Judicial Exceptions, X-142 pp., 1944.
194. Fair, Rev. Bartholomew Francis, A.B., S.T.L., J.C.D., The Impediment of Abduction, XII-122 pp., 1944.
195. Gallagher, Rev. Thomas Raphael, O.P., A.B., S.T.Lr., J.C.D., The Examination of the Qualities of the Ordinand, X-166 pp., 1944.
196. Gannon, Rev. John Mark, S.T.L., J.C.D., The Interstices Required for the Promotion to Orders, XII-100 pp., 1944.

197. GOLDSMITH, REV. J. WILLIAM, B.C.S., S.T.L., J.C.D., The Competence of Church and State Over Marriages—Disputed Points, X-128 pp., 1944.
198. GOODWINE, REV. JOSEPH GERARD, A.B., S.T.B., J.C.D., The Reception of Converts, XIV-326 pp., 1944.
199. KOWALSKI, REV. ROMUALD EUGENE, O.F.M., A.B., J.C.D., Sustenance of Religious Houses of Regulars, X-174 pp., 1944.
200. McCOY, REV. ALAN EDWARD, O.F.M., J.C.D., Force and Fear in Relation to Delictual Imputability and Penal Responsibility, XII-160 pp., 1944.
201. McDEVITT, REV. VINCENT JOHN, PH.B., S.T.L., J.C.L., Perjury.
202. MARTIN, REV. THOMAS OWEN, PH.D., S.T.D., J.C.D., Adverse Possession, Prescription and Limitation of Actions: The Canonical "Praescriptio," XX-208 pp., 1944.
203. MIKLOSOVIC, REV. PAUL JOHN, A.B., J.C.L., Attempted Marriages and Their Consequent Juridic Effects.
204. MUNDY, REV. THOMAS MAURICE, A.B., S.T.L., J.C.D., The Union of Parishes, X-164 pp., 1944.
205. O'DEA, REV. JOHN COYLE, A.B., J.C.D., The Matrimonial Impediment of Nonage, VIII-126p., 1944.
206. OLALIA, REV. ALEXANDER AYSON, S.T.L., J.C.D., A Comparative Study of the Christian Constitution of States and the Constitution of the Philippine Commonwealth, XII-136 pp., 1944.
207. POISSON, REV. PIERRE-MARIE, C.S.C., A.B., PH.L., TH.L., J.C.L., Droits Patrimoniaux des Maisons et des Eglises Religieuses.
208. STADALNIKAS, REV. CASIMIR JOSEPH, M.I.C., J.C.D., Reservation of Censures, X-141 pp., 1944.
209. SULLIVAN, REV. EUGENE HENRY, S.T.L., J.C.D., Proof of the Reception of the Sacraments, X-165 pp., 1944.
210. VAUGHAN, REV. WILLIAM EDWARD, J.C.D., Constitutions for Diocesan Courts, X-210 pp., 1944.
211. PARO, REV. GINO, S.T.D., J.C.L., The Right of Apostolic Legation.
212. BALZER, REV. RALPH FRANCIS, C.P., J.C.D., The Computation of Time in a Canonical Novitiate, X-227 pp., 1945.
213. DOUGHERTY, REV. JOHN WHELAN, A.B., S.T.L., J.C.L., De Inquisitione Speciali.
214. DZIOB, REV. MICHAEL WALTER, J.C.L., The Sacred Congregation for the Oriental Church.
215. EIDENSCHINK, REV. JOHN ALBERT, O.S.B., B.A., J.C.D., The Election of Bishops in the Letters of Pope Gregory the Great, VIII-200 pp., 1945.
216. GILL, REV. NICHOLAS, C.P., J.C.L., The Spiritual Prefect in Clerical Religious Houses of Study.
217. HYNES, REV. HARRY GERARD, S.T.L., J.C.D., The Privileges of Cardinals, XII-183 pp., 1945.
218. McDEVITT, REV. GERALD VINCENT, S.T.L., J.C.D., The Renunciation of an Ecclesiastical Office, XIV-179 pp., 1945.

219. MANNING, REV. JOSEPH LEROY, J.C.D., The Free Conferral of Offices, VIII-116 pp., 1945.
220. MEYER, REV. LOUIS G., O.S.B., A.B., S.T.B., J.C.D,, Alms-gathering by Religious, XII-163 pp., 1945.
221. O'DONNELL, REV. CLETUS FRANCIS, M.A., J.C.L., The Marriage of Minors.
222. PRUNSKIS, REV. JOSEPH, J.C.D., Comparative Law, Ecclesiastical and Civil, in Lithuanian Concordat, X-161 pp., 1945.
223. SWEENEY, REV. FRANCIS PATRICK, C.SS.R., J.C.D., The Reduction of Clerics to the Lay State, X-199 pp., 1945.
224. VOGELPOHL, REV. HENRY JOHN, J.C.D., The Simple Impediments to Holy Orders, XIV-190, pp., 1945.
225. BROCKHAUS, REV. THOMAS AQUINAS, O.S.B., J.C.L., Religious who are known as *Conversi.*
226. GRIESE, REV. ORVILLE NICHOLAS, S.T.D., J.C.L., Marriage and the Procreation of Offspring.
227. BOUDREAUX, REV. WARREN LOUIS, J.C.L., The "*ab acatholicis nati*" of Canon 1099, § 2.
228. BOWE, REV. THOMAS JOSEPH, A.B., J.C.L., Religious Superioresses.
229. DIEDERICHS, REV. MICHAEL FERDINAND, S.C.J., J.C.L., The Jurisdiction of the Latin Ordinaries over their Oriental Subjects.
230. DINGMAN, REV. MAURICE JOHN, A.B., S.T.L., J.C.L., The Plaintiff in Contentious Trials.
231. FRISON, REV. BASIL, C.M.F., M.MUS., J.C.L., The Retroactivity of Law.
232. GALVIN, REV. WILLIAM ANTHONY, M.A., J.C.L., The Administrative Transfer of Pastors.
233. GORACY, REV. JOSEPH C., J.C.L., The Diriment Matrimonial Impediment of Major Orders.
234. HALE, REV. JOSEPH FRANCIS, M.A., S.T.L., J.C.L., The Pastor of Burial.
235. HENRY, REV. JOSEPH ARTHUR, A.B., J.C.L., The Mass and Holy Communion: Interritual Law.
236. LINENBERGER, REV. HERBERT, C.PP.S., J.C.L., The False Denunciation of an Innocent Confessor.
237. LOWRY, REV. JAMES MARTIN, A.B., J.C.L., Dispensation from Private Vows.
238. LYNCH, REV. GEORGE EDWARD, A.B., S.T.L., J.C.L., Coadjutors and Auxiliaries of Bishops.
239. LYNCH, REV. TIMOTHY, M.S.SS.T., J.C.L., Contracts between Bishops and Religious Congregations.
240. MCCLUNN, REV. JUSTIN DAVID, A.B., S.T.L., J.C.L., Administrative Recourse.
241. MCGARVEY, REV. THOMAS JOSEPH, A.B., S.T.L., J.C.L., Bination.
242. MCGRATH, REV. JAMES, A.B., J.C.L., The Privilege of the Canon.
243. MARBACH, REV. JOSEPH FRANCIS, A.B., J.C.L., Marriage Legislation for the Catholics of the Oriental Rites in the United States and Canada.

244. Shimkus, Rev. Bernard Aloysius, A.B., J.C.L., The Determination and Transfer of Rite.
245. Smith, Rev. Vincent Michael, A.B., S.T.L., J.C.L., Ignorance Affecting Matrimonial Consent.
246. Wachtrle, Rev. Paul Anthony, A.B., J.C.L., The Baptism of the Children of Non-Catholics.

www.ingramcontent.com/pod-product-compliance
Lightning Source LLC
LaVergne TN
LVHW050254080826
844660LV00012B/635

* 9 7 8 0 8 1 3 2 2 4 1 7 6 *